Inhabiting the Landscape

Place, Custom and Memory, 1500–1800

Nicola Whyte

Windgather Press
is an imprint of
Oxbow Books, Oxford

ISBN 978-1-90511-924-0

A CIP record for this book is available from the British Library

This book is available direct from

Oxbow Books, Oxford, UK
(Phone: 01865-241249; Fax: 01865-794449)

and

The David Brown Book Company
PO Box 511, Oakville, CT 06779, USA
(Phone: 860-945-9329; Fax: 860-945-9468)

or from our website

www.oxbowbooks.com

Printed in Great Britain by
Hobbs the Printers, Southampton

Contents

List of Figures

Abbreviations

HER   Heritage and Environment Record
TNA: PRO   The National Archives: Public Record Office
NMR   National Monuments Record
NRO   Norfolk Record Office

Acknowledgements

....

My greatest debt is to Tom Williamson who supervised my PhD with constant enthusiasm, insightfulness and good-humour. The development of this work also owes an immense amount to time spent working with Andy Wood researching custom and memory in the early modern period. I should like to thank him for his consistent encouragement and advice. I have benefited from the criticisms and suggestions of my examiners John Finch, Alun Howkins and Rob Liddiard. I am indebted to the Arts and Humanities Research Board for a three-year postgraduate studentship in the School of History at the University of East Anglia. My thanks also go to the staff at the Norfolk Record Office and The National Archives for their assistance in carrying out research and for their permission to reproduce map evidence. Special thanks must also go to Patsy Dallas for the numerous ways she has helped me over the years. Finally, I would not have written this book had it not been for the unfailing encouragement, understanding and support of Pete Headland.

CHAPTER ONE

Experiencing the Landscape

In the closing decades of the sixteenth century the lords, tenants and inhabitants of a group of neighbouring villages around Flitcham, in west Norfolk, set about the difficult and controversial task of defining their boundaries across the open commons and heaths. Unable to reach agreement the matter was presented before the central equity courts in 1592 and again in 1602 (TNA: PRO, E178/1587). During litigation proceedings a number of oral testimonies were gathered from the elderly inhabitants of the area and a survey was made of the grounds in question (Figure 1). Seventy-year-old John Creede the elder, a husbandman, spoke about the landscape he had known since he was aged fourteen. From memory he presented a detailed account of the boundary encompassing Flitcham and Appleton common. Beginning at the 'clay pits' he described the course of the bounds extending north to a place called 'Purrells gate' near to 'Purrell stone', then to 'Sandgate' and to 'Kippestowe' before turning westwards to the north side of 'Willesdon Hill' from there to 'Purrell Well' also known as 'Redwell' and to 'Sweete Hill' then to 'Broadwater', 'Whetstone Pit' and to the mill on the river. Creede was mindful to corroborate his personal recollection of the bounds by presenting his knowledge as part of the collective memory of the village. He went on to confirm that this was the route taken during Rogation week when the parishioners perambulated their bounds, which he could remember taking place many times since the reign of Henry VIII. Creede drew attention to the significance of two boundary features in particular, noting how the 'townes of Flitcham and Babinglie did meete togither at Whetston pitt' and 'the men of Flitcham and Newton did meete at Purrell Stone'.

Creede went on to elaborate on the meaning and value of these various landmark features in relation to the complex arrangement of local farming practices, customs and land use rights. While confirming the tenants of the three lordships of Flitcham held common rights to pasture their cattle on the heath throughout the year, he also highlighted a number of internal divisions. The tenants, for example, were only permitted to common on 'Willesdon Hill' when it lay unenclosed and unsown and were allowed to take whines and furze for their fuel except from 'Willesdon Hill' and a place called 'Porters Whines'. In addition, the tenants of Flitcham had no right to pasture their animals to the north of a 'faire mencon of a broade oulde ditche' which led from the great stone known as 'Purrell Stone', in a south or south westerly direction,

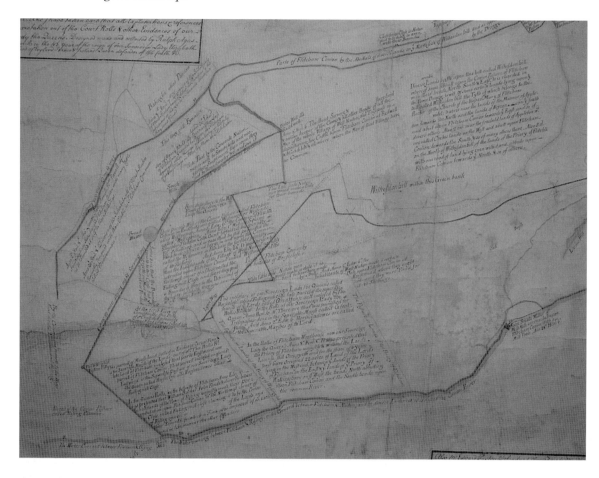

to 'Sandgate'. 'Willesdon Hill' was also employed to delimit manorial grazing rights. According to Creede the flock of sheep belonging to the lordship of Appleton were not permitted to graze any further than the south side of the hill, for that was the territory of the Flitcham flock.

John Creede's description of his local landscape illustrates well the central themes of this book. He conveys a powerful sense of the indivisibility of the physical experience of landscape and demarcation of local social and economic relations. Mapped out on the ground the intricate web of village, and intra-village jurisdictions, provided a tangible and visible medium through which Creede articulated his memories and strong attachment to the place he had known since he was a child. Creede's knowledge was deeply rooted in his conception of the past, based on his everyday experiences of working the land, his participation in public events and rituals, and also his comprehension of material antiquity in the landscape. Creede integrated a network of natural and archaeological features, surviving from various pasts, within a material language of jurisdiction and right.

Until relatively recently the focus of landscape archaeology has been

FIGURE 1. Detail of a map of Flitcham drawn up in 1601 in connection with a long running dispute concerning the course of boundaries across the open heaths shared by the lords, tenants and inhabitants of Flitcham and neighbouring townships of Appleton, West Newton and Babingley (NRO, Flitcham, 407).

predominately concerned with investigating past land use and how local environments – soils, topography, climate, availability of natural resources – shaped patterns of demography, agriculture and settlement. In order to understand the evolution of the modern landscape, research has been necessarily preoccupied with producing typologies of material artefacts and landscapes, each relating to different segments of time. Over the last two decades the emphasis has shifted, with many writers calling for greater consideration of how people living in the past experienced and perceived their physical surroundings. This move away from focusing on environment and economies towards an understanding of the landscape as a social construct, has led to innovative and exciting research much of which, as will hopefully become apparent in these pages, is enormously inspiring. Through a detailed examination of contemporary maps and court deposition evidence an important contribution can be made to our understanding of the social, cultural and economic contexts of post-medieval landscape history.

One of the principal aims of this book is to develop an interdisciplinary approach by bringing landscape history and social history closer together. Early modern social historians have spent little time thinking about the significant role the landscape played in the mediation of day-to-day social relationships. In the majority of writing dealing with this period, the landscape features only as a backdrop to social and economic relationships and construction of individual and collective identities. Yet the landscape was used as a signifying system, elements of the past were appropriated and new features were made, in order to express individual and collective beliefs and convictions regarding matters such as land use rights, local customs and traditions. As this book hopes to demonstrate, by examining a wide range of sources, many of which have not been used in any systematic way by landscape historians, an important contribution can be made to our understanding of the social context of post-medieval landscape history. This study seeks to recapture something of the ways people living in the post-medieval period valued and gave meaning to the landscape for a range of reasons other than just regarding the economic potential of the land. Of central concern is an understanding of the landscape as a lived environment imbued with multiple and diverse meanings and associations particular to the time and place.

Debating the Post-Medieval Landscape

Research on the transformation of England's rural landscape since the sixteenth century, has been mainly concerned with the development of capitalist systems of production and the 'commodification' of the landscape (Johnson 1996). Drawing on anthropological research Christopher Tilley has posited a firm distinction between the experience of landscape in pre-capitalist/non-western societies and capitalist/western societies (Tilley 1994, 20). He employs a number of binary relationships to outline the underlying characteristics of each. 'Pre-capitalist spaces' are 'ritualised' and 'sanctified', imbued with 'myth and cosmology', and 'ritual knowledge'. 'Capitalist spaces', in contrast, are 'desanctified' backdrops to rational, economic action, they are devoid of meaningful depth and 'set apart from people, myth and history, something to be controlled and used' (Tilley 1994, 21). Until recently, most post-medieval landscape studies have, to varying extents, reinforced this distinction. The subject of agrarian improvement for instance, has led many to focus on economic determinants shrouding the debate in statistical analysis concerning measurements of land productivity and crop yields (Overton 1996; Campbell and Overton 1991; Glennie 1988). In these studies the achievements of 'rational' capitalist farmers in combating the limitations imposed by nature are placed at the forefront of debate (Williamson 2002).

A pre-capitalist/capitalist dichotomy, however, underestimates the diverse understandings of place and landscape in capitalist societies (Cosgrove and Daniels 1988; Kealhofer 1999). As Kealhofer (1999, 62) points out individuals in modern capitalist societies do create 'backdrops' but 'these are evocative and symbolic, not two-dimensional and meaningless'. Research into the enclosure and re-structuring of elite landscapes clearly illustrates the symbolic and ideological meanings embodied in the physical environment in the eighteenth-century (Williamson 1995; 1998; Gregory 2005). Among the most influential writers, Denis Cosgrove has defined the landscape as 'a cultural image, a pictorial way of representing, structuring or symbolizing surroundings': a response associated with seventeenth-century landscape painting, and with the idea that the viewer is situated outside the landscape (Cosgrove 1988). The landscape therefore is not merely a physical entity, a collection of objects and structures arranged in a particular way, but also a way of seeing, which can be used to project political, social and ideological perspectives. Meaning is conveyed through a symbolic language – referred to by Cosgrove and Daniels as 'an iconography of landscape' – in which the landscape, like a painting, is analogous to a text, something to be decoded and interpreted (Cosgrove and Daniels 1988, 1). Cosgrove is concerned with the origins of the modern idea of landscape and a particular way of seeing among the wealthy elite. His approach is, however, a useful one for understanding the ways other social groups, in other contexts, may have conveyed meaning through their (sub)conscious manipulations of the physical environment (Johnson 1996).

In recent years these kinds of approach have also found favour among anthropologists and archaeologists, especially those concerned with the prehistoric past. Edited volumes by Ashmore and Knapp (1999), Ucko and Layton (1999) and Bender (1993) have, for example, emphasised the interpretation of archaeological sequences in terms of cognitive patterns, rather than simply as a consequence of mundane aspects of daily subsistence. Broadly speaking, many of these scholars would take issue with Cosgrove's premise that the 'viewer' can detach her/himself from the landscape as a subjective interpreter: in Gabriel Cooney's words, 'a person's perception or mental map of a place is what underpins his/her actions rather than the objective reality of that place' (Cooney 1994, 32). Building on these conceptual ideas the archaeologist John Barrett has proposed a theory of 'inhabitation'. He cautions against taking the meanings given to material artefacts or places as self-evident and stresses the importance of understanding the particular social and cultural contexts from which meanings were derived: 'meaning is something recognised by an observer, it is not some quality inherent to the place or the monument' (Barrett 1999, 27). Even at the time of their original conception the intended meanings attached to places, or indeed entire landscapes, could be subject to a range of interpretations and, obviously over time, the scope for re-interpretation and re-invention widens (Bender 1993).

The shift away from attempting to elucidate the origins of monuments and landscapes, to think instead about how such features were interpreted by subsequent societies, is among the most significant theoretical and methodological developments in recent years. Scholars interested in the contextual meanings of commemorative monuments have been forthcoming in adopting such approaches (Finch 2003; Tarlow 1999) but as yet post-medieval landscape archaeologists and historians have been generally slow to engage with theoretical debates taking place within the wider discipline. In the majority of work on this period, there has been a tendency to construct a linear narrative of change focused on enclosure and agrarian improvement. Understanding the landscape, as it was 'inhabited', should not be confined to prehistory; it is an effective approach for the post-medieval period.

Enclosure

Enclosure has long been a major area of enquiry and debate among scholars interested in the formation of the modern rural landscape. On this subject, Matthew Johnson's *An Archaeology of Capitalism* (1996) is among the most innovative and thought-provoking studies to date. From an archaeological perspective Johnson interprets the major structural changes implemented by enclosure as the physical expression of a deep-rooted subconscious shift driving the forces of capitalism. Johnson's objective, to look beyond economic explanations that have dominated our understandings of enclosure, is a salient reminder that for early modern societies matters of everyday life were not neatly compartmentalised. His argument, however, has been criticised on a number of grounds. Tom Williamson has discussed some of the pitfalls in adopting such a unifying approach. In particular he highlights the importance of regional variation regarding both the chronology and character of enclosure (Williamson 2000a). During the early modern period farmers enclosed and converted their arable lands to pasture in order to specialise in livestock husbandry. Outside the Midland core where large landowners undertook wholesale enclosure schemes across extensive areas, enclosure before the eighteenth century was mainly of a gradual piecemeal nature. Moreover, in prioritising enclosure as the dominant structuring force of nascent capitalism, Johnson implies that enclosed land provided the best environment for commercial farming which, as others have pointed out, was not always the case (Havinden 1961; Williamson 2000a). Within the main arable-producing regions – the wolds, downs and heaths – open field systems continued to operate within ostensibly capitalist landscapes. But both sides of the argument assume that farmers shared a common objective regarding the most profitable way to exploit the land.

Johnson's cultural model of enclosure, and the more general concern to map regional patterns of change, have both tended to underplay the confused reality of enclosure and above all its antagonistic ramifications at a local level. Investigations into the local implementation of enclosure provide a rather different story – one of conflict and dispute over the best and most profitable way to use the land. Considerable research has been carried out on the social consequences of enclosure, especially in areas, in the Fens and pastoral-industrial regions for example, where the enclosure of common land was met with strong and sustained resistance (Lindley 1982; Manning 1988, see also Edwards 2004; Falvey 2001; Hipkin 2000). Though not always culminating in the levels of riot and insurrection associated with these areas, enclosure was nevertheless an emotive and divisive issue for the inhabitants of villages located within both arable and pasture farming districts in Norfolk. This was as much the case in districts defined by piecemeal enclosure, often described by landscape historians as a consensual and straightforward agreement between neighbouring farmers, as it was in areas dominated by open field systems. As we shall see within many Norfolk villages the creation of enclosed, private landscapes was an uneven and, for a time at least, an uncertain development. In many places, until the late eighteenth century, multiple use rights and customs defined the landscape. Tensions existed between the aspirations of the individual and the moral boundaries of obligation and right set by the 'community'. Before enclosure and privatisation could be achieved this intricate web of communal rights had to be dissolved, a process of deep social and economic controversy in many villages.

Landscape and Social History

Early modern social historians have demonstrated the importance of custom as quite literally a field of conflict in the everyday life and politics of local societies (Wood 1999; Wrightson 1996, 22–25). Local customs gave authority to the claims of the inhabitants of a particular place to utilise the landscape in a number of ways: to graze their livestock on the commons and fallow open fields; to glean for ears of corn after harvest; to gather fuel and wood, and to dig for clay on the commons, for example. The authority of custom was based on continuous usage and knowledge of the past (Thompson 1991; Wood 1997; 1999). Handed down from generation to generation, local knowledge of land use rights was presented as having existed since 'time out of mind'.

In the attempt to legitimate their claims of antiquity plebeians deliberately asserted that their customs were static; that they were fixed in time and space (Wood 1997). By proving that a custom was in continuous usage, since before anyone could remember, and providing no written records were recovered to the contrary, was confirmation enough of its authority before a court of law (Wood 1997). For all that precedence was given to proving antiquity, custom was nevertheless flexible – scrutinised, manipulated and tailored to suit the needs of the present. Its adaptability was part of its enduring strength as people of all social rank endeavoured to take full advantage of their situation (Thompson 1991, 102; Wood 1997; 1999). Landowners, tenants and commoners each played an active role in transforming their lived environment through the negotiation of custom and right.

Andy Wood's study of the Peak Country offers a compelling insight into the powerful concept of custom among the free-miners of the region. He shows how custom shaped everyday social relations and, especially during periods of dispute, reinforced a common sense of purpose and identity within the free-mining community (Wood 1999). However, more attention needs to be paid to assessing the material and spatial contexts of these social interactions and developments. Local customs and land use rights were attached to the land and it is this materiality that is of great importance for our understanding of the landscape history of the early modern period. Physical space was defined by multiple layers of access rights and customs often attached to different jurisdictions – the manor, parish and township – which interlocked in various and complex ways. As John Creede's account indicates, the identification of various landmarks became intrinsic to the definition of custom and right. It was through the practical knowledge of the landscape, through the memory of the past and the ongoing physical experience of living and working in a particular place, that people defined their social and economic identities.

A stronger alliance between social history and landscape history can offer new insights on other themes and processes of the period. In an influential article written over a decade ago, Keith Wrightson examined the politics of the parish in early modern England (Wrightson 1996). Interweaving the major themes of early modern history – politics, religion, governance, and economic and cultural developments – he explored the complexities of change at a micro-level. In a number of important ways the issues outlined by Wrightson, and other historians since, are useful for our understanding of the inhabited landscape. The rural landscape was not simply an economic resource, nor was it merely a backdrop to social action; rather the landscape provided the medium through which social, political, religious and economic relations were mediated.

The Dissolution, end of pilgrimage and attack on purgatory, shaped the development of the landscape and spatial context of peoples' lives in a number of important ways, which have yet to be fully explored by landscape historians. As we shall see the Reformation had a profound impact not only on local social relations but also on the spatial configurations of religious beliefs and practices outside the parish church. In Norfolk, the closure of monastic houses, and mutilation of material artefacts, sculptures and paintings was accompanied by the closure and ruination of unprecedented numbers of religious buildings and structures: a process that fundamentally altered the spatial framework of sixteenth-century religious topographies. The material changes brought about by government legislation had further repercussions for the organisation of local administrative structures.

Religious reform was intertwined with the growing power of the Tudor State, which had important implications for local social and political relations, and also for the physicality, and meaning of place and belonging (Hindle 2000; Wrightson 1996). In the sixteenth century, renewed population growth and concomitant rise in the demand for food and high grain prices was offset by periods of economic dearth and depression. The 1590s stands out as a particularly harsh decade; badly affected by sporadic periods of harvest failures and disease, which brought distress and impoverishment to many small farmers and cottagers. The dispossessed migrated in search of work to urban centres or, as in other parts of the country, they travelled to wood-pasture and forest areas attracted by their extensive commons, which offered to them a means of subsistence. This gave rise to tensions as settled inhabitants and commoners sought to guard their rights to common resources and who frequently turned to the law courts for arbitration (Hindle 1998; 2002, 158–160). The institutionalisation of the Poor Laws at the end of the sixteenth century consolidated power and authority among wealthier settled villagers, who set about defining the moral and physical boundaries of belonging (Hindle 2000).

For villages situated in the southern lowlands of England, the growing administrative importance of the parish had a significant, yet often overlooked, impact on landscape history. Indeed, one of the major themes of the post-medieval period was the gradual rationalisation of a complex network of jurisdictions, inherited from the medieval past. Shifts in the nature and value of local administrative structures were complex and often highly contentious. In particular, the increasing influence of the parish as a social and political entity needs to be considered in relation to the changing functions and meanings of the manor. The gradual consolidation of local territorial and economic structures was mediated through the social contexts of boundary making. The tangible evidence of the past in the landscape was central to these negotiations.

Landscape and Memory

Within the discipline of landscape history the idea of the landscape as a palimpsest has long been an influential metaphor for interpreting the modern landscape. That past generations also inherited a landscape packed with elements from multiple and varied pasts, tends to be put aside in the majority of writing on the post-medieval period (Holtorf and Williams 2006). Instead, the totalising force of capitalism is prioritised as old structures and material relics are seen as being swept away in the name of improvement, progress and enclosure. Prior to the closing decades of the eighteenth century – a period of unprecedented investment and optimism in farming – the interpretation, destruction or preservation of landscape features cannot simply be put down to economic expediency, however. A central theme of this book is an understanding of the ways old apparently redundant features were assimilated and given new meanings in the development of the post-medieval landscape.

Literacy and growing reliance on written documentation constitutes one of the defining features of the early modern period: a transition, which suggests significant underlying transformations in the ways people, perceived their landscape. Much work has focused on the influence of writing, particularly printed material and rise of literacy, upon popular senses of history and development of linear time (Fox 2000, 213–258; Thomas 1984; Woolf 1988; 1991). The majority of studies have examined the integration of archaeological and topographical features within national histories and local folklore narratives. Such studies have tended to use the landscape as a framework upon which the latest historical revelation was hung, or as evidence of divine providence (Simpson 1986). While all this work is important in highlighting the ongoing interpretation of archaeological and natural landmarks, and emergence of a national historical consciousness, understanding the landscape as simply a repository of folklore narratives offers a narrow view of the significance of the landscape in shaping memory and attitudes towards the past.

In recent years, scholarly debate has focused on the erosion of oral memory due to an increasing reliance on written documents (Fox 1996; Woolf 1988). However, the emphasis placed on the codification of memory in writing overlooks the great variety of ways that systems of remembering may have operated in illiterate, and semi-literate societies (Bradley 2003, 233; Wood 1999). Perhaps the most fundamental way of creating and sustaining memory was in the interpretation and uses of the landscape. In the post-medieval period, people encountered the material environment as a complex fusion of pasts: pasts that required interpretation and re-assimilation within the changing social and economic conditions of the present. In the post-medieval period, as earlier, meaning was not inherent to a monument or landscape but was derived from the contexts of everyday life. Social relations solidified through individual experience and the shared meanings given to the landscape. Meaning was a source of potential conflict through which change – dramatic at times, at other times muted – was brought about. Understanding the material past as a fluid, dynamic concept has important implications for our understanding of the functions of the landscape in knitting together, or rupturing, local relations. Consideration of the ways meanings were derived from the everyday experience of living in the landscape turns landscape history from its linear, inevitable course. Nascent capitalism was as much about the mediation of the past as it was a forward-looking progression.

Various case studies will be used throughout this book in order to illuminate the individual and often idiosyncratic experiences of the landscape within local societies. But rather than leaving these small-scale studies to stand on their own singular merits an attempt will be made to incorporate them into the broader picture of regional and national change. The result is a multi-layered narrative that seeks to integrate the various aspects of everyday life – religion, economy, social relations and local politics – and to consider them in terms of the meanings given to the landscape. In so doing I shall not, perhaps, present a single coherent 'story'. Instead I will examine the ways in which both the landscape, and perceptions and understanding of it, were affected by the principal social, economic and ideological changes of the period – changes which were, of course, themselves connected in complex and often subtle ways. Chapter two examines the character and spatial context of the late medieval religious landscape, and the ways in which this was understood by contemporaries, before going on to examine how religious space was fundamentally transformed by the Reformation. Chapter three investigates the developing administrative and political role of the parish, and how this impacted on contemporary understandings of the physical environment, as well as examining how local people articulated a sense of place. Chapter four looks in more detail at the fragmentation of local societies, the expansion of capitalism and associated growth in power over the landscape: not only in terms of enclosure, but also in such things as the development and extension of manorial customs such as fold-course and warren rights. Chapter five seeks to draw together the various strands of this book by examining how such changes were both justified, and challenged, by reference to the material traces of the past. I would emphasise again that this book does not unfold in any simple, linear way: nevertheless, it does display a certain overall coherence, born of the fact that the matters and issues it discusses are themselves all intimately connected. As a whole this book, I hope, will serve to show how the evidence and approaches of post-medieval landscape history, if suitably informed by recent advances in archaeological theory together with modern social theory, can cast important new light on a range of old debates.

The remaining sub-sections of this chapter shall firstly outline the documentary sources used in this study and secondly discuss regional variation in Norfolk.

Sources

At the core of this study is an in-depth examination of cartographic material and records from the Westminster law courts, principally those of the Exchequer and Duchy of Lancaster covering the county of Norfolk. The equity jurisdiction of the Exchequer grew in importance from the mid-sixteenth century with the court hearing cases of relevance to the crown including matters concerning, manorial rights, tithes, and the ownership of former monastic property (Fox 2000, 273).

The records of the Duchy of Lancaster concerned the administration of the Duchy estates which sought to safeguard its rights and privileges. During litigation proceedings local people were called as witnesses to provide knowledge of local agrarian practices, customs and land use rights. Individuals from a relatively broad social spectrum were called to give evidence describing themselves as yeoman, husbandman, warreners, shepherds, labourers, wives and widows, gentlemen and clerks. These records offer a wide range of elite and non-elite perspectives but they were, however, heavily biased towards male deponents: the voices of women and the poor were considered less authoritative in the official arena of the law courts (Shepard 2003, 222–223; Wood 1999, 132).

In recent years social historians have carried out important and influential work on court depositions as a means of elucidating a range of issues including, for instance, local social and economic structures, migration patterns, gender relations and the formation of social identities (Shepard 2003; Wood 1999). In contrast depositions have been a much under-utilised resource in landscape research other than specific case studies. Heather Falvey (2001) and Peter Edwards (2004), for example, have made notable contributions by carrying out detailed analysis of local disputes concerning enclosure and access rights to common land in Berkhampsted and the Weald Moors in Shropshire (see also Yates 1981). From the perspective of the landscape historian, the thousands of oral testimonies collected during litigation proceedings provide an invaluable insight into the ways contemporaries experienced and gave meaning to their physical environs. They illuminate moments of conflict between individuals and social groups as to how agricultural and industrial practices should be organised and exploited. Studied alongside early maps, they have additional value in that they provide a unique insight into the ways the physical environment was interpreted in the past.

The development of cartography from the mid-sixteenth century, provides historians with a wealth of useful information including for instance, minor place-names, land use, the extent of common land, layout of settlements, as well as various landmark features. Students of landscape history are advised to study and analyse the maps available for their particular study area. They are necessarily cautioned as to the limitations and biases of interpreting maps and are taught to be aware that they offer distorted and idealised representations of the landscape frequently embellished with a flourish of artistic licence (Muir 1999, 67–69). However, it is precisely because of this selectivity that early maps reveal something of the ways the landscape at this time was perceived. As Harley has argued, rather than just regarding maps as a means of understanding the evolution of the landscape of a particular locality they should also be read as socially constructed artefacts and 'value laden images' (Harley 1988, 278). The idea that maps denoted knowledge and power in the organisation and regulation of space can be applied to the increasing popularity of estate maps from the mid-sixteenth century (Harvey 1993). These were commissioned by the landed elite as a means of demonstrating their control, or ambition at least, over the land

and the economic lives of local communities. In Andrew McRae's words: a map hanging on the wall 'define[d] a manor as the lord's own' (McRae 1996, 192). In parallel to this elitist agenda, the process of map-making also interconnected with the lives of ordinary people.

A number of historians have pointed out that in the late sixteenth and seventeenth centuries, maps were drawn up in relation to litigation proceedings (Bendall 1993, 107–21; Harley 1988, 285; McRae 1996, 189). The law courts often instructed that maps were to be drawn up in order to aid the judges in their arbitration of disputed territories. Though many have in more recent times been detached and re-catalogued at The National Archives, some are still to be found amongst the depositions taken during court proceedings (see for example: Binham, TNA: PRO, DL4/18/37; and Cawston, TNA: PRO, E133/1/182). These sketches appear highly schematic in contrast to the large-scale decorative estate maps commissioned by elite landowners, but the two were part of the same process of establishing boundaries and land use rights. Furthermore and to a great extent the achievement of these early surveyors was indebted to the knowledge of local residents. This was especially the case on manors where a change in ownership – following the Dissolution of the monasteries, for example – prompted landlords to set out and confirm their new territories. Contemporaries often describe their part in 'treading owt the lands' with the surveyor (TNA: PRO, E134/32Eliz/Hil20). Rather than interpreting maps as an imprint of authority from 'above' at times local people also had a significant role to play in their production. Tenants sometimes produced plans in support of their claims against seigniorial lords (see Cawston TNA: PRO, E133/1/182 p. 119 below). Beyond the park pale, the various features depicted on early maps were common landmarks, recorded because they held mutual significance for all sectors of local society.

Norfolk: Contrasting Landscapes

Any study that seeks to uncover the experience of landscape in the past must be grounded in local environmental conditions and economic contexts. For the post-medieval period agricultural historians, for the most part, have accepted a regional framework for analysis (Thirsk 1987; Wade Martins and Williamson 1999; Williamson 2002). Although the criterion for drawing the boundaries around these regions remains a matter of debate (Overton 1996, 46–62), most regional models take into account the underlying physical characteristics of an area – soils, topography, and climate – and how this range of factors influenced the development of farming and economies. However, it is important to establish that although the underlying physical characteristics of a region may represent geological stability, the nature and extent of human intervention within these environments varied over time. From the early decades of the sixteenth century renewed population growth, inflation, and advance of a more sophisticated market economy motivated farmers to develop more competitive methods of production that both suited their particular local environments and their access to market centres. In general terms light soils encouraged arable regimes and heavy clayland soils, especially in areas of high rainfall, encouraged farmers to specialise in pastoral farming (Thirsk 1967).

In Norfolk, a distinction has been made between: the light lands of the 'heathland' districts in the north and the west of the county where corn production and sheep farming predominated; the pastoral districts of the Fenlands in the west noted for cattle rearing and fattening; and the claylands in the south renowned for dairying (Thirsk 1967, 40–49). Given the limitations placed on early modern farmers due to a range of environmental, social and economic constraints, regional diversity was most marked in the early modern period, before the late eighteenth century, at which time the landscape was radically transformed by the developments associated with the 'agricultural revolution' (Williamson 2002). Eighteenth-century writers made clear distinctions between the 'wood-pasture' and 'champagne' or sheep-corn districts of Norfolk. In 1739 Blomefield described the clayland 'wood-pasture' landscape around Diss, in south Norfolk as:

> Enclosed, and abounds much with wood; it being reckoned as part of the woodland half of Norfolk. The roads are very bad in winter, especially this part by Gissing and Titshall. The lands in general are moist, occasioned by their being flat, and having a blue clay within a foot or two of the earth's surface through which the water cannot pierce, it containing 20 or 30 feet in many places. The soil is in general rich, and about half of the land is used for the plough, the other for the dairy, and grazing; it produces much wheat, turnips, clover, and all other grain in abundance, except buck or brank, and cole-seed, of which there is but little sown (Blomefield 1805, I, 211).

In contrast he described the area around Thetford as 'Champaign', the land 'being very light and sandy ... the soil is chiefly chalk under sand' which provided grazing for 'good flocks of sheep' (Blomefield 1805, I, 359).

The wood-pasture/champion paradigm has also been used to map differences in social processes, including variations in the extent and nature of poor relief. The social hierarchy of wood-pasture villages was generally dominated by yeomen, and lesser gentry: the advocates of Protestantism, promoters of strong parish governance, and founders of the parish vestry. The variegated social structure of villages fostered a greater depth of shared responsibility towards the poor. Alliances were forged between yeoman farmers and parishioners of lesser means particularly over the protection of access rights to common resources. In contrast, large estates dominated the main arable-producing districts. Here, prosperous landowners, many of whom supported Catholicism, pursued an economic and social agenda frequently motivated by self-interest. In these areas the objectives of village governance were more usually an issue of social control, often disguised as paternalism (Hindle 2002, 223–5). Broad regional dichotomies can be useful for not only pointing to the complex development of parochial governance but also the variable meaning of the parish as a social and physical entity. However, the wood-pasture and sheep-corn regions of

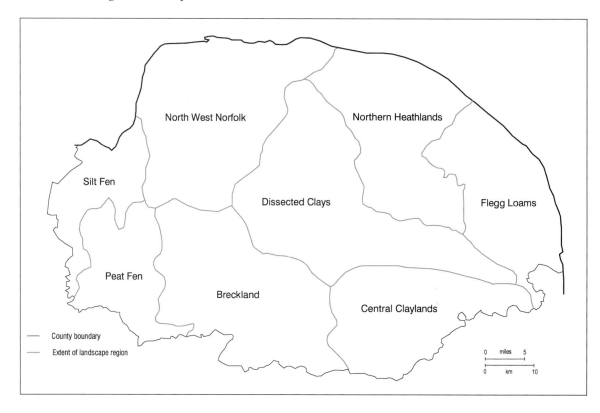

Norfolk can be divided into a number of sub-types, which are more useful for our understanding of local social and economic differences. Their basic characteristics are outlined briefly below (Figure 2).

Of the sheep-corn districts Breckland is the least fertile. Acid sands lie over porous chalk rendering the land prone to leaching and drought. The problems of soil deficiency are exacerbated by climatic conditions: low rainfall and sharp frosts, which further break up and erode the surface. Before the large-scale conifer plantings, undertaken by the Forestry Commission in the early twentieth century which effectively helped to stabilise the soils, the region was famous for its 'shifting sands' or 'sand blows' and led some commentators to compare the area to the Sahara Desert (Sussams 1996, 180–82). Francois de la Rochefoucauld vividly described the region in the mid-eighteenth century:

> As you leave the village [of Ingham] it becomes sandy and heavy on account of the large quantity of shifting sand in which the district abounds ... covered with heather in every direction as far as the eye can see – not a shrub, not a plant ... after Thetford our road continued across country as barren as that we had passed in the morning and still drier ... everywhere sand, everywhere clumps of reeds and bracken (Scarfe 1988, 72).

To the north of Breckland, the 'Good Sands' district, as defined by Arthur Young in 1804, is also characterised by light free-draining soils but, although areas of infertile acid sands are to be found, they are compensated for by

FIGURE 2. The landscape regions of Norfolk as mapped by Susanna Wade Martins and Tom Williamson (1999).

relatively fertile calcareous soils found notably along the north coast (Wade Martins and Williamson 1999, 9–10). The soils of the 'Northern Heathlands' are similarly identified but, unlike Breckland and the Good Sands, water supplies are far more abundant, the area being traversed by a number of rivers, the Bure, Ant and Wensum and their tributaries. In addition, pockets of fertile loams occur in the south of the district, which sustained areas of fenland pasture (Wade Martins and Williamson 1999, 15).

This divergent development of Norfolk's light soil regions was not just a consequence of environmental factors but also differences in social structures: large estates, increasingly dominated Breckland and the Good Sands district. For many villages, notably those located on the dry 'uplands' or 'interfluves' (Williamson 2000b), the late fourteenth and fifteenth centuries, a period characterised by demographic decline, experienced contraction as local populations migrated away from these harsh environments to take up more profitable holdings elsewhere. This unrelenting shift from large numbers of small owner-occupiers to a few large landowners continued to characterise the post-medieval centuries: a process more easily achieved in areas where land was relatively cheap and villages sparsely populated. In connection with this, these marginal settlements tended to be enclosed at an early date. Landlords who systematically bought out small landowners and thus facilitated the process of depopulation most easily achieved enclosure. In contrast, villages situated on the more fertile calcareous soils of the river-valleys, tended to be larger with complex divisions of landownership, thus making any attempt at large-scale enclosure problematical until the parliamentary enclosure movement at the turn of the nineteenth century. In addition, from a practical viewpoint the continuing viability of arable production in these areas required an open landscape in order to allow sheep flocks access to graze and manure arable lands under fallow.

In contrast, the Northern Heathlands, as defined by Wade Martins and Williamson (1999), though similarly characterised by large tracts of heath, interspersed with more fertile soils within the river-valleys, the landholding pattern was more complex as large estates were intermixed with property held by lesser gentry and yeoman. A greater degree of variation also characterised the agrarian economy of the region. Though arable was important, the prevalence of low-lying meadows allowed farmers to keep more cattle. Sheep flocks were also maintained, having the dual role of providing wool and manure needed to nourish the arable fields. The economy of the region was comparatively diverse offering craft employments, notably in the worsted wool industry. Unlike Breckland and the Good Sands, the chronology and process of enclosure differed in that many, if not the majority of villages, attempts were being made to enclose the open fields, by the gradual piecemeal consolidation of arable strips, and encroachment on the commons. Yet, enclosure was not comprehensive and large tracts of common land and open fields continued to exist until the parliamentary enclosure movement of the eighteenth century (Wade Martins and Williamson 1999, 15–16).

The 'Flegg Loam' district in the east of Norfolk is characterised by some of the most fertile soils in the country (Wade Martins and Williamson 1999, 17). Since the medieval period open fields, cultivated by relatively small landholders, dominated the landscape. On account of the richness of the loam soils land was expensive and, as a result, large estates were generally absent from the area. The farming economy of the region was further supplemented by the presence of large grazing grounds – the fens and marshes of 'Broadland' – which by this time were largely held in severalty. The inherent fertility of the arable lands, combined with the availability of extensive pastures created a diverse and rich economy based on corn production, cattle rearing, and dairying (Williamson 1997). Historians have considered that one of the key social characteristics of this region, and to some extent the Northern Heathlands, lay in the apparent independence of farmers (Campbell 1986). Free from the shackles of communal field systems found elsewhere, landholders here were able to cultivate their land as they wished. In contrast, more restrictive open-field systems operated in districts such as Breckland and the Good Sands, where strict rotations of arable and fallow had to be maintained in order to conserve soil fertility and productivity (Postgate 1973).

Like the light soil districts, the clayland areas of Norfolk gave rise to landscapes of notable variety (Wade Martins and Williamson 1999, 28). The landscape of the northern reaches of boulder clay is dissected by a larger number of rivers, the valleys of which contain lighter, more amenable soils for cultivation than the heavy waterlogged lands further south. Away from the river-valleys, the clays are overlaid with a sandy or gravely drift which, until the end of the eighteenth century, supported heathland vegetation. While piecemeal enclosure caused the gradual attrition of the open fields, arable production continued to be part of local economies, mainly to supplement fodder supplies and, as a result, fragments of open-field land survived into the era of parliamentary enclosure. The clayland districts, on the whole, supported variegated social structures comprising a mixture of lesser gentry, yeoman and small owner-occupiers. Research has shown that the creation of the 'wood-pasture' landscape of south Norfolk was largely the outcome of developments underway in farming in the sixteenth and seventeenth centuries. Early map evidence reveals extensive arable open fields within many parishes in this area, yet the majority were enclosed by the eighteenth century (Skipper 1989). Cultivation tended to be concentrated on the lighter soils of the river-valleys in contrast to the heavy, waterlogged soils of the interfluves, which were utilised as grazing either as commons or private parks.

Sixteenth-century farmers certainly considered their clayland soils to be suitable for arable production. The fields of Hethel, for example, were described as 'very fatt and good grounds for tillage' having 'born very good wheat and barely' (TNA: PRO, E178/3044). Arable production, however, required intensive inputs of labour, the demands of which small family-run farms often engaged in additional craft employments, found hard to meet. Unable to compete with the large-scale grain production achieved in light soil areas, enterprising farmers looked to develop more competitive methods of farming such as dairying, as was the case in Hethel where butter and cheese was produced (TNA: PRO, E178/3044). Specialisation in livestock required the enclosure of land, in order to protect crops growing on surrounding open fields, to improve grassland and to prevent the intermingling of livestock. By the eighteenth century, as Blomefield's description of the landscape around Diss illustrates, the claylands were predominately enclosed except for the commons, the allocation of ownership and enclosure of which, had to wait until the parliamentary enclosure movement of the late-eighteenth century. Access to market was also an influential factor in encouraging clayland farmers to specialise in livestock. In the west of the county grain was predominately transported by river and sea to urban markets, including London. Clayland farmers were, however, hindered by notoriously bad roads which made grain too costly to cart any distance to a coastal port or navigable river (Smith 1974). Lighter and less bulky products such as butter and cheese could be efficiently transported locally and livestock reared for meat could be walked further a field to market such as Smithfield in London.

In summary, one of the chief roles of the landscape historian is to decipher and classify the landscape into a sequence of phases of economic development. While many writers have recognised the significance of long-term structures in defining regional characteristics, sometimes a degree of continuity is assumed that underplays the complexities of landscape change at a local level. The post-medieval history of the Flegg region is, for example, usually based on medieval precedents. Here lordship was weak and small landholders exercised a marked degree of independence in their agrarian operations without the need for enclosure. But this flexibility should not be transferred unquestionably to the post-medieval centuries. As we will see in Flegg and elsewhere in Norfolk, particularly where local environments supported mixed farming economies, ostensibly pragmatic decisions to cultivate or enclose were deeply controversial issues bound up with custom, memory and conflicting ideas about the past.

CHAPTER TWO

Religious Topographies

....

For historians interested in the long-term ramifications of the Reformation the events of the sixteenth century constitute an unprecedented rupture from the past, marking the genesis of individualism, secularisation and capitalist mentalities characteristic of modern times (Sommervile 1992; see also Johnson 1996). Under Henry VIII the suppression of the monasteries and abolition of pilgrimage constituted a brutal break from the Catholic past. Following the accession of the Edward VI in 1547, Protestant reformers turned their attention to the superstitious beliefs and practices of ordinary people by attacking and destroying the visual imagery and ritualistic culture of parish communities across the country. Ensuing campaigns of iconoclasm transformed the richly decorative and illumine experience of going to church, replacing it with a solemn, more focused piety no longer preoccupied by material abstractions. The tangible objects of devotional practice remained a target for religious reformers under Elizabeth I, and in the seventeenth century when systematic campaigns of iconoclasm re-surfaced once more during the Interregnum. This later phase of Puritan fervour probably had the greatest impact on the appearance of medieval churches (Cooper 2001; Newman 2001, 24).

Historians concerned with elucidating the 'realities' of change at a local level have shown that popular responses to religious reform were complex and ambiguous. Drawing on a wealth of documentary evidence including churchwarden's accounts, wills and consistory court records, various strategies of resistance, compliance and adaptation to state policies, have been uncovered (Duffy 1992, 2001; Hutton 1987, 1994; Kumin 1996). Scholars have also emphasised the engagement of official and non-official strategies in destroying the tangible evidence of superstition and idolatry (Aston 1989, 2003; Oakey 2003; Shagan 2003). Others have addressed the adaptation and assimilation of traditional religious beliefs and practices within Protestant society, and have traced the emergence of a distinctive popular religious culture. Ronald Hutton, in particular, has highlighted the official acceptance for the transposition of Catholic rites into 'folk ritual': outside the Church, the beliefs and practices of the laity were considered irrelevant and, unless judged to be immoral or sinful, were generally allowed to continue. According to Hutton, 'the result was not so much an episode in the history of resistance to the Reformation as part of the process of acceptance of it, easing the transformation of a Catholic to a Protestant society' (Hutton 1996, 418).

It is in the evaluation of the subtleties of continuity and change – the establishment of Protestantism together with the assimilation of elements of the Catholic past – that the disciplines of landscape history and archaeology are particularly well placed to contribute to the Reformation debate. Among the recent literature on the subject the edited volume by David Gaimster and Roberta Gilchrist, *The Archaeology of Reformation 1480–1580* (2003), offers a valuable and wide ranging collection of papers examining responses to the Reformation, quite literally 'from below'. This volume demonstrates the importance of landscape archaeology to our understanding of the unpredictable and often confused path of religious reform. Yet the majority of studies to date remain spatially circumscribed and thematic in their design and implementation, being chiefly concerned with the structural changes inflicted upon the material fabric of parish churches and monastic houses. According to Margaret Aston, 'the Reformation for most believers meant the reformation of their parish church – it was only when they went to church that they encountered sculpture and painting (Aston 1988, 16).

There is still a need to broaden our research parameters to consider more fully the landscape history of the Reformation. Over a decade ago, Gervase Rosser stressed the need for greater topographical analysis in order to explore the close interconnections between churches and other 'holy sites' in the medieval period (Rosser 1996, 82) and, we might add, how the religious reforms of the sixteenth century impacted upon those interconnections. There is, however, a great deal of work yet to be done on the wider landscape context of religious reform, and the totality of the material and spatial consequences of changes, resulting from the combined impact of state policies and local initiatives. These issues will be the focus of the second part of this chapter. I will argue that the Reformation led to an interrelated re-structuring of spiritual topographies, a transformation which amounted, in effect, to a rationalisation of the spatial and cognitive experiences of religious life. By realising these developments we can shed new light on the complex social, ideological and economic changes associated with the Reformation. Yet in putting forward such a broad model of change care must be taken not to suggest a simple and uncontested transformation of material and conceptual landscapes: the supplanting of one spatial order by another was by no means a straightforward process. Nevertheless within a relatively narrow period, between the 1530s and the mid 1550s, the infrastructure of the late medieval religious landscape was drastically altered. The suppression of monastic institutions and the closure of pilgrimage centres, together with the widespread attack on the images and sculptures contained within parish churches, transformed the spatial context of religious life.

In order to contextualise the profound changes of the mid-sixteenth century, it is necessary to explore the ways parish communities experienced the landscape on the eve of the Reformation. The first part of this chapter then will focus on the configuration of late medieval religious topographies, and the ways in which people integrated their physical surroundings as part of a vibrant and composite expression of their religious beliefs. I will not be dealing solely or simply with religious buildings but rather with the links between church and wider landscape. Usually landscapes of agricultural practice and production are considered separately from religious topographies, something which, to a great extent, reflects the specific research interests of individual historians, and tendency to segment the study of the past into subject areas that deal independently with religion, economy and society. It is true that some attempt has been made to diminish this divide. Research on the secular uses of churches and graveyards, for example, has indicated that the distinctions made in earlier studies between the 'sacred' and 'profane' have been too sharply drawn (Davies 1968; Dymond 1999). The underlying premise of the following discussion is a simple and uncontested one: that in a religious society, many areas of practical, mundane existence were infused with sacred connotations and, as people worked in the fields or made journeys about the landscape, their lived environment formed a material context for beliefs extending far beyond the precincts of church and graveyard. The late medieval rural landscape, as it was 'inhabited', was not simply an economic resource: it was infused with layers of spiritual, social and cultural meaning.

Part One: Sacred Landscapes on the Eve of the Reformation

In England, at the turn of the sixteenth century, there were notable regional variations in the organization of ecclesiastical landscapes. These differences were the result of long-term processes and structures developing since the foundations of monasticism, the subsequent expansion of local church building, and evolution of the parochial system. The ecclesiastical functions of the parish were eventually formalised in the twelfth century, a process that effectively fossilized broad regional variations of pastoral provision and parochial organisation (Pounds 2000; Tiller 1992; Winchester 1990). In upland areas, in the north and west of the country, ecclesiastical topographies were defined by large parishes, which were subdivided into townships and chapelries (Winchester 2000a; 2000b; 1997). Here small geographically dispersed settlements, often served by subsidiary chapels, were tied into a wider system of reciprocity and obligation focused on a 'mother church'. In contrast, according to Maitland, the southern lowlands were characterised by much smaller parishes, represented by a single parish church, around which 'parish boundaries seem to draw themselves' (Maitland 1897, 15; cited in Winchester 2000a, 16).

Most studies of the religious landscape assume a rather simple spatial model: a single parish, with a single church forming the arena in which ritual activities were structured and contained. In reality religious topographies were more extensive and pervasive. In the late medieval period, individuals and communities were engaged in ostentatious exhibitions of their religiosity by supporting and embellishing a wide variety of devotional outlets (Rosser 1991;

1996). In Norfolk, a substantial number of villages contained more than one church or chapel, providing diverse arenas for devotional activities. These religious buildings were interspersed with numerous freestanding crosses, shrines and other foci for devotion. Popular belief in the intercessory role of the saints helped to sustain a dense network of sacred sites and produced a landscape defined by ritual movement which linked the more eminent centres of pilgrimage and monastic houses with a host of minor sites, such as holy wells, chapels, hermitages and local churches.

Norfolk supported 928 churches in the medieval period, a number that far exceeded any other county in England: Suffolk, for instance, was divided into 580 parishes, and Essex 415 (Batcock 1991, 1). The majority had probably already come into existence by the time of Domesday, except in areas of new colonisation mainly in the Fens (Batcock 1991; Williamson 1993, 154–163). Various reasons have been proposed to account for this proliferation of church building. Most explanations concur that the density of population and wealth of the region, in the late Anglo Saxon period, were key factors; though it has been pointed out that the number of foundations far exceeded the demands of even Norfolk's burgeoning population, the average size of parishes in the county being only 5.75 square kilometres (Williamson 1993, 158). This ecclesiastical provision added to an already complex network of overlapping territorial jurisdictions. Indeed, such was the proliferation of churches parishes were not always synonymous with villages, or vills. No less than seventy-nine villages contained two or more churches (Batcock 1991, 10). The reasons for this probably varied from place to place. In some cases population growth probably necessitated the building of a second church. The early subdivision of territories is sometimes reflected in place name evidence, for example, those villages with the prefix 'Little' or 'Great' (Batcock 1991, 10). One of the most intriguing outcomes of the county's early parochial history was the foundation of more than one church on the same piece of ground. At Reepham, for example, three churches once stood together within the same yard. Elsewhere, churches were built within close proximity to one another, often on adjoining land. It has been suggested that this may reflect competition between neighbouring lords or, possibly, the activities of freemen dissatisfied with the spiritual provision offered by their lords (Warner 1986). An alternative explanation has been posited by Tom Williamson, that the building of more than one church in the same churchyard may have been the result of the development of social and territorial divisions but the close relationship between churches was intended to maintain links with long established kinship affiliations (Williamson 1993, 159). Whatever the explanation, the long-term repercussion was that Norfolk was particularly well-endowed – perhaps over-endowed – with parish churches in late medieval times.

By the end of the thirteenth century important shifts were underway in the role of churches: no longer the exclusive territory of manorial lords, they were increasingly viewed as the responsibility of the parish community. Between 1350 and 1530 the development of religious faith, based on communion, intercession and penance, was supported and strengthened through the increasingly elaborate ritual apparatus of the Church (Hutton 1996, 413). This had an obvious impact on the material culture of the parish. In particular, the development of the doctrine of Purgatory placed ever greater stress on visual displays of religious devotion, and investment in church buildings was deemed a suitable means of fulfilling penitential work (Brown 1996, 65).

This dense distribution of parish churches was supplemented by numerous more modest religious buildings including: chapels and hermitages endowed by monastic institutions; parochial and non-parochial chapels erected to serve local communities; and private chapels owned by manorial lords. A summary evaluation of the available HER data reveals that 168 chapels, including parochial, guild and private chapels, existed in Norfolk by the sixteenth century. Broadly speaking, parochial chapels or chapels-of-ease were endowed with full rights of baptism and burial, but were obliged to pay dues to their 'mother' church. They were typically associated with regions characterised by a high degree of settlement dispersion where, as in parts of Wales and upland regions such as Cumbria and the Pennines, the chapelry rather than the parish formed the unit of pastoral care (Morris 1989, 276). But in some lowland districts too, the character of settlement sometimes warranted the establishment of additional places of worship. Communities living at least two miles away from their parish church were granted permission to build a chapel (Pounds 2000, 94; Owen 1975). In Norfolk, new chapels were sometimes built to serve Fenland settlements. In the Marshland village of Terrington, for example, a chapel dedicated to St John was built in c.1423 to serve the spiritual needs of parishioners living some distance away from their parish church (Blomefield 1805, IX, 98). But location and population pressure may only be part of the reason for the appearance of such chapels.

Religious buildings formed an important focus for a community, and helped to give it an identity, indicated by the fact that these remote or subsidiary Fenland settlements sometimes took their name from the dedication of their chapel, as at Terrington St John. Away from the Fens, an area where colonisation and reclamation continued on some scale well into the Middle Ages, it might be assumed that the comparatively small size of parishes and the sheer numbers of churches built in the early Middle Ages, would preclude the necessity of building further chapels. But subsidiary chapels did appear in numerous places. Some were erected by particular social groups: in Great Yarmouth, for example, owing to a dispute with Bishop Herbert, the men of Cinque Ports erected their own place of worship in the middle of the twelfth century (HER28931).

In an overview of chapels, N.J.G. Pounds has suggested that the majority could be easily distinguished from parish churches not only by their size but also in terms of building materials and structure, with many being timber-framed and without towers or bells (Pounds 2000, 91). This was a result of their comparative poverty, in part the consequence of the obligation of parishioners to pay tithes to their mother church (Pounds 2000, 391). A number of chapels in late medieval Norfolk, however, were probably former churches, demoted from full parochial status following the demographic and economic changes of the fourteenth and fifteenth centuries. As a result the clear structural distinctions found in other parts of the country cannot so easily be made; the chapel in Little Wacton, for instance, had a tower and that of Shelfanger was bequeathed a bell in 1518 (HER10072; HER14906).

The villages most directly susceptible to the demographic and environmental conditions of the later Middle Ages were those located on the high, waterless interfluves of the chalkland ridge running through west Norfolk. The majority of settlements here had been colonised late, and due to the poor nature of their soils, usually remained small in contrast to their neighbours living in the comparatively fertile river-valleys (Wade Martins and Williamson 1999, 9–13). Following the dramatic population crisis of the late fourteenth and fifteenth centuries the viability of these parishes as separate units was compromised and many were severely depopulated if not entirely deserted. In some places churches became secondary chapels attached to neighbouring parishes. Even after the 'Good Sands' village of Little Ringstead had been deserted, for example, the church continued to function as a chapel until the sixteenth century (Batcock 1991, 11). Clayland parishes were similarly affected; St Mary's in Little Wacton was relegated to chapel status before being finally pulled down in the sixteenth century (HER10072). In an era when the saints were allocated a special place in the landscape, individuals and local groups endeavoured to provide for and maintain such places, and only as a last resort were they actually abandoned. Some became private chapels associated with manorial complexes, used to accommodate priests whose time was devoted to praying for intercessions on behalf of their patron's family. Other private chapels on manorial sites were entirely new foundations in the late Middle Ages. In some cases they may have been used to bolster the authority of the manor not only in terms of the economic and social aspects of its tenants lives but in spiritual matters as well. This is implied in documentary evidence for North Walsham where, in the early sixteenth century, the great hall was used for the manorial court and in the adjacent chapel 'one Sir Thomas Peck a priest did then usuallie reade divine service unto the officers and tenantes of the said mannor' (TNA: PRO, DL4/63/23).

Chantry chapels were also built as freestanding structures either in, or on land adjacent to, churchyards. Church interiors are usually regarded as the most sought after location for memorial artefacts, and most academic attention has focused on the chantry chapels and altars packed into church naves (Morris 1989, 363–366). But such places of private commemoration and devotion were evidently much more widely dispersed across the landscape. Archaeological investigation has recovered structural evidence for the existence of freestanding chapels including, for example, excavation of a building surviving in the north-western corner of St Nicholas' churchyard in Salthouse, uncovered the remains of a brick altar base and fifteenth-century glass fragments (HER1578). Others have surmised that such structures were a far more common sight in the medieval period than the surviving remains would indicate (Rosser 1992). Sometimes field name evidence points to their former existence. Blomefield thus records a 'Chappel Close' in Roydon, the name given to an enclosure adjoining the south side of the churchyard, where a chantry chapel dedicated to the Blessed Virgin once stood. Founded by Robert Morley in the fifteenth century, the chapel provided accommodation for priests to sing for his soul at the altar (Blomefield 1805, I, 40).

Membership of guilds or fraternities provided less wealthy individuals with an outlet for religious expression and sociability. Founded on mutual support some groups became lucrative enough to build guild chapels outside their parish church (Giles 2003; Rosser 1994). In Pulham St Mary the brothers and sisters of St James' Guild founded a chapel situated 'a furlong distant from the church' (Blomefield 1805, V, 392). This proliferation of religious structures might, in part, be seen as evidence for competition and between different individuals and groups (Warner 1986). Alternatively, rather than representing the separation of local factions from the religious life and landscape of the parish community, the building of guild and chantry chapels suggests the complex and multifarious nature of religious belief and practice in the late medieval period which rested upon integration and reciprocity (Rosser 1991, 1994). In order to ensure the perpetuation of their memory, parishioners of all social standing were bound into this mutual relationship. This included the wealthy, who could afford to build private chapels, but were nonetheless reliant upon the prayers of the wider community (Roffey 2003). This relationship is further suggested by the spatial proximity of churches and subsidiary chapels which was, to some extent, comparable to the earlier building of two or more churches on the same parcel of land, or adjoining land (Rosser 1992, 184).

Individuals and local groups employed their physical surroundings as a visible extension of their faith, indicating a degree of spiritual separation and individual choice, while also maintaining links with their 'community', both past and present. The memories of elderly parishioners, recorded in the late sixteenth century, sometimes allude to the spiritual contours of the pre-Reformation landscape. In 1586 the inhabitants of the south Norfolk village of Tibenham recalled their lost guild chapel 'of purpose erected and buylt ... repayred and mayntened with the stock of the ... fraternities'. During the reign of Henry VIII a 'gild' or 'soul priest' had been appointed to pray for the souls of the brothers and sisters of two guilds dedicated to St Thomas and Our Lady. The apparent gender division between guilds points to another means by which people demonstrated their individuality while supporting the spiritual and material structures of their parish. This dual sense of personal faith and collective piety and responsibility was further emphasised in the geographical location of the chapel, on land adjoining the churchyard, and also its integrative social functions as the place where marriages and town feasts were celebrated (TNA: PRO, E133/4/667). Clearly for the inhabitants of Tibenham their parish church formed just one arena where they could express their faith and secure intercessions.

Information contained in late medieval wills provides further insights into late medieval spiritual geographies. A great range of religious structures and buildings were deemed worthy of their charitable investment. In Beachamwell, for example, gifts were frequently made to the various guilds and the three separate churches in the parish, and in some cases to the church of St Botolph in the neighbouring parish of Shingham (Davison 1988, 7). In 1518 Matthew Haylett of Winfarthing, as well as making legacies to the parish church, bequeathed a bell to the chapel of St Andrew in neighbouring Shelfanger (HER14906). In his will of 1456 Benedict Laweys specified his preference to be buried in the churchyard of St Michael of Braydeston, but also left 10d to the cost of repairing the chapel of St Clement's in Brundal (Johnson 1925, 204). It is not adequate to view the comparative wealth of religious buildings as indicative of their importance, rather churches and chapels, even failing ones, provided a complementary function (Rosser 1996, 77). Religious buildings and structures were not conceived of in isolation but were integrated within much wider topographies of commemoration and devotion: in Tilley's words: 'Places are always 'read' or understood in relation to others' (Tilley 1994, 27).

Monastic landscapes

A range of buildings and structures of monastic origin further increased the already dense distribution of churches and chapels in Norfolk. Monastic houses and monuments structured local and regional topographies, and a range of associated place-names attached to roads and fields provided a framework for working and moving through the landscape. Until relatively recently modest monastic houses were generally disregarded as having no real importance, either for our understanding of medieval religious history, or indeed landscape history (Gilchrist 1995; Rasmussen 2003). A number of small, relatively poor monastic houses, nunneries, chapels, hospitals, hermitages and cells existed, and whether ordinary lay-folk had regular contact with the inhabitants of these buildings or not, their presence in the landscape could not be ignored. The extent to which the lay community came into direct contact with the inhabitants of monastic houses and their affiliated institutions is not of issue here, but rather recognition of the enrichment of religious topographies through a wide-reaching geography of monastic provision.

Of particular interest here are the long-standing, recurrent connections made between monastic sites and certain kinds of places and environments. Since the earliest days of monasticism in the seventh century, there was a general preference for remote and challenging settings (Morris 1989, 128; Williamson 1993, 146–49). In Norfolk monastic communities, including those at Castle

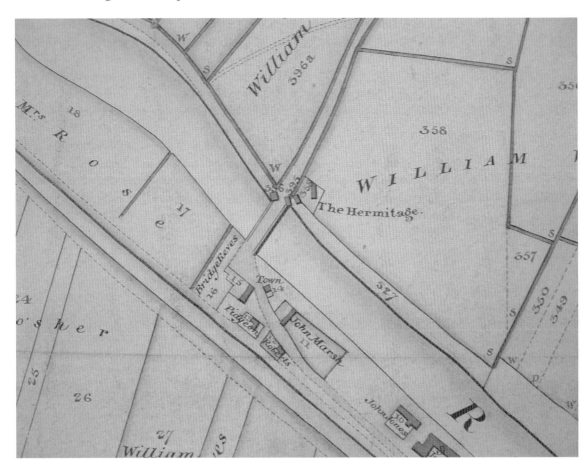

Acre, St Benet at Holme, Pentney and Langley, found isolation in areas of low-lying marsh and fen grounds. Similar topographical patterns are also evident in the location of more modest monastic houses, including nunneries, hospitals, chapels and hermitages (Gilchrist 210). Nunneries were founded in the isolated fens of west Norfolk, including Crabhouse and Catsholme, founded on an island in the fens of Methwold. In general remote, marginal or liminal places, such as topographical boundaries, river-crossings and bridges, tended to be chosen by solitary ascetics (Gilchrist 1995, 115).

Bridges were a distinctive feature of Christian theology, representing the role of Christ, bishops and popes as intermediaries to God. This symbolism may have encouraged the placing of small chapels and hermitages on bridges (Duffy 1992, 367). Certainly, there are numerous examples of the association recorded from Norfolk in both rural and urban areas (Gilchrist 1995, 173–4). Archaeological remains together with historic, and sometimes surviving, place-names suggest the former existence of such sites. Writing in 1739 Francis Blomefield recorded that the foundations of a small oratory or hermitage could still be observed at a place called 'Stonebridge' in Banham (Blomefield,

FIGURE 3. In the medieval period chapels and hermitages were commonly found on or close to bridges. Many, including 'The Hermitage' in Stow Bardolph, continued to be remembered in local place-names long after the religious reforms of the sixteenth century (NRO, HARE 6832).

1805, I, 358). Cartographic material is also useful in revealing the former locations of monastics (Figure 3). The tithe map of Acle, for instance, shows a hermitage located next to Magdalen Bridge, which carries the main road from Norwich to Yarmouth across the River Bure (NRO, 662). The site was formerly Weybridge Priory, dedicated to St Mary (Messent 1934, 9) its presence continues to be preserved in local place names as the 'Hermitage Marshes' (TG4153). In deposition evidence taken during a dispute in Attlebridge the deponents described a piece of Alder Carr as being 'by the highway by the stone bridge on the south and the hermitage ground on the west and the old River on the east' (TNA: PRO, E134/30Eliz/East25), almost certainly indicating the site of the former hermitage. There is documentary and archaeological evidence for bridge chapels in Wiveton (HER6141), Bawburgh (HER9383), Outwell (HER25839), and Kings Lynn (HER5551). As well as symbolizing the social detachment of the hermits dwelling there, bridge locations suggest the importance of finding a site that was both visible and accessible, reflecting a desire to be of service to others above reclusiveness (Gilchrist 1995, 170).

Donations received from travellers were put towards the repair of roads and bridges and other good works such lighthouses (Gilchrist, 1995, 173; Clay 1914: 50). By interweaving secular tasks with devotional practices hermits, therefore, made an essential contribution to the maintenance of communication routes, as well as tending to the spiritual needs of travellers. This was part of a wider fusion of mundane and sacred practices. As Duffy has emphasised, 'all contributions to the comfort of one's neighbours were understood as a dimension of the promotion of charity, the divine life of the community' (Duffy 1992, 368), and late medieval wills often, for example, included bequests for the upkeep of roads. In 1482 Robert Paston for example left money to the chapel by the bridge in Wiveton (Pevsner 2002a, 729; HER6141).

Similarly hospital and lazar houses occupied liminal places – outside town gates, on parish boundaries, along main routeways and bridges – although in this case a proximity to water may also have had an important practical and probably symbolic purpose (Gilchrist 1995, 43; Rawcliffe 2005). In Horning for instance the hospital, founded in 1153 to serve as the last pilgrimage stop for travellers making their way to St Benet's Abbey, was situated on the opposite side of the River Ant from the monastery (HER8444): the river formed, in effect, a symbolic barrier separating the holy arena from the secular landscape beyond. Other examples include St Mary and St Lawrence's Chapel in Ickburgh, apparently used as a leper house in the early fourteenth century, located near the bridge and adjacent to the parish boundary with Mundford (HER5083; Pevsner 2002b, 447). A leper hospital in Stalham occupied a peripheral site in the parish overlooking the River Ant, known today as 'Chapel Field' (HER8329; Messent 1934, 67).

Boundaries were particularly suitable places to house lepers, for they signified the 'liminal' status of the occupants: 'having often been obliged to relinquish his material possessions on admission, he was, in the eyes of the church, neither dead or alive, neither in heaven nor on earth, neither an outcast nor a full member of the community' (Rawcliffe 1997, 16). The location of many examples at prominent road junctions and river crossings enhanced their visual impact, suggesting that segregation of the inhabitants was not of primary concern (Rawcliffe, 2005). Conspicuous locations also provided a necessary visual reminder to travellers of the need for charitable giving. Racheness leper house in South Acre, with its associated church dedicated to St Bartholomew (the site is still known as 'Bartholomew's Hill') is situated at a junction of five routeways, as well as being adjacent to the parish boundary (TF818132). Such a location ensured that the hospital was encountered by the greatest number of travellers who were, as it was hoped, encouraged to pray for the benefactor's soul and offer donations as they passed. Moreover, physical prominence served to remind passers-by of the severity of divine retribution for sin: sexual transgressions were considered to cause leprosy, for example (Gilchrist 1995, 48, 210). Following the decline in the prevalence of leprosy from the late fourteenth century many continued to function as infirmaries, almshouses or as refuges for the mentally ill (Gilchrist 1995, 38).

It is unlikely that contemporaries viewed these buildings in isolation, but rather as part of a wider network of religious sites, not least because institutional ties often connected them. Hermits were thus often associated with larger institutions: that at Magdalen Gate in Norwich for example was affiliated to the nearby leper hospital at Sprowston (Gilchrist 1995, 175). Great Hautbois parish church, where the celebrated image of St Theobald was housed, attracted so many pilgrims that a hospital appropriated to Coxford Priory was built 200m to the south of the church in order to provide them with hospitality (Batcock 1991, 97). As well as the spatial connections made between various places, people carried with them detailed cognitive maps of a spiritual world existing far beyond parochial bounds. The links between individuals and regional, sometimes national, places of pilgrimage are revealed in bequests made in late medieval wills (Duffy 1992, 190–205). In her will dating to 1478 Alice Cooke of Horstead made special provisions to pay homage to the image of St Wandregesilus housed in the parish church of Bixley (Blomefield 1805, V, 449; Pevsner 2002b, 207); while in 1507 Agnes Parker of Keswick left money in lieu of promised pilgrimages, never carried out: 'I owe a pilgrimage to Canterbury, another to St Tebbald of Hobbies (St Theobald of Hautbois), and another to St Albert at Cringleford (Blomefield 1805, V, 297; Batcock 1991, 96).

Produced by an elite minority medieval wills, as a source of evidence, can only offer a partial view of contemporary perceptions of the spiritual landscape. There is however, corroborative material evidence, including the representation of esteemed saints within church interiors, which points to the wider integration of religious places in the popular mind. Regional cult centres provided people with focal points other than their local parish churches. One of the best known Norfolk examples is the celebrated shrine of St Walstan, housed in the chancel of Bawburgh church. Popular between the late thirteenth and early sixteenth century, St Walstan was 'a saint of the common people', and 'a petitioner for labourers' (James 1917, 264; Duffy 1992, 204). The regional popularity of the saint is suggested by the distribution of surviving images in village churches, which suggests devotion among wealthier parishioners (Duffy 1992, 200). Eight rood screens retain his image, often represented by a scythe, all located within a seventeen-mile radius of Bawburgh at Barnham Broom, Litcham, Burlingham St Andrew, Denton, Ludham, Sparham, St James' in Norwich, and possibly Beeston. The inhabitants of these parishes evidently understood their place of worship as part of a diffuse network of churches and shrines

Clearly people living in the late medieval period made connections linking together a number of religious places, shrines and images. Parish churches, monastic houses and their various affiliated structures were not viewed in isolation but were threaded together in complex and multiple ways. Descriptions of the everyday religious life of the parish as an enclosed world in which religious beliefs and practices were contained within the walls of parish churches or guild chapels, overlooks the significance of the surrounding landscape. These buildings did not exist in empty, spiritually meaningless space. Everyday tasks and movement through the landscape served to reinforce religious associations and meanings. The integration of key topographical points – such as boundaries, river crossings and crossroads – helped structure and gave spiritual context to the ordinary aspects of everyday life. At other times meanings were reinforced through collective rituals and performance. Organised processions through the landscape, during Rogation week for example, heightened the interrelationship between churches and chapels and their wider geographical and social settings (discussed below pp. 36–37). On a more extensive spatial level, the personal journeys of devotion made by pilgrims were marked by a series of material symbols and signs, which stretched across regional and even national topographies.

Pilgrimage

For the medieval pilgrim the journey itself was as symbolically important as reaching the eventual destination, and it is useful to conceptualise pilgrimage routes in the kinds of phenomenological terms as suggested by archaeologists (Tilley 1994). By considering the ways people moved through the landscape, and the material forms they encountered and took meaning from, we can begin to understand the important role the landscape played in shaping and reinforcing late medieval religious beliefs and practices. Over time, particular routes took on specific meanings in relation to the places they connected, and as a result played a significant role in structuring peoples' experiences of the places they were travelling to (Tilley 1994, 31). Pilgrims' routes were inscribed with monuments and buildings, including wayside chapels and crosses which, when taken together, deepened the spiritual experience of the journey itself. In Norfolk, the main routes leading to the famous shrine of the Virgin Mary at Walsingham were enhanced by a number of wayside chapels including: St

Catherine's in East Barsham, which has niches cut into the walls around the door probably used as receptacles for receiving donations (HER2068); St Margaret's in Hilborough (LeStrange 1973, 52; HER2711); St. James' in Hillington (NRO, NRS 21381; Figure 4); and the hospital and chapel of St Paul in Billingford provided accommodation for poor pilgrims (HER7215; Messent 1934).

FIGURE 4. The pilgrims' route from King's Lynn to Walsingham was marked by a number of modest religious buildings and monuments. In Hillington, the pilgrims' chapel dedicated to St James and two freestanding crosses (one of which is shown here, bottom left) were an integral part of late medieval religious topographies (NRO, NRS 21381).

The elaboration of routeways was of particular importance for villages wishing to promote local shrines in order to attract visitors (Lawson 1983; Webb 2000), and in a variety of ways they could act as a stimulus for local economies (Ogden 2002). The pilgrims' chapel in Litcham, reputedly visited by Henry VIII (Messent 1934, 42), attracted a major horse-hiring business for pilgrims located on Litcham Common (Rutledge 1995, 241). In Hunstanton a chapel was built to accommodate travellers who made the journey to the healing waters that bubbled up through the coastal cliffs (HER1291). Another at Stanhoe provided accommodation for people making the journey between Hunstanton and Walsingham (Messent 1934). Many of these chapels were directly associated with monasteries, such as the travellers hospice in Billingford and the hospice of St James in Horning. In West Acre a chapel dedicated to St Thomas à Becket, was used for parochial purposes by the hamlet of Custhorpe and was also regularly visited by travellers on their way to Walsingham. Affiliated to West Acre Priory, the chapel housed a small number of canons in an annexed cell. According to

Blomefield large numbers from the surrounding area attended an annual fair held here on the feast day of its patron saint, on July the seventh (Blomefield 1805, IX, 164–5). As well as being of economic advantage, the spiritual and temporal accommodation offered by a number of villages throughout the region had further importance in strengthening the collective spiritual identities of local societies.

Chapels located on the main pilgrims' routes should therefore be examined as part of the wider iconography of pilgrimage: a network of sacred places 'read' in relation to one another. Such meanings and associations were reflected, for instance, in the names given to roads. Unsurprisingly references to Walsingham occurred with some frequency, especially in villages lying between Kings Lynn and the celebrated pilgrimage centre, including Gaywood (Bradfer-Lawrence 1932) and Hillington (NRO, NRS 21381). Similar names also occur in Necton (HER2729) and nearby Ashill, where according to an early sixteenth-century survey, 'a medowe called normore conteynyng vij acr and lyeth to Walsingham wey and Bery Wey west', possibly indicating a wider geography of pilgrimage that in this case incorporated Bury St Edmunds in Suffolk (Reid 1984, 20). Likewise in Binham 'Walsingham Way' provided a spiritual connection linking the local priory to the shrine at Walsingham (NRO, Hayes and Storr 10).

Pilgrimage routes were further embellished with stone and wooden crosses. Documented examples include 'Goodales Cross' which was apparently situated on the 'Walsingham Way' in Necton in c.1427 (HER2729). The archaeological record, together with cartographic and written material (mostly dating to the post-Reformation period), sometimes allows us glimpses of the way structures related to each other in this late medieval ritual landscape. The map evidence for Hillington, for example, shows two crosses on the stretch of the Walsingham Way leading to the pilgrims' chapel of St James (Figure 4). It is notable that both crosses appear to occupy space in the centre of road junctions, suggesting a deliberate channelling of movement around the structures (NRO, NRS 21381). Villages located along the main pilgrimage routes, may have deliberately set up crosses in order to heighten the approach to Walsingham, and in the case of Hillington, for example, the route to St James' chapel. The proliferation of crosses serves to reinforce the existence of a symbolic and meaningful landscape outside the precincts of religious buildings.

We have seen how medieval pilgrims may have understood the various religious structures and buildings they encountered on their journeys: in relation to one another and in relation to their eventual destination. In this context, crosses and chapels became part of a symbolic language of material signifiers. But landscapes were interpreted in a number of ways. Crosses were integral to the visual culture of commemoration, performance and ritual; for local people they were part of a rich tapestry of spiritual outlets.

Monuments in the landscape

Stone and wooden crosses were perhaps the most ubiquitous elements in this late medieval religious landscape and yet, aside from the work carried out in the early part of last century (Cozens-Hardy 1935; Vallance 1920), they have been largely overlooked by modern historians. Representing the suffering that Christ endured in order to save Mankind the cross, is perhaps, the greatest symbol of the Christian faith. Such studies as there have been have tended to focus on elucidating the origins of this form of sculpture and it has been argued, for instance, that given the longevity of the association of stone in pagan and prehistoric ritual landscapes many early examples, in the north and west of the country at least, may have been converted from existing monoliths (Vallance 1920, 27; Wood 1987). In Norfolk, however, the lack of suitable stone ensured that monoliths were not a frequent feature of the early landscape, and the earliest crosses seem to have been erected simply to provide a religious focal point in settlements prior to the building of churches. Fragments of Anglo-Saxon crosses have thus been found at the deserted settlement site of Barrett Ringstead (HER1115); at the ruined church of All Saints in the former settlement of Wella (HER2635) later amalgamated with Beachamwell; and from the site of St Helen's church in Santon (HER5684; see also Pevsner 2002b, 520 and HER4207).

As well as preceding the erection of some churches, in the course of the Middle Ages many crosses were erected beside them, in churchyards. A Statute of Worcester II, dating to 1229, stipulated that each churchyard should contain 'a decent and comely cross to which there may be a procession on Palm Sunday' (Dymond 1999, 464). By the end of the Middle Ages, the Palm Sunday procession was 'the most elaborate and eloquent of the processions of the Sarum rite' (Duffy 1992, 23). Celebrated on the Sunday before Easter to commemorate Christ's triumphal entry into Jerusalem, the ceremony took parishioners from inside their church in a ritual procession to the churchyard cross. Just as the laity were responsible for furnishing the nave with the ritual apparatus needed to support their devotional interests so too were they involved in embellishing the churchyard. Henry Bunn of the parish of Hardley, for example, made provision for a cross to be erected in the churchyard for the offering of boughs on Palm Sunday (Vallance 1920, 13). Proximity to churchyard crosses may have influenced locations for burial. In his will dating to 1428 Robert Fayerman, of North Pickenham, requested to be interred in the churchyard 'nexte unto the Crosse ther stondyng' (Cozens-Hardy 1935, 323).

Vast numbers of freestanding crosses were also set up beside roads. Figure 5 shows the location of known examples in Norfolk, it is however a considerable underestimation of the late-medieval total. Place-name evidence for many parishes suggests that many had more than one example. Road-names in Barton Bendish, for example, indicate the former existence of 'Wilsted or Worsted

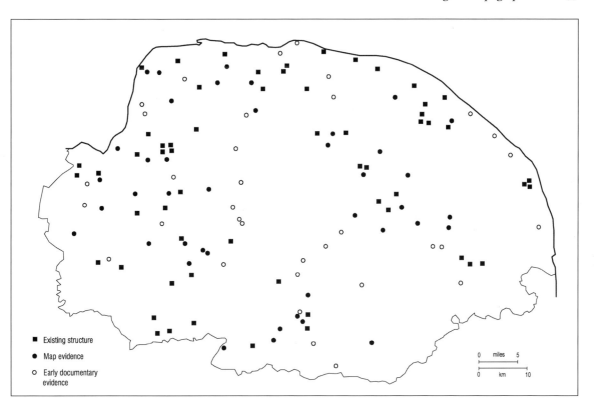

FIGURE 5. The
distribution of
freestanding wayside
crosses in Norfolk.

Cross', 'Gent's Cross' and 'Stone Cross', all located at crossroads (Rogerson 1987, 32). Elsewhere in Marham, the 'White Cross' was depicted as an extant structure on an eighteenth-century map, while the place-names 'Maiden's Cross' and 'Stub Cross' indicate the presence of two more (NRO, HARE 6814), and map evidence for Hunstanton includes place-name references to the 'White Cross' and 'Stump Cross' (NRO, LEST/OA1; Figure 6).

In its most basic form the wayside cross was comprised of a shaft recessed into a socket stone or pedestal using lead and, although no head of a cross survives in Norfolk, it probably consisted of a capital and head (Cozens–Hardy 1935, 298). Some were evidently made from wood. A document dating to 1429, for example, refers to 'repairing the Black Cross on the Highway' in Kimberley, almost certainly a wooden cross painted with pitch (HER12356). Many crosses were evidently made of freestone, their names alluding to the light colour of the limestone they were made from. 'Le whytecrosse' standing on the main highway in Horsham St Faiths is thus mentioned in a charter of 1566, and a map of Quidenham made in 1681 refers to 'Whitecross Drift' (HER26330; HER9160). The remains of the latter survive on the parish boundary with Snetterton in a plantation still named 'Whitecross drift'. Other examples include 'White Cross Lane' in Emneth included on Faden's map of Norfolk, published in 1797; the 'White Cross' in Banham, a 'White Cross' at a road junction in Hardingham, and another in Burgh-next-Aylsham (Cozens-Hardy 1935, 303).

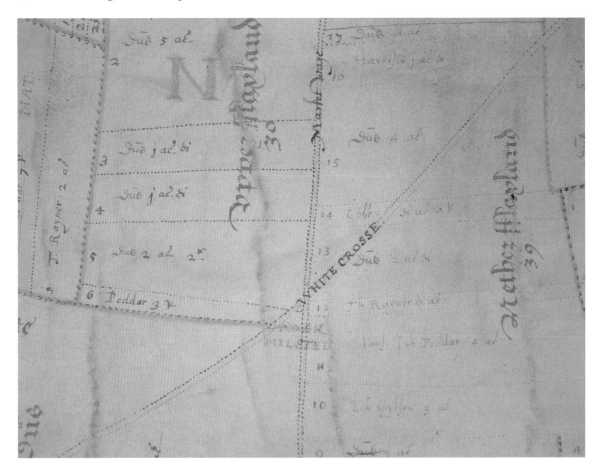

FIGURE 6. The 'White Crosse', revealed on a map dating to 1615, once marked a crossroads in the open fields of Hunstanton. Minor place-names are often the only surviving indication of the late medieval spiritual landscape (NRO, LESTOA1).

Placing them on earthwork mounds, either specifically constructed ones or existing earthworks, enhanced the visibility of crosses. For example, in 1720 John Martin recorded his journey across the open heaths of Breckland and noted the remains of a cross located on a hill between Weeting and Methwold (Cozens-Hardy 1935, 329). In Feltwell, similarly, the remains of a cross still survive on 'Cross Hill' (HER4938), and at Titchwell the base and shaft of a cross survive on a low grass mound (HER1359). In a very obvious way the use of existing mounds, many of which were probably ancient burial mounds, evokes a powerful Christian metaphor, the Hill of Golgotha. Furthermore, the apparent appropriation of prehistoric burial mounds in the Christian landscape suggests the ongoing interpretation and reuse of ancient monuments within new cultural settings, a matter we shall return to in chapter five.

There is evidence to suggest that some wayside crosses were originally set up as memorials. The ubiquitous concern in the late medieval period to secure prayers in order to ease the traumas of purgatory necessitated a series of mnemonic devices intended to remind the living of their duty to pray for the souls of the dead. For those of more humble means this usually amounted to their inclusion on the parish bede-roll, described by Duffy as a 'form of immortality' giving parishioners 'a vivid sense of the permanence and security of their place, large or small, within the community of the parish' (Duffy 1992, 334–5). As we have seen wealthier members of the community could afford to provide more conspicuous reminders by building chantry chapels, either within parish church interiors or as freestanding structures outside, and embellishing them with tombs, brasses and inscriptions. Wayside crosses were also, in some cases at least, part of this highly visual language of remembrance. The cross at Drayton, for example, was inscribed with the words 'you who pray for the souls of William Beaumont and Joanna his wife, saying a Paternoster and an Ave Maria will earn [illegible] days pardon' (Cozens-Hardy 1935, 308). In the majority of cases the natural processes of weathering, coupled with Reformation zeal, have removed such inscriptions but it seems likely that similar epitaphs were engraved on other monuments. This is certainly suggested by the way that a number of crosses were named after particular individuals or families. For example, a description of the bounds of Necton dating to c.1427 refers to 'Sparkys Cross', apparently a wooden monument erected by one Walter Sparke (HER29730).

As part of the wider geography of commemoration, individuals paid for the erection of wayside crosses, to immortalise their charitable work in repairing highways and bridges, and thus providing another means of attaining intercessions. Peter Payn of Banham, for example, bequeathed money for the repair of 'Hardewyk Way' and to set up a cross at the end of it 'where the way parts' (Blomefield 1805, I, 337). The crosses associated with bridges, like that erected on Barford Bridge in 1501 (HER12240) may likewise be associated with repairs and route maintenance. Parallels can be drawn between the decision to site chapels and hermitages at road junctions and bridges and the setting up of crosses. By utilising such locations members of the lay community ensured that the largest audience would encounter their memorials, and would in turn be reminded to pray for them. There is an interesting relationship here between the original, personal motivations for erecting crosses and their integration in wider social and cultural discourses, especially over long periods of time. Although many crosses may have been originally intended as *aides-mémoire*, a more general significance and purpose can be traced in contemporary literature.

A popular treatise on the Ten Commandments dating to 1496 emphasised the role of the symbol of the cross in keeping spiritual matters at the forefront of peoples' minds, noting: 'For this reason ben Crosses by ye waye, that when folke passynge see the Crosse, they sholde thynke on Hym that deyed on the Crosse, and worshypp Hym above all thynge' (Vallance 1920, 1). With this in mind it is noteworthy how many crosses appear to have been placed on road junctions leading to churches or chapels. Mick Aston refers to this association in relation to parishes in the West Country, where the paths taken between outlying farmsteads and their parish churches were frequently marked by granite crosses (Aston 1985, 145). Cartographic evidence from Norfolk serves to corroborate this spatial relationship. A map of 1649, for example, shows crosses on two road junctions leading to Salthouse parish church (printed in Stagg 2003, 56–7). In Marham two freestanding crosses once marked crossroads on Churchgate Way, and the 'White Cross' was situated at the junction of 'White Cross Way' and 'Maiden Cross', located some distance from the village, in the open fields (NRO, HARE 6814: Figures 7 and 8). Additional examples include Hillington (NRO, NRS 21381), Sharrington, Brandiston and Cockthorpe (Cozens-Hardy 1935).

Some might argue that the location of many crosses at road junctions was not coincidental. Road junctions were invested with a range of metaphysical associations: they were deemed to be places of magical properties and sometimes malevolent activities (Puhvel 1976, 171). In the eighth-century Penitential of Egbert, reiterated by William of Malmesbury in the twelfth century, crossroads were associated with supernatural phenomena (Morris 1989, 60). According to one early seventh-century source from the Continent attempts were already being made to curb these beliefs: 'no Christian should place lights at temples, or stones, or springs, or trees, or ad cellos (at sanctuaries) or at places where three ways meet' (Bonser 1934, cited in Morris 1989, 60). Crossroads continued to be associated with such connotations into the late medieval and post-medieval periods, most notably being used as a place to bury suicide victims (see below, p. 160). Richard Gough, in his history of the Shropshire parish of Myddle, mentioned a road junction along the way to the church, referred to as the 'crosse way', known anciently as the Setts: 'because in time of popery, the people, when they went that way with a Corps to be buried, they did sett down the Corps, and kneeling round about it did mumble over some prayers, eyther for the sole of the deceased, or for themselves' (Hey 1981, 68). There are signs of similar traditions in Norfolk: it was tradition for coffin bearers journeying to East Runton church to stop at Oxwell Cross: 'to quench their thirst from the pure cold water from the spring on the other side' (Leake 1987, 6). In these, and numerous other ways, links were forged between the parish church, and the various minor religious foci in the surrounding landscape.

By examining the geographical and social context of crosses we can begin to understand the ways monuments, originally constructed by individuals for a particular purpose, came to structure and give meaning to peoples' everyday experiences of their physical surroundings. At certain times in the year the social function of crosses was reinforced during collective events and rituals. The annual event of perambulating parish boundaries during Rogation week was among the most celebrated of these gatherings (Hutton 1996) and freestanding crosses provided a material and cognitive framework for those taking part. Before the religious reforms of the sixteenth century, it was customary to offer payers at prescribed landmarks, such as crosses, along processional routes as is suggested by the name 'Preaching Cross Fields' recorded on the tithe map of Barsham

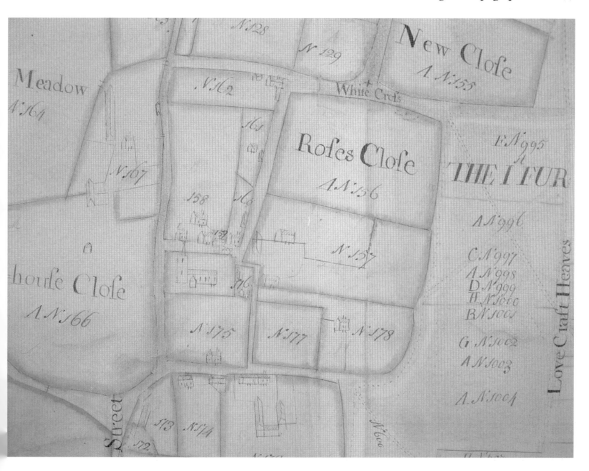

FIGURE 7. Crosses were often set up on routeways leading to parish churches. The 'White Cross' in Marham was one of two crosses erected on 'Churchgate Way' (NRO, HARE 6814). The names given to roads, and the monuments set up beside them provided tangible links between the church and wider landscape.

(HER15477). Memories of pre-Reformation rituals, recorded during a late sixteenth-century court case from Swaffham Prior (Cambridgeshire), confirm the role of crosses as elements of the ritual landscape. Maude Genne remembered that two crosses, both of stone 'wear made and sett for the particon of the severall townshipps of Burwell and Swaffhm and … the pishoners of Swaffhm did goe in pression to the said crosses and said certaine epistells gospells or other prayers at ther anncient and uttermoste bounds' (TNA: PRO, E134/28Eliz/Hil5). Given that Rogationtide processions took place over the course of several days, it is possible that some of the wayside crosses located away from parish boundaries were incorporated as parishioners journeyed back and forth from their church. The carrying of crosses about the fields was believed to be an effective way of warding off the devil: according to one contemporary 'wher soo ever the devyll … doo see the syne of this crosse, he flees, he byddes not, he strykys not, he cannot hurte' (John Longland 1535, cited in Duffy 1992, 280). The presence of crosses standing amid arable fields may have had a similar significance to the reading of prayers over growing crops. Indeed, permanent structures would have provided protection against malevolent forces on a daily basis.

FIGURE 8. The 'White Cross' and 'Churchgate Way', shown in Marham in 1723 (NRO, HARE 6814).

Crosses were not only used to mark out parish boundaries: they seem to have been used to define territorial or property boundaries more generally. It has been noted, for example, that crosses were used to demarcate monastic property (Muir 2004, 57). In Norfolk the manor of Hemsby was owned by Norwich Cathedral Priory and the 'Sellerer's Cross' was apparently set up by the Cellerer as a visible statement of monastic landownership (Cornford 1984); elsewhere Pentney Priory placed a cross, still extant and remarkable for its unusual construction, on the route-way leading between the village church and priory (HER3925). Presumably the iconography of such crosses would have been designed to distinguish them from the vast numbers encountered along the highways and boundaries of other jurisdictions. Several were used to mark out the jurisdiction of Norwich including the boundary cross, mentioned in a charter dating to 1461, situated at the junction of 'Yermouth Way' in Thorpe St Andrew or that located in Hellesdon, since removed to the churchyard (TNA: PRO, MR52; HER37469). 'Hardley Cross', set at the junction of the rivers Yare and Chet, indicated the boundary between Norwich and Great Yarmouth river jurisdiction (HER10424).

Some crosses marked the boundaries of a number of overlapping jurisdictions. In deposition evidence presented in 1609 the inhabitants of Horsey remembered that they had 'allways gone in their perambulations to the headles crosse which divideth the bounds of Horsey, Wynterton and Waxham' (Cozens-Hardy 1935, 315). The same 'headless cross' featured in an earlier document dating to 1542 as one of a series of landmarks separating the manors of Palling and Horsey and their respective customary rights to the 'wreke of sea'. This particular cross evidently provided a boundary marker for a number of overlapping units of administration: manorial, hundred, and parish:

> that should happen upon the grounds adjoining to the sea side extending from the tree called mortree standing between Eccles and Palling and so thence to a cross in Palling and from the same crosse unto a certain deke called Wynkyll dike and a crosse in the grounds called hedlasse crosse by the same dike devyding the hundreds of Happyng Eastflegg and Westflegge (Cozens Hardy 1935, 315).

Blurring the boundaries: church and landscape

The versatile function of the church itself, as a focal point for a range of rituals and beliefs, gave place to practices of which many appear to have been scarcely doctrinal in origin (Duffy 1992, 13). They also point to the fact that medieval societies did not compartmentalise the social, economic, and religious strands of everyday life as we do today, rather they were woven into a complex interlocking pattern. An illustrative example of this is the practice of keeping plough lights burning in churches, before the Sacrament or possibly the Rood (Duffy 1992, 13). The majority of evidence for the practice comes from the main arable producing areas of the East Midlands and East Anglia (Hutton 1996, 124). At Knapton, in Norfolk, each of the three ancient divisions of the parish (presumably manorial), provided a plough light for their parish church (Hutton 1996, 124; for other examples see Bolingbroke 1898, 201; Leake 1987, 16). A 'plough gallery' still survives in the nave of Cawston church its beam inscribed with a fertility prayer that makes an appreciative connection between ploughing and ale (Duffy 1992, 13; Pevsner 2002a, 429):

> God spede the plow
> And send us all corne enow
> our purpose for to mak
> at crow of cok of ye plowlete of Sygate
> Be merry and glade
> wat Goodale yis work mad.

In some parishes the significance of 'the plough' was visually expressed inside churches, where they were stored on special mounts. These were probably communal ploughs loaned out to poorer parishioners unable to afford their own equipment (Hutton 1996, 124). 'Plough Monday' fell on the first Monday after Twelfth Night and marked the commencement of the ploughing season. By the late fifteenth century it was also a time for fund-raising and included popular revels such as dragging a plough around the village to attract donations for parish funds (Hutton 1996, 125).

There is evidence to suggest that the installation of the material apparatus relating to farming activities within church interiors was mirrored in the keeping of shrines and lights in the wider landscape, particularly alongside routeways. In Witton, wills dating to 1479 and 1524 both include bequests to be made to the plough light in Nethergate Street. From the same village another will dating to 1506 mentions plough lights in Nethergate Street, Woodgate and Marshegate: roads radiating northwards, southwards and eastwards from the parish church (Lawson 1988, 85–87). In Cawston the 'plough light of Sygate' mentioned in the fertility prayer, refers to a road of the same name and strongly suggests the presence of a light kept there during the ploughing season. The road name 'Sygate' was recorded on two maps dating to 1580 and 1599 (NRO, MC 341/12 706x4a; NRO, MS 4521). Elsewhere in Salle bequests were made for four plough and virgin lights, described as 'those of Marshgate, Kirkgate, Lunton, and Steynwade' and Roger Glover apparently provided '7d for sustaining the light before the cross of Northgate on Marshgreen called Mayden Light' (Parsons 1937, 117–18). Some crosses also seem to have been focal points for votive offerings and were possibly associated with small wayside shrines. That at Aylmerton, situated at a crossroads on the parish boundary, had a niche cut into its side, which has been identified as a receptacle for offerings (Cozens-Hardy 1935, 300).

As well as embellishing the land with monuments and artefacts, existing natural and archaeological features were integrated within this already dense network of spiritual references. As distinctive features prehistoric earthworks, such as barrows for example, were often employed as boundary markers. Their practical, socio-economic functions also afforded ancient features with ritual significance as reflected in the names given to 'Gospel Hill' in Little Cressingham and 'Procession Hill' in Thetford, both possible barrows once used to mark out parish jurisdictions and, as indicated by their names, provided important focal points during annual perambulations.

Wells and springs provided other key features of the late medieval ritual landscape. The veneration of springs has a long history, dating back to pre-Christian times, although there is considerable debate over whether popular cult practices surviving in the late medieval period really represent the last vestiges of an earlier, more complex, and more prolific network of sacred sites. Many, probably most, dedications to obscure saints arose during the Middle Ages, as part of the more general development of a diffuse religious landscape already outlined. Originally some of the names attached to wells may have alluded to more mundane human interactions with their landscape. For example, the derivation of wells attributed to St. Helen may be from OE *ellern* meaning 'elder tree' (Morris 1989, 86). The etymology of Shadwell in Norfolk probably means *scead wylla* simply 'boundary well'; the extant well is situated close to the point where the boundaries of Guiltcross and Shropham hundreds meet (Williamson 1993, 142). The well became associated with the Anglo-Saxon bishop St Chad who died in 673 (Bond 1914). But it seems likely that rather than reflecting the contemporaneous veneration of the saint this was a relatively late association, developing when the parochial system became established in the twelfth century. Some writers have argued that the majority of 'holy wells' probably emerged during the period 1200–1500 (Morris 1989, 91).

The close proximity of churches to wells and springs, especially in western Britain, has also been interpreted as evidence of the Christianisation of earlier cult sites, although the need to ensure a supply of water for baptism, and for washing the chalice, was probably a factor (Hooke 1998, 16–19). 'Our Lady's Well' for example, depicted on the first edition Ordnance Survey map of Burnham Norton, provided the nearby Carmelite Priory, founded in honour of the Virgin Mary, with clean water. To the south of the remains of Coxford Priory the Ordnance Survey records the intriguingly named 'Mary Bone's Well', which strongly suggests an association with the priory of the same dedication founded in the twelfth century. Of course many holy wells were lauded for their healing properties and held an important place within the itineraries of medieval pilgrims, such as the famous wells at Walsingham for example (Warner 1879). Either way, a number of wells are located within parish churchyards in Norfolk, including St Withburga's Well in Dereham, and the wells dedicated

FIGURE 9. Natural landmarks were integrated within pre-Reformation religious topographies, particularly where there was an obvious physical connection between them and places of holy significance. 'Ladyes Well' in Appleton, depicted in 1617, linked the church to the wider landscape (NRO, BRA 2524/6).

to St Walstan at Bawburgh and Costessey (Farmer 1984). A map of Appleton
dating to 1617 shows 'Ladys Well' in the churchyard of St Mary's Church
(NRO, BRA 2524/6) (Figure 9); and St Helen's Well in Santon Downham was
associated with St Helen's Church (HER5684).

The assimilation of natural features within religious topographies extended
across a more extensive area. Documentary evidence from Wereham dating to
1450 includes a reference to 'St Margaret's Well', located on the village green
a short distance away from the parish church of the same dedication (NRO,
Paine and Brettoll acc., copy of extent). A map depicting the parish of Sedgeford
in 1634 shows 'Our Ladyes Well' situated away from the church and close to
the parish boundary (Figure 10; NRO, LEST/OC1). In Fersfield elements of
medieval religious practices survived, or were re-invented, in the eighteenth
century when the inhabitants processed from their parish church to a nearby
well (Blomefield 1805, I, 105).

The proliferation of crosses, chapels, holy wells, hermitages and other holy
places and landmarks, thus ensured that religious imagery was encountered in
a wide variety of everyday contexts, well away from the parochial 'core' of the
church; while more generally, minor place-names infused the landscape with

FIGURE 10. Detail of
a map of Sedgeford
showing 'Ladyes Well'
situated close to the
parish boundary in 1634
(NRO, LEST/OC1).

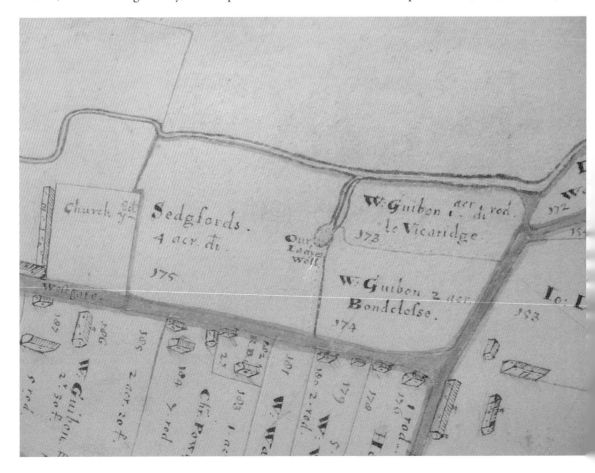

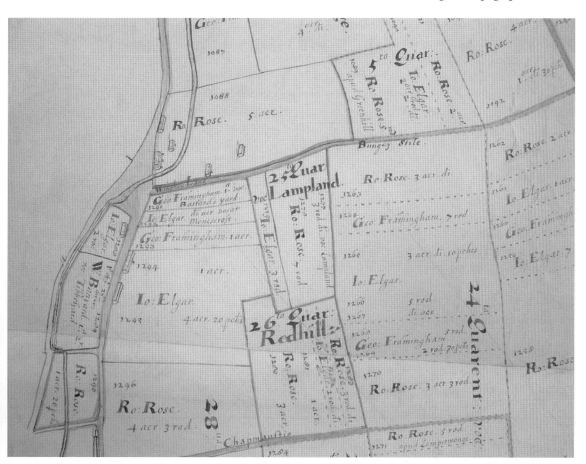

religious references. In North Lopham, for example, two pieces of land known as St John's Acre and St Peter's Acre had been named in respect of the guilds that owned them (Blomefield 1805, I, 253), while Hargham church owned two roods called 'Bell Acre' for which the rector was indebted to upkeep the bell ropes (Blomefield 1805, I, 415). In Gaywood 'Bell Rope Land' and 'Lampland' were recorded in 1486–7 (Bradfer-Lawrence 167; 176) the latter reflecting the purpose of keeping a lamp burning in the church paid for from the profits acquired from the land in question. 'Lamp Acre' in North Lopham, and 'Lampland' in Sedgeford (Figure 11; NRO, LEST/OC1) presumably have the same explanation. By naming land in respect of their prescribed purpose, such identification served as a persistent reminder, and confirmation, as to its religious and social functions.

We have seen how the farming landscape became both an extension of personal expressions of faith, as well as providing an interrelated framework for the perpetuation of the Christian world-view. Beyond the precincts of monastic houses and parish churches, a landscape rich in religious meaning and symbolism shaped peoples' lives. As people moved through the landscape they encountered shrines, lights and crosses. At certain stages in the agricultural year particular routeways, such as those leading across arable open fields, were viewed with heightened significance for local communities as they ploughed the land, blessed their crops during Rogation week and brought the harvest in. In this sense the landscape can be seen as having an active role to play as both a repository of religious beliefs and also in providing a series of signposts for the perpetuation of customary practices and beliefs. The everyday landscape sustained, moulded and intensified religious experience. The process of religious reform fundamentally altered this diffuse religious landscape of the early sixteenth century.

Part Two: Re-forming Religious Topographies

Studies of the Reformation landscape have been predominately concerned with the material and spatial reform of parish church interiors. According to Margaret Aston: 'the Reformation for most believers meant the reformation of their parish church' because 'it was only when they went to church that they encountered sculpture and painting' (Aston 1988, 16). Such arguments tend to assume a rather simple spatial model: a single parish, with a single parish church forming the arena in which ritual activities were structured and contained. As we have seen, in reality the religious landscape was more extensive and pervasive. Alongside the attack on the ritual paraphernalia of the late medieval church, the work of reformers and iconoclasts assisted in reshaping religious topographies far beyond the parish church. The ruination of monastic houses, or their conversion to 'secular' use, and the closure of pilgrimage centres, was accompanied by the dilapidation of a wide range of modest religious buildings and structures that lined the routeways of rural Norfolk. These former channels of devotional practice were ruthlessly removed from the landscape, not only altering the physical parameters of religious beliefs and practices, but transforming the ways people experienced their physical environs.

The religious landscape of the late sixteenth and seventeenth centuries is generally equated with material neglect: 'Puritans had dismissed the concept of the holy place as idolatrous' (Morris 1989, 437), something which 'had an impact on the entire Protestant establishment' (Newman 2001, 25). According to this view there was an unprecedented level of disregard and, as a result, decay of religious buildings across England. This lack of respect for holy sites would appear to confirm the arguments put forward by those historians who regard this period as a time of unrelenting 'secularisation' and 'individualism'. According to one proponent of this view 'by the Restoration, the issue did not seem to be Christian orthodoxy so much as the bare presence of religion in England' (Somerville 1992, 185). But the extent to which this apparent disregard for hallowed ground reflects a more general decline in religiosity has been questioned. Religion continued to remain a central element of English society far beyond the seventeenth century although perhaps, as Martin Ingram suggests, the compulsory nature of religious duties coupled with the concern for order fostered a minimalist approach to overt religious practices (Ingram 1995, 100–15). Similarly, although a large number of religious buildings were abandoned over the course of this period, this does not mean that all were considered with indifference. For the majority of early modern villagers, the enduring presence of their parish church stood as a testament to the collective enterprise of members of their local community, past and present. However, in parishes containing two or more churches one was often taken down in order to repair the other. The initiative came from within local communities, unable to bear the financial costs of supporting subsidiary churches and chapels. As we shall see this process of 'rationalisation', in terms of the spatial context of religious practices, has interesting implications for current debates in social history.

Historians interested in the impact of the Reformation on material culture have focused on the behaviour of iconoclasts in attacking and destroying the objects and images of devotional practice (Aston 1988; Duffy 1992; Philips 1973). Eamon Duffy has described the vandalism as a 'celebration of the sacrament of forgetfulness in every parish in the land' (Duffy 1992, 480). Duffy's eloquent words invoke a profound sense of change, but the material relics of late medieval religious life had a more complex and at times ambiguous role to play in promoting change. Iconoclasm was a visual language intended not simply to obliterate but to leave behind visible traces as a constant reminder of the overthrow of corruption and superstition (Aston 2003). However, the intentions of a small minority of zealous reformers are one thing, the measure of popular opinion another: an issue that lies at the heart of modern debate. The necessary repair and maintenance of parish churches, especially during the restoration schemes of the nineteenth century, has given away the hiding places of sacred relics. Revealed beneath floors, walled up in stairwells and recesses, these artefacts were initially stored presumably in the hope that one day the old religion would prevail (Tarlow 2003). Archaeological investigation has shown how the concealment of sculptures and relics, the shattered pieces of which were often carefully placed, indicates one way in which local individuals and groups offered outward acquiescence to the authorities while hiding their true religiosity.

The following section will consider the broad geographical implications of religious reform and its consequences for contemporary relations to religious space and the post-medieval development of local territorial structures. We will examine the impact of government statutes on local landscapes and their subsequent, often unintended, spatial ramifications.

'The Great Sacrilege' – the Fate of the Monasteries

I am now come out of the rivers into the ocean of iniquity and sacrilege, where whole thousands of churches and chapels dedicated to the service of God in the same manner that the rest are which remain to us at this day, together with the monasteries and other houses of religion and intended piety, were by King Henry VIII, in a tempest of indignation against the clergy of that time mingled with insatiable avarice, sacked and razed as by an enemy (Spelman *The History and Fate of Sacrilege*, quoted in Hoskins 1976, 122).

Writing in the 1630s Sir Henry Spelman, a Catholic propagandist, saw the previous century as a period blighted by the country's sacrilegious offences. In his critique of Norfolk families he found that, of those who had acquired monastic property in the aftermath of the Dissolution, all had succumbed to terrible misfortune. He related a number of tragedies which befell the Townshend family soon after they became owners of Coxford Priory. Following his father's death in a duel, Sir Roger Townshend was further aggrieved when, during the demolition of the steeple of the abbey, a workman was killed and the foundations of his new house inexplicably cracked. For Spelman these were unequivocal statements of Divine judgement upon those who would profane sacred property (Hoskins 1976).

In 1536 an act was passed to suppress lesser religious houses, whose revenue did not exceed £200 a year (Cook 1965, 256). Royal commissioners were instructed to 'pull down to the ground all the walls of the churches, stepulls, cloysters, fraterys, dorters, chapter howsys and the like' (Doggett 2001, 166). Notwithstanding such royal injunctions, the quantity of surviving evidence shows that in Norfolk, as elsewhere (Airs 1995; Doggett 2002; Howard 1987), monastic houses were rarely levelled to the ground. The extensive remains at Castle Acre, West Acre, Weybourne, North Creake, and Binham and until the early nineteenth century, at Wendling were only the more prominent landmarks. The official procedure was to remove materials of any value, before defacing the church and rendering the domestic buildings uninhabitable (Doggett 2002). Blomefield includes documentary evidence for the money paid in the case of West Acre Priory to:

> Dyverse other persons for taking downe of the belles and wayeng of the same, plucking down of the leade, melting and weying of the same, and defasyng, and pulling downe of the church dortre and other howses, as by the boke appereth … The commissioners for their costes and expenses ryding from London to the sayd late monastery, and there being with dyverse with them for the suppressing, dissolving, and defasyng of the same for five weeks, and for their costes and expenses in returning to London (Blomefield 1805, IX, 165).

The presence of the commissioners from London, in overseeing the work brought the arm of royal authority into local communities. Their work was accompanied by what must have been for many a shocking spectacle brought about over an intense period of, in the case of West Acre, five weeks. Lead taken from the roofs was melted on site, thus rendering it a more convenient shape and size for transportation. Such industrial activity illuminated the process of demolition against a backdrop of blazing furnaces and smoke. The remains of a furnace have been found in the presbytery of Langley Abbey, its location representing blatant disregard for catholic sensibilities (NMR TG36260285). In the densely settled county of Norfolk few monasteries were geographically isolated from lay communities and the sights and sounds of destruction must have been an inescapable presence in the daily lives of local inhabitants. Nor did they merely stand by and watch. There was also much looting, often clandestine,

FIGURE 12. Langley Abbey depicted in the early seventeenth-century, evidently a number of service buildings were still standing and presumably still in use. Note also the remains of a cross on Langley Green (NRO, NRS 21407).

on the part of local populations. Shagan has argued that by engaging in such activity ordinary people contributed significantly to the reformers' agenda (Shagan 2003).

The 1536 Act contains a certain degree of ambiguity regarding how far monastic houses were to be defaced and destroyed (Howard 1987, 139). Certainly, the purchasers were 'bound by authority of this Act ... to keep, or cause to be kept, an honest continual house and household in the same site or precinct, and to occupy yearly as much of the same demesnes in ploughing and tillage of husbandry' (Cook 1965, 260; Howard 1987, 139). Judging from the available map evidence for Flitcham and Langley, substantial numbers of monastic buildings were still extant at the beginning of the seventeenth century (NRO, MS 4290 and MS 4294; NRO, NRS 21407: Figure 12). While at West Acre two early sixteenth-century barns, once part of the monastic complex, still survive (Pevsner 2002b, 760). Providing the religious buildings were rendered unusable there was no need to abandon the site entirely, and in consequence the secular function of monastic properties, as places of agrarian production, was maintained.

In places like Hertfordshire, large numbers of new gentry-owners converted monastic complexes into fashionable country houses (Doggett 2001; 2002; Howard 1987, chapter 7). In Norfolk, however, conversion was rare, with Horsham St Faith's, where the refectory range was converted into a house, being the only exception (Pevsner 2002a, 566). The reasons for this are complex and due to a number of interrelated factors, including the condition of the monastic buildings, their location, and the volatile land market created by the Dissolution (Swales 1963). But, it seems that in Norfolk local environmental and topographical factors probably played an important part in dissuading landowners to attempt costly conversion schemes. Here the majority of monastic houses were located on low-lying, damp land adjacent to rivers. Castle Acre (Figure 13), West Acre and Pentney, for example, were situated on the River Nar; West Dereham Abbey occupied a site surrounded by land that remained waterlogged until it was drained in the eighteenth century; Hickling Priory and St Benet's Abbey occupy very low-lying sites on the edge of the Broadland marshes. Leaving aside the potential threat from flooding, contemporary opinion regarded such sites – not without justification – as unhealthy, and likely to harbour ague or malaria. Furthermore, landowners at this time were increasingly interested in the location of their residences, and preferred places with potential for laying out a park and garden and, if possible, with extensive prospects over well-cultivated terrain (Hunt, 1986). For the new owners of monastic property the decision to convert for residential use was thus determined less by the character of the buildings themselves, than by that of the landscape in which they were set.

Old monastic buildings were, nevertheless, used in a range of ways. Some simply became quarries for materials used to construct houses located elsewhere. In a county noted for its lack of stone, the reuse of monastic material in the fabric of new buildings was an important visual statement of any occupant's social pretensions. In Old Buckenham the existing fabric of Abbey Farmhouse, dating to the mid-sixteenth century, incorporates stone from the adjacent priory (Pevsner 2002b, 579). Fragments of Peterstone Priory in Burnham Overy were incorporated into Peterstone Farmhouse (Pevsner 2002b, 233). As mentioned earlier the map evidence for Langley and Flitcham points to the reuse of domestic buildings. The case of Flitcham is particularly interesting. In 1614 a

FIGURE 13. The ruins of Castle Acre Priory.

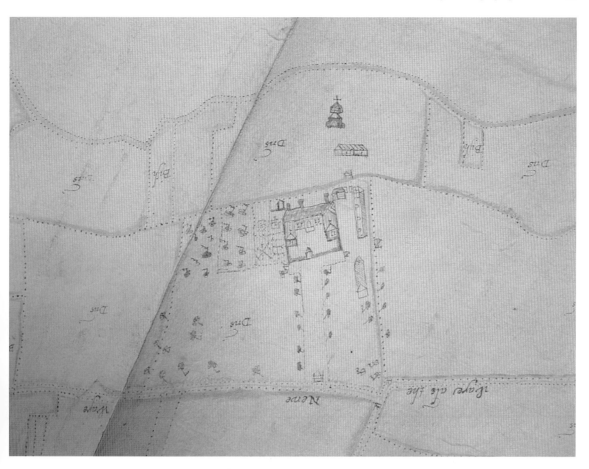

FIGURE 14. Flitcham Abbey in 1655, converted at a relatively late date into a courtyard house with gardens and dovecot, thus completing the image of an aspiring gentry landowner (NRO, MS 4295).

payment was made for 'repairs to ye old buildyngs at ye Abbey' (NRO, Flitcham 449) and judging from map evidence, it had by the mid-seventeenth century been developed into a residence (Figure 14).

Stripping the landscape

Under Henry VIII the suppression of the monasteries was accompanied by a campaign against idolatry and superstition, as the royal commissioners dismantled shrines, and destroyed holy relics. In 1538 parishes were instructed to remove images from their churches: 'such 'feigned images as ye know of in any of your cures to be so abused with pilgrimages or offerings of anything made thereunto, ye shall, for avoiding that most detestable sin of idolatry' (cited in Cummings 2002, 185). A number of the most 'abused' images, including those from Walsingham and Ipswich, were taken for ritual burning in London, with Hugh Latimer looking forward to a 'jolly muster' in Smithfield (Philips 1973, 75).

The closure of pilgrimage centres and attacks on relics and images ruptured traditional networks of religious practice (Duffy 1992, 385). Influenced, perhaps, by the scale of the upstanding remains, studies of the Dissolution have tended to focus on the most eminent monastic houses, such as Fountains and Rievaulx or, in Norfolk, Castle Acre and Walsingham. The denigration of saintly relics and symbols had far wider repercussions for the spatial contexts of religious practice than a focus on the larger sites would suggest. For religious reform found further expression, or clarification, in the closure and ruination of the chapels that had been 'an essential part of the physical, economic and symbolic landscape' of the late medieval period (Gilchrist 1995, 2). In Hillington for example, the pilgrims' chapel dedicated to St James, which had formed one of a series of landmarks along the route to Walsingham, was in ruins by the seventeenth century (NRO, NRS 21381). Similar fates befell the pilgrims chapels at Stanhoe and East Barsham, while in Hunstanton St Edmund's chapel was likewise abandoned: its roofless remains left standing amid the arable open fields of the parish (NRO, LEST/IC 68: Figure 15). Hospitals dedicated to the care of pilgrims were also closed including, those at Billingford, Horning, and Boycodeswade hospital was dissolved with Coxford Priory (Messent 1934, 18). Indeed the end of monasticism saw the closure of a number of affiliated sites, such as the chapel of St Nicholas in Whitwell, formerly affiliated to Pentney Priory (HER13296). People did not have to travel to places like Walsingham to witness the effects of government legislation.

Subsequent statutes caused the further dislocation of religious topographies. The Henrician Chantries Act of 1545, though not carried out systematically until the reign of Edward VI, covered a wide range of religious buildings and organisations – 'colleges, free chapels, chantries, hospitals, fraternities, brotherhoods, guilds, and stipendiary priests having perpetuity for ever' (Kreider 1979, 5). Following Henry's death in 1547, the government ordered the destruction of all shrines, paintings and sculptures purported to have superstitious uses. In that year the state decreed that all endowments of chantries, religious guilds and perpetual obits be relinquished on the grounds that Purgatory was a fabrication (Hutton 1987, 147). Not only did this alter the symbiotic relationship between the living and the dead, it amounted to the condemnation of a way of life: 'the elaborate rituals and practices, colours, lights, symbols and artistic representation from and in which this relationship had been expressed' (Roffey 2003, 341). In its wake, large numbers of religious buildings were shut down. Though hospitals were to be exempted under Edward, the closure of 'free chapels' and detached chantry chapels, continued apace (Kreider 1979, 5). St John the Baptist's chapel in Barton Bendish, once affiliated to West Dereham Abbey, was dissolved in the first year of Edward's reign, as was St Nicholas' chapel in Diss (HER12056). The chapels dedicated to St Botolph in Ditchingham, and in Broome, both apparently in ruins by 1558 (HER10635; HER14911) while St Margaret's chapel in Hilborough was dissolved in 1550 and allowed to fall into disrepair (Messent 1934). In addition, the Chantries Act of 1547 also outlawed guild chapels. In 1586 William Herne, born in 1516, remembered the guild chapel in Tibenham: 'wherein the guylde hath ben kept used (for) marriages and feasts havinge been kept here for the

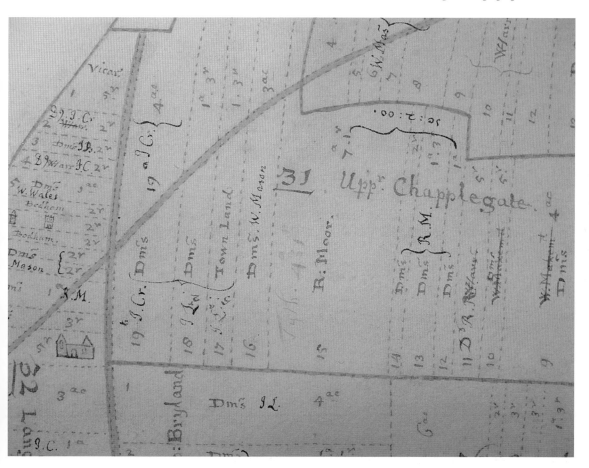

FIGURE 15. The ruins of the former pilgrims' chapel dedicated to St Edmund stood amid the open fields of Hunstanton in the seventeenth century. The lead roof, the most profitable acquisition, had been stripped away leaving the walls to crumble (NRO, LEST/ IC 68).

towne and that the same howse is adioyninge to the churchyard of Tibenham'. The chapel had since been converted for use as accommodation for the poor (TNA: PRO, E133/4/667).

There is, however, some evidence to suggest the continuation of religious activity at least in some of these places, after their official abandonment. In particular, a number of crucifix pendants of post-medieval date have been recovered from the site of the free chapel dedicated to St Giles in Topcroft (HER10197). Furthermore early map evidence illustrates that these sites continued to be incorporated within local geographies and were in some places commanding features of the landscape. Branstone Chapel in Marham, for example was depicted as an imposing ruin in the arable fields of the village in the late sixteenth century (NRO, HARE 6811; HER4511). By c.1723 it seems there was little left of the site, only the hill on which the chapel had once stood, nevertheless its former existence was preserved in the road and field names, 'Branstone Way' and 'Chapel Hill' (NRO, HARE 6814).

Some chapels were converted to new, secular purposes, though often at a relatively late date, presumably after the memory of their pre-Reformation functions had diminished. The chantry chapel of St Mary in Walpole Fen in the parish of Walpole St Peter, appropriated by Henry VIII in 1544/5 and conveyed to secular ownership (Blomefield 1805, IX, 119), had by 1609 been converted into a cottage (HER19803). Similar conversions took place in Stow Bardolph, where Stow Chapel, which had previously been supported by the guild of St Botolph, was converted to a small farmhouse (HER14904); and a fourteenth-century wayside chapel in Litcham was reused as a house sometime in the late sixteenth century (HER4072; Messent 1934, 42). The sixteenth century also saw the reuse of the leper house in Ickburgh as a bridge toll house, probably in effect a continuation of its main pre-Reformation function: it continued in this role until converted into cottages in 1739 (HER5083; Pevsner 2002b, 447). Others were reused for civic functions, as schoolhouses and accommodation for the poor, such as the guild chapel in Tibenham, and were thus assimilated once again into the social terrain of village life (TNA: PRO, E133/4/667). In 1670 a school was founded in St James' guild chapel in Pulham St Mary (HER10778): given the time-lapse between dissolution and reuse – over a century – this strongly suggests maintenance of some kind in the interim period. An earlier example comes from Wymondham where the former guild chapel dedicated to Thomas á Becket was converted for use as a school in 1559 (HER9439).

Many chapels and hospitals were simply converted into barns, such as the chapel dedicated to St James' hospital in Horning. In Old Buckenham monks from the nearby priory served St Andrew's church until 1536 when it was closed (Batcock 1991, 53), map evidence reveals it was in use as a barn by c.1580 (NRO, MC 22/11). In Little Wacton the tower of St Mary's church, which had been relegated to chapel status by the early sixteenth century, was closed and used as a dovecot presumably until it was demolished some time before 1655 (HER10072). The profane use of these former religious buildings amounted to an irreversible statement of closure.

As we have seen, the medieval population exercised a great deal of freedom in their choices concerning investment in the religious landscape, frequently incorporating sacred places outside their home parishes. Popular pilgrimage routes had been kept alive through continual use, material elaboration, and in social memories. The suppression of the monasteries and dismantling of pilgrimage networks not only disrupted local economies but also forcibly undermined the spatial context of religious beliefs and traditions. The decaying elements of the Catholic past were an inescapable presence in rural Norfolk. At a regional level the onslaught on the material culture of religious practice, dramatically altered the scope of peoples' spiritual geographies.

The reformation of the parish

What has not, perhaps, received sufficient attention from historians is the extent to which the transformation of the religious landscape involved more than the simple abolition of certain kinds of shrine and building. The remaining ecclesiastical provision – parish churches, and their associated territories – was also substantially altered with, in particular, a marked reduction in their numbers. The abandonment of churches was certainly not new to the sixteenth century. Research carried out by Batcock has shown that between 1100 and 1600 a steady rate of closure took place with an average of seven disappearing every fifty years (Batcock 1991, 7). Except in the second half of the fourteenth century when, during a period of particularly severe demographic contraction and economic climate, this rate doubled. In contrast, the sixteenth century saw the closure of no less than 112 churches (Batcock 1991, 6). The majority were abandoned as a result of the Act of Consolidation in 1535/6, which permitted neighbouring parishes to be united and for one church to be closed, providing the churches were less than a mile apart, and where one was valued at less than £6 a year (Batcock, 1991, 7). The proceeds gained from the closure of one church, such as the sale of lead roofing, were put towards the upkeep of the other, as in the case of Guist Thorpe for which the Inventory of Church Goods of 1552 recorded:

> The churchwardens certify thatt there were ij Chyrches in Gests and on' paryche and on paturne and on person and both Chyrches in grett decae. In concederacyon whereof the paturne and person Sir Roger Touneshend wyth the consent of the Inhabitantes there hath unyd on' Chyrche to Repare the other ij daye of October laste paste (Walters 1941, 13).

Given the ecclesiastical peculiarities of Norfolk – the multiplicity and over-provision of churches – the results of this act were, in village after village, a radical streamlining of religious topographies. In Congham, a village divided between three parishes, All Saint's church was abandoned in c.1550 and St Anne's, also known as St Mary's, was closed soon after (Batcock 1991, 53). All Saint's had apparently been suffering economic hardship for some time and, in the late sixteenth century, members of the local community gave account of its subsidiary status:

> Of anncyente tyme there have ben and lately weare two churches eche of them wth a steple and channcell in ether of the said parishes of Congham St Andrewes and Congham St Maryes but onely a chappell wthowte steple or channcell in Congham All Sayntes ... there is verye lyttle arrable lande within the said pishe of all Saynts and that the parishners of Congham all Saynts have allwayes ben and yet be fewer and poorer than the parishners within either of the other two parishes (TNA: PRO, E134/25&26Eliz/Mich22).

Following the closure of All Saints, the farmer of the rectory took away 'two little belles in the gable ende' presumably signifying its abandonment. By the time of the court case in 1583, St Anne's had also been abandoned. Robert Mendham, a resident of the township, indicated what this closure and that of All Saints, meant in terms of the religious terrain of local life, as gradually the parishioners of the three parishes came together to worship under one roof:

> After the dacaye of all Sayntes the pishioners of the same pishe dyd reporte unto the pishe churche of St Annes to here servys beinge wthin the tyme of this his knowledge and that ... there is no other churche nowe to reporte unto wthin the said three pishes to heare servyce but onely the churche of St Andrewes (TNA: PRO, E134/25&26Eliz/Mich22).

Another illustrative example comes from the south Norfolk village of Stratton. Until the mid-sixteenth century the village supported two churches, St Michael's and St Peter's, located 'not a bow-shot distant' from one another. St Peter's became a chapel in 1444 when the parishes were consolidated. Yet they continued to operate as separate parishes for almost a century more, the rector apparently holding service in both churches on Sundays. Again there appears to have been great tenacity on the part of the local community in preventing the closure of their subsidiary church. Their support continued until the chapel was finally demolished and both parishes merged in the mid-sixteenth century (Blomefield 1805, V, 198).

Government policy had undermined the multifarious nature of late medieval religious culture, but also encouraged impoverished parishes to take the initiative to abandon their subsidiary churches and chapels and invest in one place. It is important to note, however, that while the act of 1535/6 was crucial in the rapid disappearance of so many churches, there is some evidence that it was only one aspect of a more organic process. In Wacton, for example, St Mary's church (referred to as 'Wacton Chapell' in the sixteenth century) was situated less than half-a-mile from the present parish church and was abandoned in the 1520's although it was not demolished until the official consolidation of the two parishes in 1575 (Batcock 1991, 55). It was reported in the manor court rolls that 'unknown people had stolen lead from the roof and broken windows and it was agreed that Richard Lavyle could take the residue of the lead and the iron window bars' (Barringer 1977): clearly the site presented a financial opportunity for those who could procure the goods.

The late medieval religious landscape was altered in other important ways, with the dilapidation of a host of other, minor foci of religious devotion. Churchyard crosses were targeted probably due to their function in parish processions, especially at Easter. All parish processions, in church and churchyard and other places were abolished following a set of Injunctions made in 1547 and in 1559 (Aston 1988; Duffy 1992, 453–4). But the result was not always complete destruction. Once the offensive imagery of the cross itself had been taken down, and the structures thus divorced from their liturgical associations, churchyard crosses were allowed to remain (Aston 1988, 16). This extended to wayside crosses more generally, because of their actual or potential association with processional rituals, especially at Rogationtide. The priest of a parish near Doncaster in Yorkshire recorded in 1548 that at Rogationtide: 'no procession was mayde abowtt the fealdes, but cruell tiranntes dyd cast downe all crosses standynge in oppen ways dispittefully' (Duffy 1992, 462). Many wayside crosses however, like those in churchyards, were reduced to 'stumps' rather than completely destroyed. Judging from the surviving examples practical ease dictated that they were usually broken off at an accessible height.

No longer part of an overt religious culture, the destruction or vandalism of crosses and other revered landmarks such as holy wells, can be viewed as part of the broader shift in the spatial re-orientation of religious practice on a single parish church. The suppression of the monasteries and attrition of churches and chapels served to reinforce the rationalisation of religious topographies.

Conclusion

The first part of this chapter considered the wide variety of devotional outlets individuals and communities supported and embellished in the medieval period (Rosser 1991; 1996). In Norfolk, a substantial number of villages contained more than one church or chapel, providing diverse arenas for devotional activities; while the landscape was further enhanced with freestanding crosses, shrines and other natural and archaeological foci for devotion. Popular belief in the intercessory role of the saints helped to sustain a dense network of sacred sites and produced a landscape defined by ritual movement which linked the more eminent centres of pilgrimage and monastic houses with a host of minor sites, such as holy wells, chapels, hermitages and parish churches.

Studies of the Reformation, and especially of the changes in material culture associated with this process, have concentrated on the physical structure of the church, and to some extent on its immediate surroundings. But equally important were two associated developments. Firstly, the symbols of the state were now present in the church in a way that they had never been before: most dramatically, the royal arms replaced the rood, at the junction of nave and chancel. The church became in one sense an arm of the state with, for example, statutes and orders regularly read out there on Sundays, and in administrating the poor laws. Secondly the church, and associated churchyard, came to be regarded for the first time as purely religious spaces. In late medieval times churches had served a wide range of social and economic functions, as places for popular revels and feasts: such profane uses were now gradually, yet inexorably, curtailed.

An examination of the wider landscape context throws additional light on the significance of this latter change, in particular. As the church building was simplified with the removal of internal chantry chapels, shrines, and images, so the surrounding countryside was stripped of its overt religious connotations and associations. Of course this change was not affected overnight. As we shall see, the relics of the pre-Reformation landscape continued to structure and to give historical context to local social and economic geographies, but the meanings attached to them gradually altered over time. Even when relic features disappeared without trace, place-names and folklore narratives continued to remind people of their former existence. Nevertheless, the change was real enough. A wide, diffuse religiosity was replaced, in the course of the early modern period, by something more focussed, and at the same time more controlled.

These spatial changes had an obvious chronological parallel. The late medieval year had been punctuated with innumerable religious festivals: these were now suppressed or abandoned (Cressy 1989). Once again, of course, the process was gradual and partial. A range of old rituals and customs continued to survive for a while: indeed, Hutton has discerned something of a revival of festivity in the late sixteenth and early seventeenth centuries, the authorities generally tolerant of them providing they did not violate the church and its precincts (Hutton 1994, 237). But ceremony had largely been stripped of spiritual meaning, and while (as we shall see) saints' days continued to structure the pattern of the farming year, the calendar beat, for the most part, to a very different rhythm – that of the Sabbath. Under Elizabeth, all parishioners were obliged by law to attend their parish church on Sundays. The sermons preached from the pulpit, 'had replaced the confessional as a source of guidance on moral and economic conduct' (Hill 1969, 34).

The transformation of religious geographies discussed in this chapter also involved, in Norfolk especially, a drastic simplification of older systems of ecclesiastical organisation, with the disappearance of many parishes and a growing tendency for each village to have but one church. Yet this in itself was part of a wider development, witnessed throughout England. The re-formation of religious topographies in the late sixteenth century had important implications for the structures and processes of governance at the local level in the seventeenth century. The parish now became increasingly important in the secular as well as the religious life of the nation, used as part of the apparatus of the state and eclipsing, in many respects, that other key element of medieval social organisation, the manor. The parish church provided the forum for select groups of 'chief' inhabitants, or the 'better' sort, to orchestrate the governance of local life (Hindle 2000; 2001). This was a change with wide ramifications, and with its own particular implications both for the landscape, and for social geographies.

CHAPTER THREE

The Early Modern Parish:
A Landscape History

The neighbourhood itself ... was a shifting and unstable entity, constituted by
processes of inclusion and exclusion which were not infrequently occasions of contest
(Wrightson 1996, 22).

To understand the profound changes that brought about the re-structuring
of early modern religious topographies, it is necessary to engage with wider
debates dealing with contemporary social and political changes. By looking at
the gradual encroachment of the Tudor state on local life, in conjunction with
the process of religious reform, it is possible to achieve a deeper understanding
of how contemporary perceptions and experiences of the landscape developed.
Over the course of the late sixteenth and seventeenth centuries the increasing
interest of the state in local affairs placed greater emphasis on the parish, rather
than the manor, as the basic administrative unit. As Wrightson points out,
the politics of 'state formation' should be considered jointly with the process
of religious Reformation, although this involves the bringing together of two
vast though essentially independent historiographies: 'they can be conveniently
taken together, however, since from the perspective of the parish, with its
overlapping civil and ecclesiastical functions, they had a good deal in common
in their impact' (Wrightson 1996, 26). In spatial terms the re-alignment of
religious topographies on a single place of worship, had a significant role in
providing a central place and basis for the civil adminstration of the parish.
While the secular functions of the medieval church have already been noted,
under the Tudors the church was no longer a focus for popular revels and other
such denigrated customs, but the seat of local governance and order.

The establishment of the Poor Laws under the Elizabethan government
was intrinsic to the development of the civil functions and responsibilities of
the parish. At the turn of the sixteenth century poor relief was regarded as a
personal concern deeply entrenched in the belief that it was possible to acquire
salvation through material acts of benevolence (Duffy 1992, 359–362). The
poor were cared for by a number of charitable means including: outdoor relief
distributed by monasteries and religious guilds; hospitals devoted to serving
the needs of lepers, pilgrims and travellers; and almshouses, which catered for
the poor more generally (Gilchrist 1995, 9). The Dissolution brought an abrupt
end to these charitable institutions, a development that not only left an obvious
void in the means to provide for the destitute, sick and aged, but also threw

into sharper relief the social proximity of the poor. Renewed population growth in the sixteenth century, high agricultural prices and unemployment further aggravated the problem. In search of work and relief the destitute left their rural villages and travelled, often long distances, to urban centres. The perceived problem of vagrancy – of the masterless young men and women wondering the countryside, "debase pilferers" and prostitutes living outside the geographical confines of parish jurisdiction and control – stood at odds with the social ideal of the parish community based on respectability and order (Amussen 1988).

The Poor Laws, instituted in 1598 and 1601, placed on the parish the responsibility of caring for the old, sick and destitute. Relief was bound up with notions of social obligation rooted in what was deemed to be acceptable membership of the parish (Wrightson 1996, 21). The administration of poor relief was essentially the duty of wealthier villagers who were responsible for paying rates. Consequently the regulation of migration – the politics of 'inclusion' and 'exclusion' – rested within the interests of the local 'middling' and 'better' sort of inhabitants (Hindle 2002, chapters 6–9; Hindle 1998, 67–96). The decision as to who should receive aid was measured on the basis of a 'criteria of belonging', and as a result attempts were made to return the thriftless poor to their place of birth (Hindle 1996; 2000). One important implication of these territorial constraints was that they served to reinforce the geographical ties of the poor to a parish. The politics of welfare provision can be seen as a manifestation of the growing polarisation of society not only between the poor and the 'better sort of the parish', but also between the deserving and undeserving poor (Wrightson 1996, 21).

At a local level the nature and mechanics of change were not propelled in any straightforward way by central government. The political and cultural changes of the late Tudor and early Stuart periods were the result of complex social dynamics originating from within local communities. State policies were not simply imposed from 'above' but were the subject of internal conflict on all social levels, often for protracted periods of time. Indeed, the establishment of welfare provision, following the passing of the Poor Laws, was by no means universally accepted. Studies of the impact of religious reform and government policy have shown that the chronology and extent of change varied from parish to parish (Wales 1984).

This chapter seeks to relate the growing socio-economic pressures experienced in the late sixteenth and early seventeenth centuries to the strengthening definition of the parish as a physical entity. Steve Hindle has recently argued that Rogationtide processions were appropriated by the parish elite – clergymen, churchwardens and affluent tenants – as part of a process that saw the 're-casting' of social relationships within local communities (Hindle 2000). In contrast to the medieval period when it is usually assumed that beating the bounds represented 'a corporate manifestation of the village community' (Thomas 1971, 74), the event was seized upon as a means of denoting the authority of an oligarchic elite over the territory of the parish – 'the little commonwealth'.

In this context, perambulations provided an opportunity for village elites – on whom the responsibility for contributing to the poor rates fell – to delineate the extent of 'settlement and entitlement' (Wrightson 1996). Knowledge of parish boundaries thus represented the enclosure of social space, which was vital in regulating the migratory patterns of the poor. However, such arguments assume the post-medieval parish to be a stable and uncontested physical territory but, as we shall see, the politics of the parish was as much about local attempts to define and fix parochial bounds. The politics of local governance was mediated over a contested landscape of custom, right and the material boundaries of belonging.

The growing authority of the civil parish in the late Tudor and early Stuart period constitutes an important, yet often overlooked phase in post-medieval landscape history. This chapter will look at the history and meaning of parish boundaries in the post-medieval period: starting with their physical definition before moving on to examine their role in defining local social and economic relationships both within, and between neighbouring parishes. The discussion will concentrate on the intent and purpose that lay behind the ritual of beating the bounds; an event that belied a range of personal interests, loyalties and allegiances within local societies. We shall focus on the practical priorities and motivations among those taking part, and the role of the landscape in defining a parish 'community'. Post-medieval landscape history can develop in new ways by considering the physical terrain over which these power relations were mediated.

'For the Continuwence of the Bownds'

> It has long been the custom of officialdom to while away idle hours by tidying boundaries and removing enclaves, meanders, etc. These tinkerings, though seldom of practical advantage, destroy some of the meaning, which has to be recovered from nineteenth-century maps. Even the first edition 25-inch Ordnance Survey does not always show the true course of boundaries (Rackham 1986, 19–20).

Oliver Rackham makes an important point regarding the history of parish boundaries – what we see today is not necessarily what people saw or experienced in the past. However, his statement implies that until the nineteenth century parish boundaries were static lines drawn across the landscape. Rackham's work, like the majority of research to date, has focused on the origins of parochial territories, which has tended to assume long-term patterns of continuity. Bonney for example has suggested that in Wessex a substantial proportion of boundaries, or at least sections of them, were inherited from very ancient patterns of territorial division (Bonney 1972; Gelling 1978; Winchester 1990). It is generally accepted though, that from the end of the thirteenth century the network of parish bounds solidified, with the number of parishes and their boundaries remaining broadly consistent until the local government reforms of the nineteenth century (Rosser 1991,

174; Morris 1989). There were, however, some notable exceptions to this, including in Norfolk the late partition of Marshland discussed earlier, while research carried out by Angus Winchester on the moorland landscapes of northern England has shown that in many upland districts parochial division occurred at a relatively late date (Winchester 2000, 16–33). In Norfolk, away from the Fens, there were no great tracts of intercommoned land to compare to upland areas. But there were numerous common grazing grounds shared by the inhabitants of two or more parishes, the boundaries across which remained ambiguous, sometimes well into the post-medieval period. Indeed, the 'truth' and 'meaning' Rackham proposes to recover from nineteenth-century tithe maps negates the often controversial and contested nature of boundary preservation and delineation in earlier periods.

The precedence given to researching the origins of boundaries, and the belief that they were stable and incontrovertible features of the landscape, has led to a general lack of interest in their development in later historic periods. Citing tithes to be one of the principal causes of altercation, N.J.G. Pounds has recently argued that 'boundary problems continued to arise throughout the Middle Ages, but generally ceased to be of importance after the Reformation' (Pounds 2000, 73). As the number of court cases brought before the church and equity courts amply demonstrates, tithe disputes did not end with the Reformation, and nor did the contests over the 'true' course of parochial bounds. The allocation and payment of tithes continued to prove a source of contention within local societies, especially among the new lay owners of monastic land determined to maximise their profits, and the clergy for whom tithes often formed a major part of their income (Evans 1976; 1985, 389).

It is often assumed that boundary disputes were resolved with the growth of written and cartographic documentation from the late sixteenth century. According to Adam Fox 'much which had always been preserved in memory and practice was now entrusted to paper and parchment' (Fox 2000, 297) and, similarly, Pounds has suggested that mapping boundaries diminished the value of 'folk' memory (Pounds 2000, 79). However, it is simplistic to assume that the shift from oral traditions to written record followed a straightforward linear progression (Wood 1999). In his study of archival sources from Kent and Devon, David Fletcher found that very few parishes in the eighteenth century kept written records of their boundaries (Fletcher 2003, 177–97). Rather boundary preservation relied on the transmission of oral memories, reinforced during prescribed rituals such as the annual event of beating the bounds (Bushaway 1982, 84; Fletcher 2003, 177–97; Hutton 1996).

Rogationtide processions took place during Ascension week over a number of days, obviously depending on the size of the parish. In New Buckenham, a small parish, it apparently took three days to walk the bounds (NRO, PD 254/171). The occasion was defined by both religious and secular activities, the balance of which is best seen as shifting over time (Hutton 1996, 277–287). In the medieval period it was a communal occasion, a progression made behind a portable cross and banners depicting Christ and the saints. There was a particular emphasis on hospitality, the giving of food, sometimes money, to those who took part, a theme that was resurrected in later periods (Hutton 1996, 278–279). Songs were also sung, seventy-six-year-old Thomas Neave of New Buckenham recalled how he often went on the perambulation for he was a 'singing boye' and 'used to helpe to singe the procession' (NRO, PD 254/171). The parishioners paused at various designated points where gospels were read and crops were blessed. According to one sixteenth-century commentator gospels were read in the open fields 'amongst the corn and grass, that by the virtue and operation of God's word, the power of the wicked spirits which keep in the air may be laid down, and the air made clean, to the intent the corn may be unharmed' (Richard Taverner cited in Hutton 1996, 279). The occasion also provided an opportunity to collectively inspect and confirm ancient territorial limits set out between neighbouring villages (Thomas 1971, 72). Such issues were given precedence with reference to biblical passages such as 'thou shalt not remove thy neighbour's mark, which they of old time have set in thine inheritance', and 'accursed be he who removeth his neighbour's doles and marks' (Bushaway 1982, 82).

The notion that parish boundaries ceased to cause any friction after the Reformation implies that perambulations achieved their primary function in maintaining an orderly society in which everyone knew and respected their geographical limits. Along the same lines, others have viewed post-Reformation rituals as nothing more than pale imitations of their medieval predecessors: ultimately stripped of meaningful context, yet surviving to give local inhabitants respite from the mundane aspects of their lives (Cressy 1989, 24; Underdown 1985, 45). In contrast to the later sixteenth and seventeenth centuries, research has so far only assembled relatively scant evidence for the existence of Rogationtide ceremonies in earlier centuries. Ronald Hutton has suggested that this may be a reflection of the investigation of mainly diocesan records, which only noted cases of neglect (Hutton 1996, 278; 1994, 35). A lack of documentation would thus indicate not 'widespread acceptance and enactment so much as for widespread indifference, with reluctance to report those who neglected the custom' (Hutton 1994, 35).

It is sometimes possible to extrapolate from sixteenth- and early seventeenth-century court records evidence for perambulations being carried out in the early part of the sixteenth century. In one case Edmund Cosen recalled his childhood experiences of going the bounds of Thorpe in the 1530s, and Richard Jubye could remember the perambulation of New Buckenham taking place in King Henry VIII's time (TNA: PRO, E178/7153; TNA: PRO, E134/38Eliz/Hil24). Sometimes deponents remembered pre-Reformation ritual elements of the ceremony. Seventy-year-old Thomas Chapman confirmed his knowledge of the parish boundary of Binham by relating his first-hand experiences of partaking in the procession: 'and for better testimone of his knowledge therein saythe that in that same procession he this deponent hathe carried about the holywaterstoppe' (TNA: PRO, DL4/18/37). Others recalled the reading of prayers at specific points along the procession route, with freestanding crosses frequently providing conspicuous landmarks at which to pause and pray (TNA: PRO, E134/28Eliz/ Hil5). In the closing decades of the sixteenth century evidently, many elderly inhabitants could still remember the vibrant nature of pre-Refomation rituals but, by the time their knowledge was recorded, the function and value of perambulations had changed. At the turn of the seventeenth century local inhabitants were using their knowledge of the ceremony in order to confirm, or to contest, the course of boundaries in the present. Beating the bounds became intrinsic to the political and economic life of local communities.

Historians have charted the subsequent development of the custom through the confusion of the mid-sixteenth century when, despite the hard line attempts of Protestant reformers to extinguish them entirely, the rituals received government sanction under Elizabeth I (Hutton 1996, 281; Thomas 1971, 73). In 1559 the government ordained that 'the clergy shall once a year at the time accustomed walk about their parishes with the Curate and other substantial men of the parish' (Beresford 1984, 29). The early Stuart period saw renewed enthusiasm for elaborate celebrations, and it became popular among parishes to spend more on providing refreshments. A further resurgence of popularity occurred after the Restoration, but following a peak of activity around 1700, the custom entered a protracted phase of decline, lasting a century (Hutton 1996, 285).

As I have mentioned, this decline in popularity is usually attributed to the combined impact of advances made in cartography and also the spread of enclosure (Thomas 1971, 74). According to Pounds, 'beating the bounds had become a time-wasting ceremony of little or no practical value: by the later eighteenth century boundaries were unlikely to be lost' (Pounds 2000, 79). Keith Thomas has stated that the 'ritual was well designed for open-field country', and that enclosure would have 'impeded anything so cumbersome as a perambulation around parochial boundaries' (Thomas 1971, 74; Bushaway 1982, 82; Cressy 1989, 24). There are, however, a number of problems with these arguments, neither of which provide particularly adequate explanations.

A number of early maps dating to the sixteenth and seventeenth centuries record 'perambulation' or 'procession' ways, and there is considerable evidence that perambulations were still being carried out regardless of the fact that the line of parish boundaries had been cartographically recorded. 'The Purrell Way' in Cawston is one such example: recorded on a series of early maps (NRO, MS 4521; NRO, MC 341/13; NRO, NRS 21404), it was also the focus of a protracted boundary dispute lasting into the late seventeenth century (TNA: PRO, E134/43&44Eliz/Mich7: see below pp. 73–74). Clearly the matter of recording boundaries on maps was not in itself considered sufficient for the preservation and maintenance of parochial bounds.

The connection between enclosure and the decline of perambulations is not straightforward either. David Underdown's research in the West Country found that there was a marked decline of perambulations in wood-pasture parishes (Underdown 1985, 80–2), but this does not appear to have been the case in Norfolk (Figure 16). Even on the heavier clay soils in the south of the county, where early piecemeal enclosure was extensive, there is much evidence for the continuing importance of perambulations, including seventeenth- and eighteenth-century references for New Buckenham, Brooke, Diss, and Redenhall with Harleston (NRO, MC 22/11; NRO, MC 1209/1, 808 x 1; NRO, MS 4525). Perambulations were being carried out in Newton Flotman and Aldburgh in the eighteenth century, both parishes were already enclosed by this date (NRO, Dun (c) 82, 499 x 6; NRO, PD 196/82). Enclosure did not necessarily make the course of a parish boundary clear or self-evident. In the seventeenth century confusion over the correct course of boundaries, between a group of enclosed parishes around Stockton in south Norfolk, led the court commissioners to conclude: 'every Towne doe severally walke their pambulations once evry yere but differ in diverse places upon their walkinge and therefore we cannot sett downe justly their distincte Bounds' (TNA: PRO, E178/4289). Farmers owning land on either side of a boundary could arrange their fields irrespective of the course of parochial bounds. An illustrative example comes from Diss, for which a map dating to 1727 shows a single tree growing within an enclosed field evidently preserved to mark the 'Perambulation Way' (NRO, MS 4525; Figure 17). Diss continued to be perambulated as late as 1825 when the Reverend William Manning led thirty-nine parishioners on a perambulation accompanied by music and, at the end of which, each participant received 'a shilling for dinner, a shilling to drink' (Bushaway 1988, 85).

David Fletcher has found that it was not until the 1830s and 1840s that parish boundaries were extensively mapped, initially by the tithe commissioners and later by the Ordnance Survey (Fletcher 2003). In Norfolk, for many parishes, the work of the parliamentary enclosure commissioners was an important precursor to these government initiatives. As well as providing a detailed written account of the grounds to be enclosed, the enclosure awards for Norfolk parishes began with a comprehensive description of the boundaries of the parish, paying particular attention to describing various landmark features, both old and new. Where parish boundaries crossed former tracts of common land it was necessary to set out newly created boundary marks, the course of recently set fences and hedges, while field-names and the names of landowners were documented to provide further reference points. The importance of recording old or instating new boundary marks was made all the more crucial in the face of accelerating agricultural change. On the claylands of Norfolk, farmers were steadily transforming their landscape by implementing land drainage schemes and field rationalisation, associated with the conversion of pasture closes to arable (Williamson 2002, 83–103). Judging from later Ordnance Survey maps the boundary trees, many of which had once been incorporated within hedgerows, were now left to grow isolated amid arable fields. It is possible that the official capacity of the enclosure

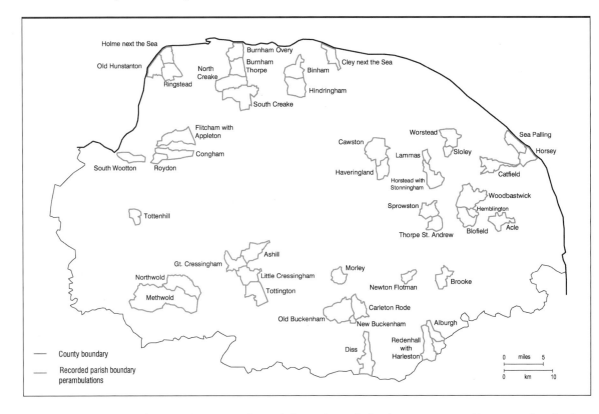

commissioners in confirming the route of parish boundaries helped to preserve such boundary features in otherwise awkward locations seemingly at odds with agrarian improvement. John Chapman has argued the achievement of the enclosure commissioners is too often overlooked (Chapman 1993, 51–55). Indeed, perhaps we should add their work in documenting, often for the first time, the boundaries of many parishes, in Norfolk at least.

The reasons for the continuation of perambulation rituals, and the meanings invested in them by individuals and social groups, are complex and have no single, straightforward explanation. By the eighteenth century, the overt holy connotations of the event had been stripped away, and in their place, the practical and social importance of preserving boundaries was highlighted. Bushaway (1982) and, more recently, Fletcher (2003) have argued that perambulations were carried out as an expression of local solidarity and parish identity. The underlying balance of interests – economic, social and political – shifted over time. The purpose and weight given to beating the bounds in the late sixteenth century was not entirely the same as beating the bounds either a century later, or at the end of the eighteenth century. Lurking behind the quaint façade of the old fashioned ritual, as imagined by some commentators, there was a vital social and political edge (Hindle 2000; Wood 2002, 101–103) – parish boundaries offered an essential point of contact where diverse aspirations were pitched. To take Hutton's argument a plausible step further, the apparent lack

FIGURE 16. Sample of recorded perambulations c.1550–1800 from deposition and cartographic sources. The distribution covers a mixture of 'wood-pasture' and 'sheep-corn' landscapes.

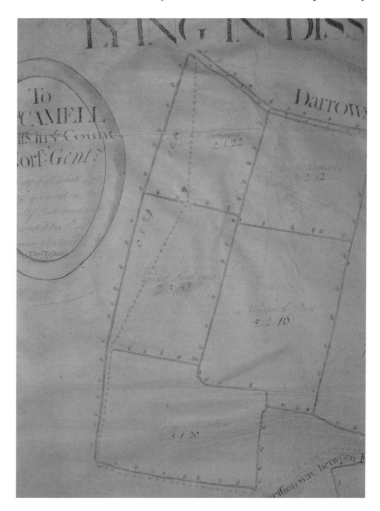

FIGURE 17. Detail of an eighteenth-century estate map showing the route of the 'Procession Way' between Diss and Roydon, villages located in the wood-pasture district of south Norfolk. In all parishes, whether located on light or heavy soils, the continuity of boundaries relied on the preservation of landmarks, such as the tree marked on this map (NRO, MS 4525).

of evidence for the practice of perambulating in the Middle Ages was perhaps countered by a growing interest in, and relevance of, the ceremony in the post-Reformation period, albeit now for rather different reasons.

Points of Contact: Old and New Landmarks

Modern maps allow landscape historians to follow the course of boundaries as linear features in the landscape. Until the comprehensive documentation of parish boundaries and growing accessibility of maps in the nineteenth century, for the majority of people boundaries were not thought of as linear constructs but were visualised as the routes taken between 'fixed' or 'nodal' points in the landscape, with each being remembered in relation to the next. Even when a boundary followed a linear feature, such as a road or river, the various boundary markers along its course prompted movement indicating for instance a change in direction. Landmarks structured peoples' cognitive maps rather than the spaces between. David Rollison's discussion of the difference between 'official' and 'popular' orderings of space is useful here. He describes the static nature of the official cartographic gaze, in contrast to the 'moving tour' of the latter (Rollison 1999, 7).

The ways early modern people conceptualised their physical bounds without the visual aid of maps, contrasts yet more strongly with the modern imagination when we consider that perambulations took place over a number of days. As a result, boundaries were not always learnt as continuous circuits, but rather as radiating out from a central point. The words of seventy-six-year-old Thomas Neave from New Buckenham convey this patterning of thought particularly well. In 1589 he recounted how on the first day of the perambulation the parishioners went from the town or borough of Buckenham to the Castle garden where they joined the inhabitants of Old Buckenham and walked with them as far as Dambridge. On the following day they left the borough to fetch in Buckenham Park and St Andrews church, they processed through the old church of St Andrew's, which had since been converted into a barn, Kings Close and Watts Close before returning to the town. On the third day they left the borough of Buckenham and walked to a place called Ostrocke, on the north side of the common, from there they travelled along a green way to Buckenham Haugh before returning through the Castle Meadows and ending their journey at Buckenham church (NRO, PD 254/171). Neave's memory of the bounds of New Buckenham provides an important insight into contemporary conceptualisations of boundaries. Cognitive maps were structured in relation to the experience of moving through the landscape rather than written or cartographic documents (Rollison 1999). In Neave's version of events, the journeys made to and from the centre of the town or borough were remembered with comparable importance to the outer bounds of the parish.

Research on boundary markers has usually focused on elucidating their origins by extracting evidence from early written sources such as Saxon charters. It is well attested that the special character of certain landmarks, such as ancient trees, burial mounds, and unusual topographical features, led to their incorporation within boundaries at an early date. The longevity of such features is usually taken for granted. Yet the enduring recognition of boundary marks was deeply embedded in the social and economic needs and processes specific to the time and place. In the post-medieval period material antiquity was not necessarily a given fact, but rather a matter of ongoing negotiation and contention.

The legitimacy of apparently permanent natural features, such as 'Broad Water' in Flitcham and 'Derbies Well' on the Hindringham/Binham boundary (NRO, Flitcham 407; TNA: PRO, DL4/18/37) became the focus of dispute in the late sixteenth and seventeenth centuries. Other natural landmarks were similarly contested. Glacial erratics such as the 'Cowell Stone' which marked the point where three parishes met, those of Marham, Swaffham and Beachamwell (NRO, HARE 6814) or the 'Trunch Stone' shown at an exaggerated scale on a late sixteenth-century plan of Congham (NRO, NRS 21377). The ritual significance and longevity of boundary landmarks was often indicated in the names attached to them, such as the 'procession mere' of Thetford', (TNA: PRO, E134/33&34Eliz/Mich29), and that of Hunstanton (NRO, LEST/IC). 'Gospel Hill' recorded on a map showing the perambulation route of Great Cressingham suggests a place where prayers were read (NRO, WLS LXI/I/7); as does 'Preaching Hill Close' in Morley situated on the parish boundary with Deopham (NRO, PD3/108 (H)). The hills indicated in these latter examples, probably refer to barrows, the perceived antiquity of which gave them particular significance as boundary markers in post-medieval landscapes; a subject explored in greater depth in chapter five (below pp. 146–154).

In between these prominent landmarks there existed an array of features – stones, earth, mounds, wooden stakes – which, while perhaps less visually obvious, nevertheless provided a material framework of reference points to be learnt by each generation. It is worth noting that the significance of boundary features, in whatever form they took, was not immediately apparent to outsiders. The identification and functions of landmarks, knowing which way to go next, was a social phenomenon, which the young together with newcomers were required to learn. In the late sixteenth century, Robert Rydde of South Wootton could remember the bounds 'by reason that he hath gone the pambulacon of the town' and was 'towld the same by his father and other anncient men of the said towne' (TNA: PRO, E134/34&35Eliz/Mich7). When he went to live in Woodbastwick, sixty-year-old John Rudd learnt the ancient perambulation route by the 'credible reporte' of his neighbours (TNA: PRO, E178/7153). As the keepers of local knowledge and memory, elderly residents were called upon to verify the authenticity of boundary features. The maintenance of boundaries did not rely on map evidence alone, but relied on local experience of the landscape and an understanding of the relational sequence of landmarks.

The written testimonies produced during court proceedings offer a valuable insight into the complex inter-relationship between the written and cartographic record, oral memory and the material evidence on the ground. For example, the inclusion of the 'Whight Stake', on what is a large and ornate map of the city of Norwich and its environs, indicates its significance as a landmark for commoners and manorial lords alike (Figure 18). Its specific use as a boundary is not obvious from the map evidence alone, however. During litigation proceedings of the late sixteenth century, Edmund Cosen, a fisherman and inhabitant of Thorpe, regarded the 'Whight Stake' to be a feature of some antiquity. Having known it for fifty-two years, its value was imprinted upon his memory as a child when:

> in company with the inhabitants of Thorpe in their pambulacon made for the continewance of the bownds of the sayd towne ... and about the second tyme of (his) goinge ... came to a bownd called the White Stake (he) beinge but a child his father came behynd him and tooke him by the eare and bad him remember the Crosse waie there because it was the uttermost bownd of there Towne goinge towardes the White Stake (TNA: PRO, E178/7153).

Contemporary descriptions such as this, offer a sense of the ways boundaries were conceived in predominately oral societies. Landscape and memory combined, and boundary features became intimately associated with peoples' own life histories.

Frequently referred to as 'dooles' – a generic term for boundary mark in Norfolk (Forby 1830) – boundary marks took the form of such relatively ephemeral features as stakes, stones, earth mounds, and cross-shapes dug into the soil. A 'special doole stone' for example marked the point where the boundaries of Westwick, Sloley and Worstead met (TNA: PRO, DL4/49/3). The bounds of South Wootton incorporated 'a stonne lying in Walsingham way' (TNA: PRO, E134/34&35Eliz/Mich7). In other villages, doole stones were afforded names such as the 'Pearle' or 'Pirle Stone' which marked the boundary of Flitcham and Appleton (NRO, MS 4293; Figure 19). For marking the stretches of boundary on open commons a particularly favoured motif was that of a cross dug into the ground: a symbol reminiscent of the use of freestanding crosses. This device had a practical use representing the need for a mark that would be distinguishable from the hollows and pits made by commoners extracting clay for brick-making (on Mousehold Heath, for example, TNA: PRO, E178/7153) or digging for rabbits (such as Cawston, TNA: PRO, E134/43&44Eliz/Mich7).

Some 'dooles' may have been very ancient features, but many had been introduced in relatively recent times as a result of the growing concern to stabilize ambiguous sections of parish boundary notably across stretches of open countryside, or in periods when new farming regimes required enclosure. Indeed, taken at face value certain boundary markers appear to have been relatively impermanent features in contrast to major topographical features, in the sense that they could be easily moved, ploughed out, or chopped down and therefore relied heavily on collective participation for both recognition and preservation (Figure 20). As a result they often became highly contentious points in the landscape. This was particularly the case across tracts of common and heath, where in the past boundaries had been less carefully delimited. In a court case of 1586 the inhabitants of Swaffham Prior in Cambridgeshire were accused of setting up new, and false, boundary markers: Robert Manning claimed that they had made 'two crosses within thies six or seaven yeres last paste uppon the ground uppon the top of the said highe bancke ... wher never was any before made' (TNA: PRO, E134/28Eliz/Hil5). Similar boundary markers were appearing on Mousehold Heath in the second half of the sixteenth century and on Roxham common, where the 'digged cross' a supposed boundary was strongly refuted (TNA: PRO, E178/7153; NRO, PRA 470 380x6). During the dispute over Flitcham common and attempts of local inhabitants to verify the legitimacy of boundary features, it was reported that a 'dole of a cross ... did plainly appear but it was filled up before the next year' (NRO, MS 4291). The deliberate choice of the cross-motif may have been intended to tie in with common ideas about the past, and the long-term association of freestanding crosses and boundaries.

The features used to mark the course of parish boundaries were not therefore

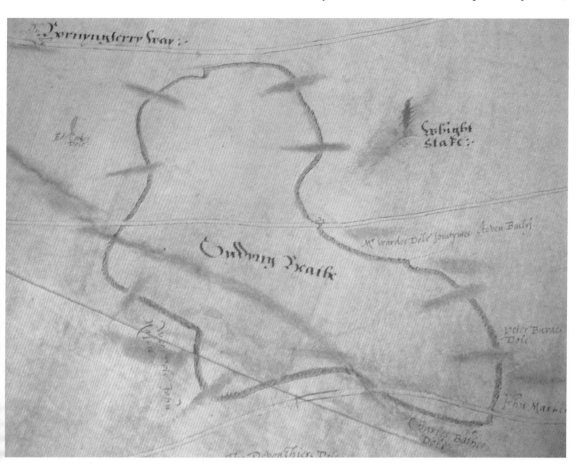

FIGURE 18. The 'Whight Stake' depicted on a map of Mousehold Heath dating to 1589. The map was drawn up in association with litigation proceedings concerning the division of the heath between adjoining villages (TNA: PRO, MR52).

simply fixed points but required constant recognition and maintenance, a process that in itself lent otherwise movable objects a degree of permanence and gave substance to claims that they had existed since time immemorial. The often humiliating and sometimes painful education of children, the provision of beer and food, and before the Reformation the saying of prayers and gospels, all took place at historically and collectively revered landmarks. In Worstead the company of parishioners paused for refreshments at one such doole stone, which marked the corner of an enclosed field. According to Nicholas Russell the owner of the ground provided beer in acknowledgement of the course of the parish boundary:

> To a doole stone fixed at the corner of a close called hasts close and further saith that in the tyme of their goeing the said purrell the said Mr Leverington hath come out and brought them beare not disalowing or gaynesaying the goeing of the said purrell (TNA: PRO, DL4/49/3).

The parishioners of Worstead undertook routine maintenance of the 'dooles of stone or boundaryes' that marked out their common. Henry Wright, husbandman, deposed that he had walked 'the purrell' of the town of Worstead for sixteen years and that the way adjoining Brockley Heath was 'dooled with stoones on eyther sydes' and 'in their purreling' they 'goe in the said waye and to make bare the said doole stones on the north side of the said waye when they are covered' (TNA: PRO, DL4/49/3). The inhabitants of Burnham Overy and Burnham Thorpe were likewise involved in the ritual re-construction of boundary marks. Robert Swan a husbandman living in Burnham Thorpe explained that during their respective perambulations the inhabitants of both towns built stone mounds to mark their sides of the boundary:

> The inhabitants of Burnham Thorpe yearelie at soche tyme as they go their pambulacon laie a heape of stones at the upper ende of that waie by Holkhams bordere as a marke to pte and devide the bounds of their towne from the bounds of Burnham Overy and he thinketh that the inhabitants of Burnham Overy laye also a heape of stones on the other side of that waie against the said heapes laid by Burnham Thorpe (TNA: PRO, E134/37Eliz/East17).

Such regular acts of maintenance were an essential part of the ongoing process of sustaining local memory, as well as a requisite for the preservation of the physical features themselves. The premise behind the remaking, or adding to an existing structure, was to demonstrate social cohesion: their efforts recognised and substantiated the actions of past generations and sought to build for the future.

The social context of Rogationtide has been widely discussed, often from the perspective of an inward-looking community: according to Underdown perambulations were 'a welcome relief from toil; they also brought neighbours together and affirmed the links that bound them to each other and to the world of nature' (Underdown 1985, 45). But there is evidence to suggest that the process of recognising and remembering these individual, often idiosyncratic boundary features had more complex roles to play in the social life of villagers. There was, for instance, the possibility that neighbouring villagers would meet one another during their respective processions. Indeed, some festivities were coordinated in this respect, so that meetings would take place at certain designated points in the landscape. As we have seen, on the first day of the Rogation week celebrations, the inhabitants of New Buckenham joined with their neighbours from Old Buckenham in the castle gardens and walked the section of bounds together as far as 'Dambridge' (NRO, PD 254/171). Elsewhere, in a court case concerning Mousehold Heath, Richard Lathe of Thorpe remembered encountering the inhabitants of Sprowston on the heath during their perambulation and met the inhabitants of Postwick 'at a certain place called Gargate hills' (TNA: PRO, E178/7153). From Flitcham, John Creede's account is also revealing. As mentioned in chapter one, the inhabitants of Babingley and Flitcham met at Whetstone Pit while the inhabitants of West Newton and Flitcham met at the 'Purrell Stone' (TNA: PRO, E178/7153).

Given the importance of perambulations in maintaining parish boundaries, their prohibition under the Edwardian regime, had serious consequences in some villages. In 1547 a set of injunctions commanded that no procession

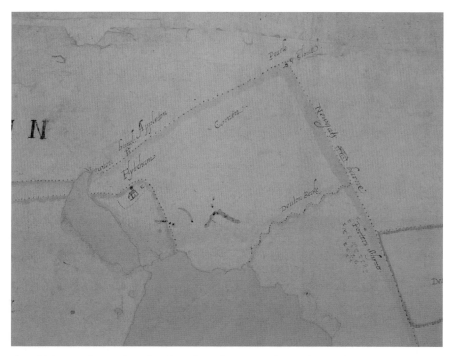

FIGURE 19. The parish boundary across Flitcham Common was marked by a range of modest features among them the variously spelt 'Pearle', 'Pirle' or 'Purrell' Stone (presumably named in reference to the annual event of 'purrelling'). Note also the curious, apparently purposefully built structure referred to as the 'bund' or 'bound' of Appleton (NRO, MS 4293).

should be made in church, churchyard or anywhere else in the parish, a ruling that probably extended to the Rogationtide ceremonies (Duffy 1992, 452). This interlude, in what were purportedly unbroken customs, lasted until the accession of Mary, and was later recalled by Edmund Cosen who stated that: 'he hathe knowne the same pambulacon made and used for the towne of Thorpe for the space of fyftie yeres saving in the tyme of Kinge Edwarde the Sixte it seased and begane agayne in queene maries daies' (TNA: PRO, E178/7153). It is possible that the suspension of the custom, albeit for a relatively brief period, gave rise to a degree of ambiguity, opportunistically exploited on occasions, concerning the 'ancient' course of boundaries, particularly where they ran across areas of open common land shared between neighbouring communities. In New Buckenham, for example, deponents held the religious and political upheavals of the mid-sixteenth century responsible for the surreptitious movement of boundaries. John Miles remembered that before the 'comosion' and 'Ketts Camp' in 1549: 'He never heard that the inhabitants of Old Buckenham did in their pambulation fetch in any parte of the waste ground lying on the east side of the Borough of New Buckenham but since the comosion time' (TNA: PRO, E134/38Eliz/Hil24).

Perambulation routes and boundary landmarks were evidently not static features etched onto the landscape since time immemorial. Court cases from the late sixteenth and early seventeenth centuries include frequent allegations of fabricated routes. During the litigation proceedings from Flitcham, concerning the rights of the inhabitants to access heathland intercommoned by a number of neighbouring parishes and manors, it was deposed that:

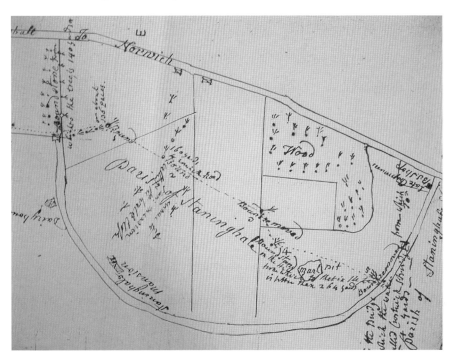

FIGURE 20. The parish
boundary of Staninghall
recorded in the late
eighteenth century.
Despite the enclosure of
land in the parish, the
bounds still required
careful deliberation and
in places restoration.
Evidently some boundary
features had been
removed. In an effort to
'fix' the boundary, care
was taken to measure
the distances between
boundary stones and
boundary trees and their
relationship to Norwich
Road, which was deemed
to be a permanent feature
(NRO, PD 597/77).

Appleton men goe in the pambulacon with Flitcham for certeine parte of the
boundes aboute purrell gate and so oughte Newton men to go there But ... of late
yeares the inhitants of Newton have of late come further ... southward with theire
pambulacon (TNA: PRO, E178/7153).

This case and others such as Mousehold Heath, involved tenants, parishioners,
and in many cases manorial lords, who attempted to shift the course of parish
boundaries in order to gain a greater share of local resources. But in some places
the natural terrain prevented access to sections of perambulation route. In the
late eighteenth century the perambulation of the 'Broadland' parish of Catfield
could not be undertaken without 'boates and bootes' (NRO, PD 531/1). Robert
Morley of Tottenhill remembered how 'the grounde was so weete and full of
dikes that he could never make pambulacon that waye, but he was always
mynded if he could have passed drye' (TNA: PRO, E134/20Eliz/Trin5).

The highly local and deeply problematic context of boundary preservation,
especially across open landscapes, was alluded to in a court case concerning grazing
rights to Mousehold Heath. During the 1590s a survey was made, apparently in
the presence of diverse credible inhabitants of the bordering villages, and a map
was drawn up to distinguish the true bounds of the waste. Such was the enormity
of the task and potential for ambiguity the surveyors sought 'not to distinguishe
the pambulacon or lymitt of any Towne upon Musholde nor the Bounds of
severall fouldcorses or such like leaste we shoulde make litigiouse any mans
interest' (TNA: PRO, E178/7153). This reluctance, on the part of the surveyors
to enter into a dialogue with neighbouring villagers, confirms the difficulties of
setting out boundaries within predominately oral societies without giving rise

to argument and controversy. As a result the map represented Mousehold Heath as a homogenous territory and yet clearly a network of boundaries existed, as suggested by the depiction of various isolated features including the Whight Stake: the status of which rested in the minds of local people.

Because sections of boundaries were not 'fixed', to the extent that they are now, and because the large majority of local societies had a vested interest in their upkeep, they were the subject of constant surveillance and interrogation. Ascertaining the 'true' bounds of a parish was made more problematic by the transient nature of many boundary features. As indicated in the court cases from the Burnham's and Worstead, at this time the upkeep of boundaries was part of an ongoing process of adding to what was already there, a process that required collective participation. There were also moments in the 'life histories' of parish boundaries when old landmarks were removed for some reason. To guard against destruction or surreptitious movement was a major reason for perambulations, but another was to endorse new markers.

A sketch map of Cawston, dating to c.1600, refers laconically to 'the place where the elme stod', evidently a prominent, although now lost, landmark (Figure 21). But it is only the details provided by a slightly earlier Exchequer court case that reveals the full extent of its importance as a former boundary mark (TNA: PRO, E134/43&44Eliz/Mich7). In this one of the witnesses John Jegoe stated that, for the previous twenty years, the inhabitants and ministers of Cawston had 'gone ther pambulacon unto the said elme and so back againe through the said lane unto a purrell waie lyeth betwene a close of the defendt next adioyning to his howse in Heverland and the feild in Cawston'. John had been employed to fell the tree, explaining to the court that:

> Ther did stand in the said lane an ould decaied elme which … was the bound betwene Heverland and Cawston and saith that by reason of the narrownes of the said lane as also by reason of the … ould elme the … lane was … noe good foote waie for men to travel through.

The tree was to be replaced by a new boundary stone, John described how he felled the tree and 'did place and sett downe in the same place … a fayre doleston' at the defendants own cost. According to John the lane was made 'much fayrer and better for passengers than in tymes past it hath bene'. During the replacement of the established landmark there was a strong emphasis on collective participation. Before grubbing out the tree John notified 'diverse of the tenants of Cawston … to come and see the dole stone sett and placed in the stead thereof'. The incident was also amerced in Cawston manor court which, as well as documenting the replacement of the boundary mark, was another means of disseminating the news of the event and thus substantiating the validity of the new 'dole stone'. However, documentation and public notice did not dissipate local tensions regarding the course of the boundary.

With the removal of this particular landmark the inhabitants of Cawston were concerned to confirm and to remind others as to the correct course of the parish boundary. John Sewell, speaking in the same court case, recalled that some twenty five years previously he had heard 'old Loame' and 'ould Bulman' say 'that the purrell waie devyding Cawston and Heverland did lye through the orchard of the defendt and so by the backhouse and next his howse in Heverland from the Elme'. John Sewell went on to describe how a wall, recently constructed by the defendant was situated: 'soe nere the ... tree where ... the anncyent purrell waie laye through soe as they can neyther goe nor see into the said orchard'. Until that time the orchard had apparently been enclosed with a bank and 'an ould pale'. Undoubtedly the tree was removed because it was an obstruction to the line of the wall. However, the wall, the boundary stone and the course of the parish boundary through this property, continued to be an acrimonious issue throughout the seventeenth century.

Coloured in bold red the wall is clearly shown on an otherwise monotone map dating to 1674 (Figure 22). The map shows the route of the perambulation or 'purrell way' passing by 'Stantling Cross' on the left. During their perambulation the parishioners followed their customary route, walking to the 'dowle stone' situated by the wall, before commencing with their circular route of the parish. In recognition of the correct course of the boundary Mr Hirne, owner of the mansion house, was expected to provide hospitality at the stone, 'in acknowledgment of their civilty in not passing in their perambulation through his mansion house' (NRO, BL IC/2/17). But in 1676 the parishioners found the gate locked and the owner away from home, nevertheless they set about making their customary mark upon the wall. Whether this was intended as an act of antagonism or not, as the parishioners maintained they had made marks in previous perambulations, their actions provoked Hirne who came out of his house and allegedly 'with much fury' ran at John Lamb and 'violently laid him over the pale with an oaken stick, then gave him a second blow'. When asked to account for his actions he replied 'he would strike him for digging downe his walls' (NRO, BL IC/2/17). Evidently, an earlier compromise had been reached between the property owner and the parishioners, which involved their meeting at the stone. In rejecting his established role in the ceremony Hirne denied local knowledge and, as is apparent from the deposition evidence, this knowledge could be traced to the mid-sixteenth century at least. Boundaries, in terms of their function as 'nodal' points, were thus not simply fixed since time immemorial. They required ongoing and collective mediation achieved through the oral and material culture of the parish.

Tithable Territories

It is generally accepted that one of the main reasons for the longevity of perambulations was their essential role in defining and safeguarding the rights of clergy to claim tithes (Bushaway 1982, 86; Pounds 2000, 77). The subject of tithes was fiercely contested over the course of the seventeenth century (Brace 1998; Evans 1984, 395). The vagueness of the biblical justification for the system was used to denounce the legitimacy of the obligation. Others questioned its

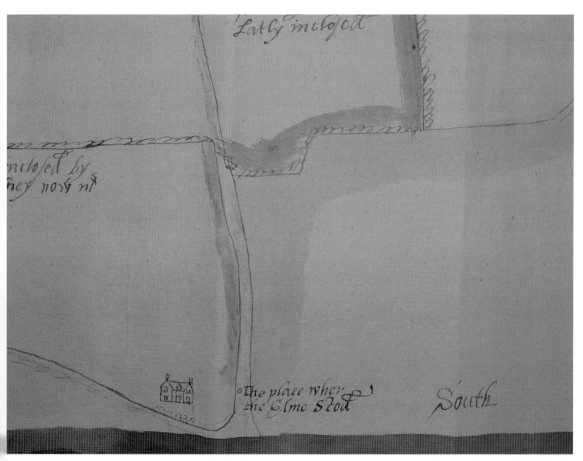

Latly inclofed

inclofed by hey now nt

The place wher the Elme Stod

South

FIGURE 21. Detail of a sketch map of Cawston dating to the late sixteenth century, drawn up in connection with a dispute over land use rights during which various 'ancient' landmarks, including an old elm tree, became fiercely contested (NRO, MC 341/13).

expediency to society and economy, condemning tithe customs as constituting a break on agrarian improvement and the advancement of the Commonwealth (Brace 1998, 46–59). At a local level tithes were hotly contested, but often for different reasons. The provision of tithes secured for many impoverished clergy a basic income, especially in parishes where there was little glebe land (Evans 1976, chapter 1). However, following the Dissolution and subsequent re-distribution of monastic lands a substantial proportion of tithes, as much as one third of the total, was transferred to lay landowners or their lessees (Evans 1976). This transferral of ownership was met by dissatisfaction and in some places outright hostility within parish communities. Some tithe payers refused to accept the new lay owners, claiming that produce from land formerly belonging to the monasteries was exempt from the tithe tax. In Wymondham, for example, the tenants refused to pay their tithes from 'Downham shift' as it was believed 'by diverse of the towne of Windham that it was for that the same were sayed to be Abbey landes' (TNA: PRO, E134/35&36Eliz/Mich5). Often owned by wealthy landowners, such disputes unravel to reveal complex territorial interests.

In the medieval period ecclesiastical territories were part of a complex, overlapping web of jurisdictions – the township or vill, the manor and the parish – together they formed the basis of the social, economic and religious terrain of local life. Shifts underway in the post-medieval period simplified this territorial complexity however, as gradually 'the parish' superseded the manor and township as the primary unit by which local society was organised. This re-alignment of interests was far from straightforward, and warrants further discussion later on. At the turn of the seventeenth century these antecedent administrative structures were still giving rise to confusion and disagreement, conflicts that were often manifest in the competition for tithable territories.

Historians have paid some attention to the origins of this complexity, especially in Norfolk where the manorial network – the basis for agricultural organisation – rarely corresponded to parochial boundaries. The introduction of the tithe system in the tenth century prompted churches to define their geographical territories (Winchester 1990, 10) but in East Anglia, and in Norfolk in particular, social idiosyncrasies ensured that ecclesiastical arrangements often took an unusual form, with some communities supporting more than one church in the same churchyard, of which there are twelve examples in Norfolk alone. Warner has demonstrated that the arable lands belonging to each parish could be extremely intermixed in the open fields, so as to render any attempt at perambulating the bounds impractical (Warner 1986). The 'two churches in one yard' phenomenon, moreover, was only an extreme version of a much more common occurrence, where a single village, with a single name, possessed two or more parish churches (as at Barton Bendish, where there were three churches strung out along the main street of the village: Rogerson 1997). Some, at least, of these distinct parishes were likewise extensively intermingled in the arable of the vills in question. Even communities more conventionally separated in space, but united by a shared name – the various 'Greats' and 'Littles', 'Norths' and 'Souths' – often had some intermixed tithable land. In a number of places, moreover, the boundaries of adjacent parishes were so tangled that particular strips and parcels in the fields were allocated to one, or the other, in spatially complex ways. In Garboldisham, where two churches stood only a quarter of a mile apart, the tithes were so intermixed that disputes arose 'on all sides' (Blomefield 1805, I, 270). Similarly the tithes of Framingham Pigot and Framingham Earl were apparently 'so mixed that every autumn disputes were caused' (Pounds 2000, 75).

The lack of correlation between tithable land and parochial boundaries occurred between groups of neighbouring parishes more generally. In the 1630s, during a dispute regarding the allocation of tithes in Ashill and Great Cressingham, it was reported that it was 'an ordinary thing in Norfolke' for a parson to receive tithes from land lying within the bounds of another town (NRO, PD 131/40). In the south Norfolk village of Thurlton confusion also resulted in litigation: 'because there hathe bene contention betwene the parsons of the sayd pishes' regarding the tithes pertaining to 'diverse acres' of land lying in the parishes of Thurlton, Barrowe and Chedgrave (TNA: PRO, E178/1585). In some parishes novel attempts were made at avoiding future litigation. In Middle Harling a fourteenth-century court insisted that the parishioners dig a

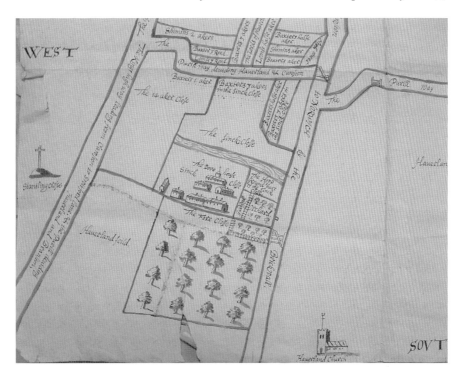

FIGURE 22. Cawston in 1674. The map shows the route of the 'purrell way', the controversial section of wall by the orchard, and the new doole stone placed next to it (NRO, NRS 21404). Enclosure often served to heighten tensions rather than diminishing them.

Saint Andrew's cross on each parcel of land before crops were sown – a symbol to represent their church dedicated to St Andrew (Blomefield 1805, I).

In places where tithes were owed to more than one proprietor idiosyncratic measures were often put in place for the distribution of produce. In Congham, for example, which had until the late sixteenth century supported three churches, it was customary for the tithe corn of the whole township to be gathered into the tithe barn where it was divided into three equal shares and allocated to each parish accordingly. Though a smaller proportion may have been given to one of the parishes, All Saints, because its inhabitants were 'fewer and poorer than the pisheners within either of the other two' (TNA: PRO, E134/25&26Eliz/Mich22). In a court case concerning the matter one witness, Thomas Skott, gave a detailed account of the procedure:

> The tythe corne yerely growinge wthin all the sevall pishes and whole towne of Congham hathe then yerly used to be equallye devided into ther several ptes and fyrste gathered by one man and layed into a bearne and after the same beinge threshed devyded by the bushell unto everye parson or there fermors severallye a like quantytie and proporcion and the strawe and chaffe likewyse and all the resydewe of the tythes wthin the said three severall pishes and towne of Congham vidz the tythe wooll tythe lambe tythe pygges and geese and other severall tythes hathe ben used to be payed to the parson of St Andrewes and the parson of St Maryes and he never did knowe itt otherwyse ... he hathe allwayes payed theme in that maner durynge the tyme of his abode in ... the towne of Congham. (TNA: PRO, E134/25&26Eliz/Mich22).

In the closing decades of the sixteenth century friction was caused within the township by the actions of James Dewhurst, parson of the parishes of St Mary's and St Andrew's, who 'by violence or constraynte (did) take awaye certayne tythes from the parsonage of all Sts' (TNA: PRO, E134/29&30Eliz/Mich35). In order to clarify its status as a tithable unit, attempts were made to ascertain the ancient bounds of the parish of All Saints. Humphrey Camme, a sixty-six-year-old yeoman, provided two versions of the bounds. The first he confirmed with reference to his father, former farmer of the parsonage, who had likewise been taught the bounds when he was a boy by 'Old Mannes', believed to be over one hundred years old when he died (TNA: PRO, E134/25Eliz/East12). Thus Camme presented the parish as an ancient territorial unit, which had been in existence for over three generations of inhabitants. However, even when the precise line of a boundary was mapped or described on paper, problems still arose when such accounts no longer related to what was on the ground. Consequently Camme was required to give a second description. Expanding on the details of the first he included details of new landownership, and the hedges and ditches of recent enclosures, which thus brought the bounds up-to-date.

The situation in Congham illustrates well the difficulties facing tithe owners and parishioners in disentangling inherited jurisdictional structures. Camme's detailed explanation of the bounds was not recognised by everyone. As attested by eighty-year-old Thomas Skott (husbandman): the 'certenyne bowndes meetes and lymytts of the said three severall pishes hathe ben and yet be unknowne or doubtfullye knowne' (TNA: PRO, E134/25&26Eliz/Mich22). Skott's uncertainty suggests that either Camme could claim privileged knowledge of the bounds or, as it was not unusual for the tithes of closely related parishes to be intermixed and bearing in mind the extent of recent landscape changes brought about by enclosure, he fabricated them – presumably encouraged by Dewhurst. Dewhurst was accused of coercing others into supporting his claim. William Swanton claimed that George Barrett, who had testified at Norwich Consistory Court regarding the issue, told him that: 'James Dewhurste both terryfied and threatined him' to the end that he might:

> reword and recante that which before he had sworne and deposed menasinge him further that unlesse he would so doe he the sayd Dewhurste would take awaye from him the sayd Barret certayne lands which the sayd Barret had in fearme of the sayd Dewhurste and ... if he would so doe he should still retayne and enioye them (TNA: PRO, E134/29&30Eliz/Mich35).

Changes in parochial organisation – the decline of small parishes particularly following the Act of Consolidation in 1536 – thus compounded problems anyway inherent in the complex system of ecclesiastical organisation that characterised Norfolk. But other changes could serve to engender disputes over the boundaries and the allocation of tithes, most notably changes in land use. When land remained under pasture or heath the exact line of a parish boundary was a matter of some indifference to tithe owners. Tithes owed for sheep and cattle were easily assessed and extracted and were not directly related to precise areas of land. In contrast, where land was cropped it mattered greatly whether a particular parcel lay in one parish or another. In 1598 a further level of complexity was added to the Congham dispute. Ralph Waller, from neighbouring Roydon, claimed the tithes owed from fifty acres of barley, lying in the West Field of Congham, which he had sown three years previously. Apparently for the first two years the tithes had been 'quietly' gathered and divided into the three customary portions pertaining to the three parishes of Congham. But following the last harvest, Waller carried away the entire crop. Humphrey Pollard, who had been appointed to gather the tithes, accused Waller of attempting to deceive the parsons of Congham, alleging that his servants: 'did take and carry awaye the barley growing upon the said lands and did not cast nor set forth the tythe thereof accordinge to the accustomed manner ... or if he did ... it was so secret and couenouse that the sayd parsons of Congham or there servants could not have any notice thereof' (TNA: PRO, E134/40Eliz/East3).

Local opinion was deeply divided on the issue. Edmund Chartres of West Newton could remember when fifty years previously sheep and rabbits grazed the West Field, until twenty-five years ago when Mr Waller's farmers broke up and cultivated outlying portions of heath or 'brecks'. Attempts to establish the perambulation route only served to heighten the controversy, with inhabitants from both sides of the boundary remembering taking in the heath grounds in question. According to sixty-five-year-old Alice Swanton 'the landes so sowen with barley ... doe leye wthin the precinct and pambulacon of Congham', conversely fifty-year-old Ellen Norrys remembered when she was 'but a girle of thage of 10 yeares' walking with the inhabitants of Roydon in their perambulation at which time they encompassed the grounds called Roydon Field alias Congham Westfield and the tithes of the grounds 'ought to belong to the parson of Roydon onelye'. The dispute became yet more complicated, to judge from the statement of eighty-year-old John Pond, husbandman from Castle Rising. He claimed that the tithes from the lands within Congham, 'commonly called Roydon Field and Congham West Field', when sown had usually been taken away by the parson of Castle Rising (TNA: PRO, E134/41/East5).

In territorial and spatial terms, therefore, this particular part of the dispute was between the jurisdictions of the township of Congham, taken to be the principal tithable unit as the tithes of the three parishes were gathered together, and the territories of manors – those of Roydon and Castle Rising. Whilst the land was under rough heathland grazing the tithe wool had apparently always been paid to Congham. Breaking up the heaths for cultivation was a particular feature of periods of population growth and buoyant grain prices, such as the late sixteenth century (see below p. 108). Once under the plough and more profitable, the hostility to the tithe system became more intense, particularly where a manor was expected to yield ten percent of its profits to another jurisdiction – manor or parish.

Controversy arose for similar reasons in the heathland parish of Ashill. In the first half of the seventeenth century disagreement ensued when eighteen acres of the sheep-course was broken up and converted to arable 'which never was ploughed before in the memory of man' (NRO, PD 131/40). The land in question was divided by the parish boundary of Ashill and Great Cressingham, which resulted in ambiguity over the payment of tithes. Whilst under pasture the tithe lamb and wool was paid to the parson of Great Cressingham except for one year when it was remembered that the parson of Ashill 'got away one lamb by violence and weakness of the other's deputy'; yet the portion of cultivated heath named Windmill Close was apparently situated within the perambulation of Ashill. Subsequently the question arose as to 'whether the nature of the profit changed doth inferre a change of the parson's right'. In other words should the parson of Ashill receive the tithe corn or, as the parson of Cressingham had always enjoyed all other tithes produced on the land, should he continue to enjoy this right. Elderly inhabitants recalled that when the breck was first ploughed some forty years previously the tithe was paid to Great Cressingham. Such a distribution was tolerated at least when the land was under rough grazing, but clearly changes in land use in conjunction with rising grain prices led to altercation.

In places demarcated by complex manorial and parochial jurisdictions, the identification of the correct course of parish boundaries was often ambiguous. In another case involving the allocation of tithes, the parishioners of Burnham Overy (also known as Burnham St Clement's) and Burnham Thorpe were locked in intense dispute over the arrangement of their local territorial structures (TNA: PRO, E134/37Eliz/East17). The dispute concerned the tithes due from land belonging to the manor of Lathes, situated close to the parish boundary. Today the parish boundary simply follows the road leading from Burnham Market to Holkham. In the sixteenth century, however, the perambulation route was a matter of controversy. Giving an account of the perambulation of the town 'in Quene Maries daies', William Peapes confirmed the location of the manor house within the parish of Burnham Overy. He remembered leaving the common way and encircling the manor house and enclosed grounds of Lathes. According to Peapes, in more recent perambulations the inhabitants of Burnham Overy interrupted the route taken by their neighbours of Burnham Thorpe, forbidding them 'to go their perambulation on the north side of Lathes'. The cause of the dispute was the allocation of tithes from twenty acres of land lying in diverse pieces in 'South Field' belonging to the manor but owed to the parson of Burnham Thorpe, which the inhabitants of Burnham Thorpe claimed within their parochial perambulation. For as long as he could remember sixty-five-year-old Robert Swan had known the several furlongs belonging to Lathes to lie in the parish of Burnham Thorpe. Uncertainty surrounding the correct course of the parish boundary continued to be a source of dispute. In 1635 it was noted that forty years previously the vicar of Burnham Overy 'did sometimes leave out to the parson of Thorpe and sometimes take in part of the landes belonginge … to the …towne of Overy', in consequence the perambulation 'hath not binne rightly gone this threescore yeares' (TNA: PRO, E134/10Chas1/Mich51).

The origins of this anomaly, like so many in Norfolk, are uncertain, and lost in the medieval past. But in the context of the later sixteenth century the dispute acquired a new and significant meaning. As the tithe was paid to their church, the inhabitants of Burnham Thorpe claimed common grazing rights especially after harvest during the period known as 'shack' (TNA: PRO, E134/37Eliz/East17). According to them, the inhabitants of Burnham Overy were entitled to graze their cattle in the South Feild at just two places called 'brakewonge' and 'water meeres'. Such restricted rights were not recognised by the inhabitants of Burnham Overy and they continued to graze their stock on South Field and within their perambulation. The dispute became increasingly acrimonious when the 'men of Burnham Thorpe' impounded the cattle belonging to their neighbours. This is a complex story but one that illustrates well the interweaving of several points of interest. The dispute over the allocation of tithes was certainly the reason behind the court proceedings. However, delving deeper into the roots of the conflict a further underlying issue emerges, one that concerned the allocation of resources between the inhabitants of neighbouring vills. In other words, the complex relationship between manor, vill and parish inherited from the Middle Ages provided opportunities for disputes regarding one kind of unit or jurisdiction to be used as a way of contesting customs and land use rights which really pertained to another.

Examining the causes of tithe disputes can thus recover intricate stories comprising a number of perspectives and ulterior motivations. The economic concerns of seigniorial lords are clear in their attempts to extend control over the landscape. But also as in the case of Congham and Burnham Thorpe, manorial interests sided with parochial interests as local solidarity was demonstrated among those taking part in Rogationtide processions. Occasionally the poor were implicated in local disagreements, revealing that they, too, had an active role in tithe disputes and boundary preservation. An excellent example concerns the depositions from Ashill and Great Cressingham. Here, the breaking up of portions of heathland for arable gave rise to altercations over gleaning rights between the poor of the two villages. In 1623 it was remembered that the parson of Ashill entered the field with a company of 'unknowne hired desperate rogues' and took away part of the tithe, and afterwards 'the poore of each towne (in great number of all sorts) went to gather by the eares (even to blood-shed) for the right of gleaninge'. The interaction between tithe collectors and gleaners is worth noting: in 1634, when the land was sown with rye and wheat, the tithe was collected 'in a skrambling and violent manner' apparently four sheaves of rye were 'plucked to pieces' and as a result were cast to the gleaners. The scuffle between the tithe-owners was replicated in that the 'poore gleaners of either towne fell to quarrelling' in their attempts to catch the corn. This suggests that either the sheaves were damaged to such an extent that it was only worth giving them to the poor or, more probably, there was some connection in the popular mind between the land that was tithable to a particular parish, and the rights of the parish poor to glean over it.

In 1634 the rules of gleaning were written down for the parish of North Elmham, it was stated that 'none gleane before the corne groweinge and the rakings thereof carrid awaie by the owner and the Tithe by the parson' (NRO, PD 209/210). Amussen has recovered further references from the Quarter Sessions at Swaffham and Fakenham which ruled that gleaning could commence only when the tithe corn had been allocated: 'The permission of the churchwardens and minister was necessary to glean, affirming patronage and deference between governors and governed' (Amussen 1988, 157). The obligations of the church, and perhaps of landowners more generally, in relieving the poor – and indeed the expectations of the poor themselves – were visibly articulated through the uses, and perceptions, of the landscape. The resident poor had a vital interest in the boundaries of their customs and rights.

The subject of tithes was thus connected with a complex raft of social and economic issues that drew together tithe-owners, tithe payers, and at times the poor, into a web of affiliation and conflict. Disputes about tithes had implications for the farming community, and for the poor. At a time of rising population, pressure on resources, and widespread land use change, it is hardly surprising that the precise line of parish boundaries was a matter of increasing importance, or that Rogationtide perambulations should be a matter not only of social concern but also, a matter of economic interest.

The Politics of Parish Boundaries

The event of beating the bounds drew on the repository of local memory; memories that to some extent cut across local social structures and extended the boundaries of belonging to include the resident, respectable poor. Elderly residents were given a special place, their perceived knowledge of local landscapes and customs giving them weight of authority above their otherwise economically marginal status (Fox 2000, 261; Shepard 2003, 225–30; Wood 1997). According to some historians the politics of place and memory was gendered. Women were excluded from the political terrain of local life, which was manifest in their prohibition from the Rogation ritual of beating the bounds (Hindle 2000). Government statutes stipulated that the chief male inhabitants or 'better sort' of the parish were to attend perambulations. Quantitative research appears to support contemporary advice. Andy Wood's comprehensive survey of equity court depositions for Derbyshire, for example, found that not one woman referred to her participation in beating the bounds (Wood 1999, 172). However, insufficient attention has been paid to the broad differences between administrative jurisdictions in upland and lowland areas and the variable importance of the parish as a unit in defining contemporary senses of place and belonging (Winchester 1997; Whyte forthcoming). In Norfolk, women took part in perambulations well into the seventeenth century. As we have seen, neighbours Ellen Norrys of Roydon and Alice Swanton of Congham gave contradictory accounts of the boundary across the open heaths lying between their parishes (TNA: PRO, E134/41Eliz/East5). Elsewhere at Worstead, for instance, 'diverse men, women and children' attended their perambulation (TNA: PRO, DL4/49/42), as they apparently did at Binham and Hindringham (TNA: PRO, DL4/18/37).

Though more usually discussed in terms of social inclusion and exclusion, the examples discussed so far in this chapter demonstrate the fragmentary and contentious process of setting out parochial territories in the sixteenth and seventeenth centuries. The opinions and motivations of those taking part in perambulations were not homogeneous; nor did these diverse inhabitants necessarily regard the entire circumference of the parish with the same degree of importance. Individuals living within the territory of Gimingham Soke in north-east Norfolk, for example, were amerced for ploughing up 'purill ways', and for non-attendance of their ancient perambulation 'as their ancestors had done' (Hoare 1918, 335). Martin Ryse, for example, was accused of encroaching 'with his plowe upon a pambulacon meare devidinge Northrepps and Southrepps at a place commonly called Millhill' (Hoare 1928, 337). In 1632 during a dispute between the owner of the Rectory and manor, and tenants of Hickling Netherhall, the court heard how the boundary meere separating the tithes pertaining to the parishes of Hickling and Sutton had been ploughed up and 'defaced' (TNA: PRO, E134/7Chas1/Mich18). These are interesting cases, for they not only point to the constant issue of maintaining perambulation or 'purrill' ways, and not just at Rogationtide, but also the divergence of interests between local inhabitants, especially perhaps when farmers held land in manors outside their home parish.

Certain sections of boundary probably provoked greater depth of emotion than others, in particular those dividing open tracts of common land. When asked to describe the parish boundary of New Buckenham, his place of residence, Peter Underwood was uncertain as to the course of the boundary to the south of the town, but he remembered very well the route of the perambulation across the common land:

> whether the pambulcan have gone to St Andrewes churche and from thence to Cundalls greene and so by Watts Lane under Harlinge woode (he) doth not now well remember but he ... remembreth the procession and pambulacon have gone ... by a Greene Waye nere Goldelockes Corner and Sheepemeare to a place called Hawghead and so fetched in Buckenham hawge ... the drinkings in that pambulacon were made ... upon the comon there (TNA: PRO, E133/8/1234).

The route of the boundary across the common held special significance for Underwood: as a resident of the village he would presumably have utilised the various resources the commons provided. It was in his personal interests, and a part of his responsibility to his neighbours, both present and future, to commit to memory the bounds of their common rights. He described the provision of refreshments upon the common, which highlights another important aspect of perambulation festivities – that as well as being enjoyable 'neighbourly' occasions, they were also mnemonic events of social and economic importance. We have already seen that in Worstead and Cawston beer was drunk at contentious boundary marks: a clear and visible statement of claims to customary rights (TNA: PRO, DL4/49/3; TNA: PRO, E134/43&44Eliz/Mich7).

It is in this context that women's involvement – as members of the household unit and commoners often in their own right – in preserving the course of boundaries becomes clear. Eighty-four-year-old Cicely Hunford, for example, described the perambulation route along the stretch of boundary separating the commons of Carleton Rode and New Buckenham, confirming that the inhabitants had time out of mind pastured their livestock there: 'Because it hath ben so used during her owne tyme and she hath heard her father and grandfather affirme it to have ben so used in ther tymes' (TNA: PRO, E178/1538). If examined qualitatively the evidence suggests that although women's knowledge was marginalised in the central law courts elderly women were considered to be the guardians of local custom and memory just as their male neighbours were (Shepard 2003, 225–30; Whyte forthcoming).

The boundaries that crossed common land represented a fusion of interests and, to a great extent, it was the addition of the Poor Laws that helped consolidate these interests. The statutes gave overseers a range of responsibilities, including the construction of poor houses on manorial wastes in order to house the destitute and deserving poor. A survey of Stockton Soke in 1625, for example, recorded the building of four small cottages on waste in Geldeston, two in Stockton and one in Gillingham for the use of the poor (TNA: PRO, E178/4289). For ratepayers, common land boundaries thus took on special significance, as they defined not only the jurisdiction of the poor rates, but also the land by which the poor could support themselves. It was not until the middle of the seventeenth century that a systematic relief system emerged in Norfolk, but even after this it made sense for local inhabitants, charged with contributing to the welfare of the poor, to allow and encourage them to use the commons, as a way of keeping their monetary obligations to a minimum (Birtles 1999, 78; Wales 1984).

It is clear from the examples given in this chapter that Rogationtide continued to be an important event in Norfolk villages in both light-soil and clayland districts. In many places this enduring importance had perhaps more to do with underlying political and economic tensions than with merriment and hospitality: tensions that permeated local social relations on a daily basis. The accountability of the parish in supporting the poor gave grounds for the policing of parish boundaries at times other than Rogation week. As we have seen in the predominately oral culture of the sixteenth and seventeenth centuries, parish boundaries were not simply fixed features of the landscape. The modest nature of many boundary features and vulnerability of oral memory dictated their constant observance on a daily basis. This process is usefully illustrated, for example, in the deposition of John Nadfield, who described himself as a husbandman and inhabitant of Woodbastwick. When asked in 1589 about his knowledge of the section of parish boundary that ran across Mousehold Heath he gave an account of his experience of the bounds as a young man:

About fyftie yeres sithens beinge then married unto his wife at Bastwick Church the inhabitants of Bastwick did take uppon them for to have carried the bride unto Hemblington where (his) dwellinge howse … was then scituate and when they had carried her to a certon waie called Walsham waie the inhabitants of Blowfeld mett them there and did there receive her and wold not permitt the said inhabitants of Bastwicke to carrie her any further because the uttor bownds of Bastwicke aforesaid went no further as the inhabitants of Blowfeld then affirmed (TNA: PRO, E178/7153).

Clearly, the inhabitants of Woodbastwick did not want an extra burden placed on them, and felt strongly that the couple should move to his place of residence in the nearby parish of Hemblington. It is striking, however, that the 'inhabitants' of the adjacent parish of Blofield prevented the progress of the party any further than the bounds of Woodbastwick. Such actions were presumably intended to safeguard their parish from an influx of young couples, desiring to take up residence there and potentially becoming a burden on local resources. This example conveys a strong sense of the landscape defined as a series of bounded spaces, across which movement for the poor was tightly regulated. The processes of inclusion and exclusion had a strong spatial context: in Hindle's words 'the poor should know their place in a geographical sense and in the social-structural relations to their betters' (Hindle 2000, 99).

The consequences of the marriage of John Nadfield is an obvious example of the day-to-day need to observe parish boundaries, but regulation of a different kind manifested itself at other times in the life-cycle of villagers. During a court case concerning the division of resources on Mousehold Heath, John Marker recalled the circumstances of his uncle's death which occurred outside his home parish of Little Plumstead. Richard Marker died in neighbouring Rackheath and, arrangements were made to convey his body to Little Plumstead where he was to be buried. His body, however, was not carried to the parish church, but to the parish boundary. On this occasion the exact place of exchange became a matter of contention, when the parishioners of Rackheath carried his body:

in a waye leadinge from Wroxham to Little Plumstead a little further than the crosse towards Little Plumstead to be buried there and the townesmen of Little Plumstead by appoyntment betwene the two townshipps metinge them in the said waie neere foxhooles where uppon by consent of the inhabitants of both the said townes he was caried backe to the said crosse as to the extreame bownds of both townes and the said dead bodie was there left by the townesmen of Rackheath and received by the townesmen of Littel Plumstead (TNA: PRO, E178/7153).

The extent to which the carriage of Richard Marker's body to 'Foxholes' was a deliberate act on the part of the townsmen of Rackheath, and to what extent an unwitting oversight, is open to speculation. However, it is possible that the inhabitants of Rackheath were laying surreptitious claim to heathland that fell within the bounds of Little Plumstead. If the inhabitants of Little Plumstead had received Richard's body at 'Foxholes' it is feasible that an opportunity would have been created for future ambiguity regarding the correct course of the parish boundary. Should the precise line of the boundary fall into question at a later date the attempt at instating a false boundary mark may have been reinforced through the collective memory of the events that took place there. In a sense therefore, whilst boundaries can be seen as exclusive terrain, they also had a part to play in receiving people back into the 'community': they were utilised as a symbolic expression of 'inclusion', as well as 'exclusion' (see also TNA: PRO, E134/28Eliz/Hil5).

In Norfolk, the particular importance of boundaries that ran across open commons and heaths is suggested by the number of disputes brought before the central law courts, and also in the various deponents' personal accounts of them. This is most evident, for example, in the cases of John Nadfield and Richard Marker, whose memories bore the imprint of deeply personal and familial experiences. In both instances these were made tangible through the deliberate use of the landscape, and by tapping into the range of meanings that boundaries already carried. As we shall see in chapter five, perhaps one of the most profound uses of boundaries was for the burial of the dead. The ephemeral nature of many boundaries demanded the continual maintenance of landmarks not just at Rogationtide but also throughout the year. We have seen how boundary features became part of peoples' life-histories when shown the bounds as children, and even in death their bodies were claimed and re-integrated within parish society. These were collective events designed to perpetuate and re-affirm local geographies of inclusion and belonging.

'Forryners Hathe Alwaies Ben Punished'

The evidence for the tightening-up of parochial bounds, and renewed vigour for perambulations, may thus reflect in spatial terms the institutionalisation of the Poor Laws and the emergence of the parish as the unit of jurisdiction for settlement and entitlement (Hindle 2000; Wrightson 1996). Common land, especially the tracts shared by more than one parish, provided a point of contact where a range of interests interconnected and allegiances were formed. Perambulations were often as much about negotiating the range of customs and rights attached to the land as they were about defining the 'parish community'. Of particular significance in all this was the shifting balance of interests between manor and parish.

Norfolk is well known, among local landscape historians at least, for its complex manorial structure, which frequently produced landholding patterns uncontained by parish boundaries. It was common for individuals to hold land belonging to more than one lord, and in a number of townships (Campbell 1986, 243; Rogerson 1995, 371–372). Some writers have suggested that despite this complexity a degree of village identity might nevertheless have been maintained during the medieval period through, for instance, the holding of manorial leet courts. In townships characterised by more than one manor the head manor assumed overall authority, and dealt with broader intra-village issues, other than those concerned with the individual manor, including the regulation of common land (Rogerson 1995, 348–349). The extent to which such arrangements existed prior to the mid-sixteenth century is, however, unclear. Cord Oestmann for example found that it was in the sixteenth century that the leet court in Hunstanton was more rigorously organised (Oestmann 1994, 118). Christopher Harrison has argued that rather than declining in the later sixteenth century 'manorial courts were central to the governance of rural England', remaining so until at least the mid-seventeenth century (Harrison 1997, 43–59). As we might expect, at a local level the authority of manorial courts varied from place to place. Jane Whittle's study of villages in the Northern Heathland district, for example, found manorial courts to be in decline as places for hearing criminal offences and petty pleas: their role increasingly taken by the county courts (Whittle 2000, 46–56). By the late sixteenth century, however, the increasing popularity of the Westminster law courts in adjudicating local land disputes had a further impact in shifting the balance of power away from manorial courts. Indeed, manorial lords complained bitterly at the loss of revenue this cost them. Richard Beckham, lord of Narford Manor in 1579, allegedly said to his tenants that they were intent upon 'disinheriting' him, by presenting 'dyvers things in the quenes courte which ought to be presented in his courte' (TNA: PRO, E134/21&22Eliz/Mich31). In many places, however, manorial courts continued to operate, not only dealing with questions of manorial property but also regulating other aspects of village life, such as the use of common land (Harrison 1997; Whittle 2000, 58–63).

The complex relationship between manors and vills in Norfolk ensured much uncertainty over precisely who was entitled to use particular commons, which aggravated tensions both within and between settlements. There was uncertainty in Shernborne, for example, over whether Ling Common lay within Shernborne Manor or Snettisham Manor: for the tenants of Snettisham dwelling within Shernborne, together with the tenants and inhabitants of Shernborne, were both said to have collected fuel and grazed their animals there (TNA: PRO, DL4/18/6). In Stratton Strawless the tenants of Stratton Manor together with diverse inhabitants of the town, some holding their tenements of the manor of Buxton and others holding them from the manors of Hevingham, Catts and Hainforth, together enjoyed common of pasture on the 'great heath' of Stratton 'time out of mind' (TNA: PRO, DL4/57/47). Yet in nearby Felmingham it was only the tenants of Suffield Manor living within the bounds of Felmingham who were entitled to graze their livestock on Stow Heath, and not the tenants of Felmingham Manor (TNA: PRO, E134/26Eliz/East13). In Wacton both the tenants of Forncett Manor and the inhabitants of Wacton had 'tyme out of mynde' common of pasture during all seasons of the year on Wacton Great Green (TNA: PRO, E134/37Eliz/East4).

Competition over resources was not, therefore, just a contest between neighbouring parishes, but also between the tenants and lords of neighbouring manors. This does not necessarily mean that the influence of the Poor Laws, or sensitivity towards poverty, was not also a motive driving ratepayers to assert their social and economic territories. Moments of apparent solidarity arose out of the common interests of manorial lords, tenants and commoners. William Warde, who described himself as an inhabitant of Roughton, declared during one dispute that:

> Every fermor and owte dweller thoughe he had londes within the towne of Roughton oughte to be debarred and secluded from kepinge of any shepe or cattell uppon the saide great comon and that dyverse have bene amercyed in Salgrave leate for so doinge (TNA: PRO, DL4/12/6).

The words used to describe individuals from neighbouring settlements were often xenophobic in tone (Hindle 2000). In the Norfolk examples the image used is frequently that of unknown, faceless 'strangers' or 'foreigners'. In the Queen's leet of Shernborne, for example, 'dyverse strangers' from the nearby parishes of Bircham and Fring had been duly punished for trespassing on Shernborne Ling (TNA: PRO, DL4/18/6). In many respects, the concern to limit the use of common land to local residents would appear to confirm the growing importance of the parish as a focus of local identity. Steve Hindle has argued that: 'the intensely localised basis of taxation fostered competition between parishes as community identities were forged anew in opposition to the demands of poor migrants' (Hindle 1996, 126). In Norfolk, however, the extent to which such disparaging language reflected animosity towards poor migrants was probably less of a significant factor, where begging tended to be highly localised (Wales 1984, 360). A situation that stands in contrast to other parts of the country, such as forest areas, where extensive areas of waste attracted squatters from far and wide; or districts such as Hertfordshire, where the migration of poor vagrants to urban centres, especially London, placed unprecedented demands on social and economic resources (Hindle 1996, 129).

In Norfolk, it was a consolidation of interests between lords and tenants, at a superficial level at least, that helped reinforce the importance of the parish as the basic territorial division. This was most clearly expressed in the recurrent use by deponents in court cases of their knowledge of 'ancient' perambulation routes, and especially in the fact that on some occasions the manorial context of perambulations was explicitly referred to in the division of common land. In Felmingham, for example, manorial divisions and tenants' rights were physically mapped out on the ground. John Eyllyard deposed that in 1584:

> The Quenes tenants of Suffield have alwaies used to make their pambulacon and purlue abought the bounds of Stow Heath and the Quenes maiesties tenants in the right of the mannor of Gymmingham hath alwaies a pambulacon and purlie of the est northest of the said towne and comon called Stow heath (TNA: PRO, E134/26Eliz/East13).

In Flitcham, seigniorial interest in establishing grazing rights coincided with the desire of commoners to segregate and secure their rights from adjacent villagers. As discussed in chapter one, the owners of Flitcham Manor exercised grazing or 'fold course' rights on Flitcham common across which the lords of Appleton were accused of encroaching with their fold course by grazing their sheep beyond the south side of Willesden Hills. But parallel hostility had also surfaced between the inhabitants of Flitcham and their neighbours from West Newton. The heath in question was a large tract of intercommon to which the inhabitants of Flitcham, Appleton and West Newton, claimed common rights. In the late sixteenth and seventeenth centuries attempts were being made to delineate the physical boundaries that ran across it and to confirm the allocation of resources between villages and manors. Allegations were made against the inhabitants and townsmen of Flitcham that during their perambulation they 'alter in there goinge sometymes going in one place and sometymes in another' (TNA: PRO, E178/1587). This territorial ambiguity was probably added to by the fact that Appleton, which by this time had suffered a considerable measure of depopulation, was generally thought of as being annexed to Flitcham – as 'the parish constable of Flitcham was always that of Appleton' (TNA: PRO, E178/1587). 'The men of West Newton' were accused of grazing their stock and cutting furze upon Flitcham common, while the inhabitants of Flitcham had been 'disturbed and denied' in their attempts to take furze on the north and north west side of an old ditch, taken to be the division between West Newton and Appleton. The demarcation of fold courses in respect of parish boundaries again draws attention to the consolidation of manorial and parochial interests. Comparatively small tracts of common could also become the focus of controversy between neighbouring villages, such as that shared by the inhabitants of Binham and Hindringham. In the late sixteenth century both sides claimed that the route of their perambulation took in the greater part of the common (TNA: PRO, DL4/18/37).

Conclusion

The boundary disputes and subsequent alteration of boundary routes described in this chapter, may only be minor alterations to us, but were for contemporaries a highly contentious matter. Contention was clearly about establishing the correct and 'ancient' course of parish boundaries, but in particular the disputes were about the boundaries across open commons and heaths. Set within the context of welfare reform – as a combination of state legislation and 'unofficial' measures introduced by resident ratepayers – the significance of common boundaries becomes evident. In permitting the poor to collect fuel or to graze a cow or flock of geese those responsible for their maintenance under directives of the Poor Laws could reduce their contributions to the relief system (Amussen 1988; Hindle 2002, 232; 2004; Neeson 1993; Wales 1984). In view of this, the continuing post-Reformation importance of old Rogationtide rituals becomes clear: perambulations were as much about the articulation of rights to access local resources, as they were about defining parish boundaries for the purposes of assessing tithes or the new responsibilities of the parish towards the poor.

The 'tinkerings' that Rackham has declared for modern times were as much an issue in the early modern period and, as a result, the 'truth' he seeks from nineteenth-century maps, certainly with regards to parish boundaries across common land, would not necessarily have been recognised as the truth for village communities living in previous centuries. Added to this, even when boundaries were documented cartographically in the late sixteenth and seventeenth centuries, we should not assume that their representation reflected the 'truth' on the ground. As we have seen in the case of Cawston, maps could be at variance with local knowledge relating to the 'ancient' course of parish bounds. As landscape historians are well aware, early maps should be treated with caution – they were commissioned by wealthy landowners for a range of purposes that changed over time, but were basically designed to represent a simplified, often idealised version of the world. Court records provide invaluable access to the knowledge and memories of local people which, when used in conjunction with cartographic material, highlights the powerful meanings and associations attributed to various landmarks. The depiction or indeed omission of the features discussed during court proceedings points to the complex interplay between elite and popular understandings of the landscape.

Another important point to emerge from the foregoing discussion is the very different way the physical boundaries of place were perceived in this period compared to our modern conceptualisations. Boundaries were identified in terms of the landmarks that defined their course – their recognition relied on local knowledge, most obviously created and sustained in the event of perambulating the bounds. But they also featured in peoples' lives at other times as well, most strikingly illustrated in the conveyance of dead bodies at parish boundaries and, as we shall see, sometimes their burial. It is by looking at the treatment of such landmarks and their integration within people's life-histories, that we gain an insight into contemporary concerns regarding the ephemeral nature of boundaries, especially across tracts of open common and heath. This is evident in the deliberate destruction of old boundary markers and the creation of new ones, both actions were contentious and could lead to a great deal of confusion as to the correct course of the boundary. The ongoing preservation of boundary features relied on collective participation in what amounted to a shared dialogue between the present and knowledge of the past, expressed in terms of a material language of memory.

In spatial terms the sixteenth and seventeenth centuries were characterised by the growing importance of the parish. But the concept of the parish as a fixed physical entity, posited by social historians, overlooks the complexity of maintaining and fixing parochial territories. Added to this, the contests over parochial bounds were part of a wider process that saw the steady rationalisation of territorial structures inherited from the medieval past. Just as the diffuse religious topographies of the late medieval period, were radically streamlined following the Reformation, an intricate network of overlapping jurisdictions were gradually disentangled, eventually leaving the parish as the primary administrative unit.

CHAPTER FOUR

Geographies of Custom and Right

Upon the evening of 'Martlemas' in November 1600, a long festering dispute between the tenants and warreners of Snettisham manor erupted in violent altercation. Presented as a witness before the Duchy of Lancaster court, Thomas Burrow, a husbandman of thirty-three, described how he accompanied the warreners of Snettisham Manor, John Doughty and his son Thomas, to a close called Horsewell Furlong lying within the warren, to trap and kill conies. Here they found William Baynard, Thomas Stone, William Farror and Thomas Wraske setting and pitching their nets. On entering the ground Thomas Doughty enquired 'whome have we hear' whereupon Stone, Banyard and Wraske without speaking assaulted the warreners. The men were armed apparently with more substantial weapons than the apparatus required for trapping rabbits. Stone was described as having 'a long field pyke disguysed with a skarfe about its neck', the others held long staffs, and Baynard wore 'a headpeece upon his head and a souldiers coate upon his back'. As it appears this was a planned and deliberately heavy-handed attack intended to scare and deter the warreners from entering the tenants' lands. John Doughty was so badly beaten about his head that 'some parte of his chawe bone afterwards rotted out', as a result, he was forced to keep to his house for eighteen weeks and 'was not able to goe about and follow his busines'. But this was by no means the end of the matter.

Early in January the following year, Robert Bunting, a sixty-year-old yeoman, witnessed a further assault upon the warreners. He recalled meeting John and Thomas Doughty, and Thomas Borrowe, as he drove his horse out to pasture. They entreated him to join them on their way to Down Close which lay within the bounds of the warren where they had heard John Cremer, William Banyard, Thomas Stone, Thomas Wraske, Jeffery Cremer, John Cremer the younger and Henry Cremer, and others were 'hayinge with two hayes to take and kyll conneys'. Bunting was not easily persuaded, saying he was loathed to go with them for he was concerned there 'wold growe some quarrell'. To which John Doughty assured him otherwise commenting that 'they had no such meaninge for he wold take tenne blowes before he wold gyve one'. Bunting agreed to go with them. On entering Down Close, John Doughty went to John Cremer 'putting of his hatt and gyvinge hym the tyme of the daie' and said 'goodman Cremer I marvayle you will ... Kyll our game knowinge that we are poore men and are farmors of the warren'. But to this apparently deferential appeal, John

Cremer responded with angry words 'out villayne what doe you here I am an hundred marks the worse for you' and with that shouted 'downe wth hym boyes for I will defend you'. What happened next was another brutal attack on John Doughty. John Cremer allegedly drove at him with his walking staff 'of twoe yards longe' and continued striking him 'tyll the staff flew out of his hand' he then attempted to take Doughty's staff from him but failing, kicked him 'upon the privities so vehemently' the force caused Doughty to cry out 'O goodman Cremer you have spoyled me', which made his son think 'he should never have recovered' (TNA: PRO, DL4/42/41).

The altercation over Snettisham warren has been outlined in detail as it encapsulates well the central themes of this chapter. It points to the situated context of local disputes that took place literally in the field, and highlights the interweaving of social and economic territories as a source of internal division within parish societies. The landscape of early modern Snettisham was clearly a contested terrain. Eighteen acres of heathland located next to Down Close was used as a breeding ground for rabbits, and their numbers had increased to such an extent that they regularly strayed onto nearby arable land. Local inhabitants described the extent of the destruction caused 'by such a multitude of conies wch are so abundantly increed as they doe straye thereby into the errable lands of John Cremer and other inhabitants of Snetsham being sowne with corne and thereby distroy the corne theron growinge' (TNA: PRO, DL4/43/12). Contest was not only focused on the incompatibility of rabbit farming and corn production, it was also about the control of space, the status of enclosed land and the continuance of additional access rights claimed by other parties, in this case the warreners.

In their investigations of the political and social complexities of local land disputes, social historians have tended to view the landscape as a backdrop against which these socio-economic grievances were played out. However, the landscape was clearly more than that, it carried layers of meaning, inspired deep emotion and was a focal point where the boundaries of human relationships were physically tested and negotiated: social and economic relationships were literally mapped out on the ground. While parish boundaries were clearly important in defining the social and administrative terrain of village life in the sixteenth and seventeenth centuries, the shift away from the importance of the manor was a protracted development. The emphasis placed on Rogationtide in recent writing has overlooked the significance of other, often less well documented, jurisdictions that played a significant part in structuring the social and economic landscape and in forming the boundaries of belonging (Winchester 1997). In Snettisham and other Norfolk villages, manorial lords, tenants, commoners and warreners as individuals and collectively sought to reinforce their claims to access the land and exploit their rights and customs. A consideraton of the material contexts of custom and right has great importance for our understanding of the physical and conceptual development of the post-medieval landscape.

Enclosure: Defining the Boundaries of Custom and Right

The archaeologist Matthew Johnson has proposed a theory of 'closure' as a means of understanding the development of individualism, and of capitalist ideology. For Johnson, enclosure is the physical manifestation of deeper social and cultural processes, involving a radical re-structuring of community and gender relations. Johnson draws parallels between the changes made to the internal organisation of domestic space and the enclosure and privatisation of agrarian landscapes. At home and in the field, the spatial context of peoples' lives became increasingly compartmentalised and bounded. According to such arguments enclosure, as well as being the physical manifestation of these social and cultural changes, also had a major impact on the physical and cognitive experiences of landscape, as local communities were effectively disconnected from their ancient customs and traditions, their systems of knowledge and memories (Johnson 1996; Rollison 1992, 67–84). These changes have been linked to the growing assertiveness of the 'middling sort' in bringing about change through their involvement both in local politics and in the development of 'improved' farming practices and enclosure. According to Steve Hindle:

> In their role as the policemen of migration, in the piecemeal enclosure of rural England ... in their pre-eminence in the rituals of Rogationtide ... the chief inhabitants of rural communities turned the landscape into emptiable space, and dictated the order of human territoriality (Hindle 2000, 109).

The idea that enclosure represented an underlying structural force has been criticised by Tom Williamson. He reminds us that the decision to enclose was primarily about farming, and that it was not some 'subliminal desire throughout the post-medieval period' that motivated farmers to enclose regardless of local environmental conditions and economic necessities (Williamson 2000, 58). It should also be noted that piecemeal enclosure was often a slow process, taking several generations to complete, which makes the attempt at ascribing it to some coherent cultural movement even more difficult to substantiate. As social historians have been careful to caution against using expressions like 'community' which conceal a range of contradictory perspectives and antagonistic relationships (Withington and Shepard 2000), so perhaps greater care needs to be taken when using enclosure as a blanket term of unequivocal meaning, a point made by Joan Thirsk forty years ago:

> [Historians] cannot make sense of the seeming contradictions without recognising first that the word 'enclosure' was a very loose general term for a number of different dealings concerning land and changes in land use, and secondly, that the economic advantages and social consequences of enclosing and engrossing differed profoundly from one region to another (Thirsk 1967, 200).

The efforts of some scholars to provide a progressive model of landscape and cultural change encounters further problems when we consider that a large portion of Norfolk remained 'open' until the late eighteenth century. Landscape historians have shown that there were marked regional and local variations in the extent and nature of pre-parliamentary enclosure, resulting from a combination of factors including environmental conditions, local antecedent structures (such as tenurial arrangements and the strength of manorialism) and demographic and market structures. Open field systems of various kinds could, in the Middle Ages, be found in both sheep-corn and wood-pasture districts. In the latter districts they were gradually removed in the course of the sixteenth, seventeenth and eighteenth centuries, a consequence of the shift from mixed farming to specialisation in dairy and beef production. In contrast, the main arable districts of Norfolk, the Brecklands and Good Sands regions of west Norfolk and the eastern Flegg district, continued to farm open arable into the late eighteenth century, but were nonetheless heavily engaged in commercial production for the strengthening market economy. Elsewhere, in the Northern Heathlands and on the more amenable soils of the dissected boulder clays, the extent and chronology of enclosure varied from village to village; those dominated by single landowners tended to be enclosed at an early date, but for others substantial portions of arable open fields were retained often well into the eighteenth century. The emphasis placed on enclosure as a single cohesive movement thus tends to skew the 'reality', as far as we can judge it, of what was happening on the ground.

Indeed, in a whole raft of ways the 'structural' interpretation of enclosure suppresses a highly complex situation, and a diverse range of practices. It is well attested that contemporary commentators made a distinction between 'good' and 'bad' enclosure, the latter being associated with depopulation and deprivation, the former deemed to be beneficial to the diligent farmer, and to the realm (McRae 1996; Thirsk 1990). At a local level, needless to say, attitudes towards enclosure were by no means homogeneous: individual tenants, seigniorial lords, even cottagers, supported and carried out enclosure when it suited them yet simultaneously opposed it when it did not. Pred makes the point in his discussion of eighteenth-century enclosure in Skåne, Sweden, that the process of enclosure was locally constituted. He argues that a dialectical relationship existed between external influences, such as state policy, and the agency of individuals who in turn were influenced by specific environmental and social conditions which gave rise to localised variations in the chronology and character of enclosure (Pred 1985, 360).

The contention that the physical enclosure of land was directly related to emerging capitalist mentalities, infers that those farmers still operating open fields were less capitalist in their outlook, and opposed to change: such arguments cannot easily account for the fact that, as already noted, in many districts farmers clearly operating along 'capitalist' lines were apparently content to continue cultivating their land in open fields (Williamson 2000). Above all, farming landscapes were frequently a complex mixture of open-fields, commons and 'anciently' enclosed and recently enclosed land. As illustrated by an early map of Cawston the ancient enclosures, taken to be above forty years old, and the lands more recently enclosed were not considered to mean the same thing (NRO, MS

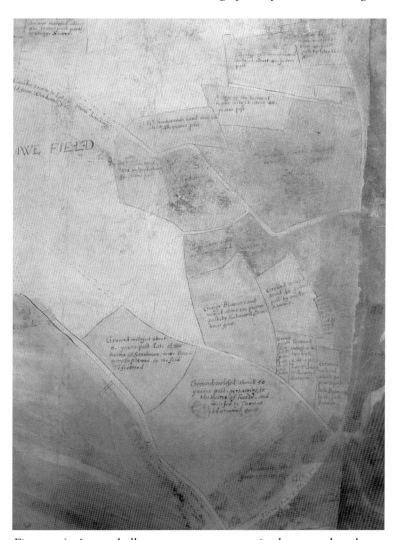

FIGURE 23. The
landscape of Cawston
in 1599, a mixture of
anciently enclosed,
recently enclosed and
open fields. The ancient
enclosures (made within
the previous forty years)
were exempt from
manorial grazing rights,
in contrast the recent
enclosures continued
to have common access
rights attached them
(NRO, MS 4521).

4521, Figure 23). As we shall see, contemporary attitudes toward enclosure were most obviously contradictory in areas where local environmental conditions had the potential to support mixed farming economies, such as the Northern Heathlands, where seigniorial interests in sheep farming ran into direct conflict with farmers engaged in enclosure and specialisation in cattle farming.

It is important to emphasise the extent to which early piecemeal enclosure did not necessarily create parcels that were fully 'private' property in the eighteenth- or nineteenth-century sense. Johnson has suggested that 'hedges and ditches shifted power over the land from the manor and community to the individual household':

> Power over the land was no longer embedded in common practices … to socially embedded ideas of cutom and tradition; now it was solely Man, or more accurately the owner of the estate, or the gentleman or yeoman farmer, in direct confrontation with Nature (Johnson 1996, 75).

But this does not give us the full story. Full rights of private possession were often only gradually asserted. As we have seen, local communities exercised the right to walk through private landscapes during their Rogationtide perambulation of the parish bounds. More importantly, the physical enclosure of open-field land did not necessarily extinguish all rights of use and access – their abolition often had to be negotiated, sometimes resulting in arbitration before the central law courts. In most cases there was an extended transitional phase, *via* a farming system which permitted a degree of communal access, such as warreners rights and common grazing or 'shack' rights, to unequivocal private ownership. In his discussion of the meaning of custom in the eighteenth century, E.P. Thompson has argued: 'how could enjoyment be exclusive if it did not command the power to exclude from property's physical space the insolent lower orders' (Thompson 1993, 141). But in many villages customs and access rights were not just the preserve of tenants, commoners and the lower orders they were also manipulated and exploited in equal measure by wealthy landowners.

All this serves to undermine any simple, monocausal or 'structural' argument regarding the progress of enclosure: rather than being the outcome of some hidden, underlying cultural process, the decision to enclose, or not to enclose, was guided by a combination of inter-related factors, of which local environmental conditions and the practicalities of farming different soil types was paramount (Williamson 2000). But enclosure was also deeply connected with the ongoing struggle over customary practices and the right to access and control local resources. The re-organisation of the post-medieval landscape along 'capitalist', 'rational' lines involved a number of spatial re-configurations of which piecemeal enclosure was just one aspect. Other important elements of this process, especially in areas of light land, included the standardisation of manorial fold-course systems; the extension of warren rights; and the attempts to rationalise access rights to commons and heaths. Though the rapacious activities of a minority of landlowners and wealthy farmers are an inescapable presence in the history of the post-medieval landscape (Aston and Bettey 1998; Williamson 2000b), the sources, and especially the evidence of court depositions, allow us to see something of how landscape change was experienced by tenants and commoners. There emerges an undercurrent of discontent and bitterness towards the landowning elite, but there was also resilience and enterprise. Local allegiances were forged that cut across social boundaries and the physical terrain of parish and manor.

Manorial Rights and the Fold-Course System

The 'Good Sands' and the Breckland districts of Norfolk were areas characterised by 'sheep-corn' husbandry. By medieval times, agriculture was based on the organisation of the infield/outfield system, where the more fertile soils of the infield were more intensively cultivated than the 'outfield' – land which was tilled regularly, but allowed to revert to heathland after a few years of ploughing, in order to allow the soils to rejuvenate. Beyond this arable land, the heaths remained largely unploughed, only occasionally cultivated to supplement grain supplies, particularly when demand was high. Soil fertility was maintained through the rigorous and systematic folding of sheep; flocks were grazed on the heathland during the day, then folded or 'tathed' on the fallows by night, to enrich the soils with a constant supply of manure (Allison 1957). In parishes owned by more than one manor, land was divided into blocks or 'fold courses' each containing contiguous portions of open-field and heathland pasture, units which often traversed parish boundaries. This system operated under the supervision of the manorial lord, who preserved the right both to restrict the number of animals owned by tenants and the right to fold the manorial flock on the fallow lands at night. Research has shown that such arrangements were well established by the middle of the thirteenth century, if not earlier (Hassell and Beauroy 1993). But it was really only in the course of the fifteenth and sixteenth centuries that fold-course management and communal cropping arrangements became more clearly and rigorously defined (Bailey 1989).

Mark Bailey has raised some important questions regarding the development of the fold-course system in the late medieval period. He has argued that during this period a distinct regional dichotomy evolved between the operation of field systems in light soil and in wood-pasture districts, systems which had hitherto been broadly similar. The geographical scope of Bailey's study focused on a district of north west Suffolk that encompassed the sandy soils of the Brecklands to the west and the heavier loams of high Suffolk on the east. Of particular interest here is Bailey's emphasis on the 'rationalisation' of fold-course arrangements in Breckland. In the medieval period the fold-course system was not the seigniorial monopoly it was to become by the end of the sixteenth century. The right to erect folds was exercised by individual tenants, which permitted them to manure their own lands. This could be obtained for a limited period, under licence from the manorial lord, but in some cases more permanent fold rights were attached to particular tenements. Bailey argues that 'the presence of so many peasant folds can only imply that the medieval fold-course system operated in a more fragmented and flexible manner' than the model put forward by Allison, which had been based largely on post-medieval documents (Bailey 1990, 44). It is also possible that 'fold-course' arrangements were once more widely dispersed outside light soil districts, on the heavier soils of the claylands, although a distinction needs to be made between the rights of 'liberty of fold' – commonly found in East Anglia – from fully developed fold courses: the former term refers to the lord's right to fold his land, the latter (which tended to be confined to lighter soils) comprised a more extensive range of rights, and importantly, a strong degree communal cooperation (Campbell 1981, 22–26; Bailey 1990, 44–45).

Shifts in landowning structures, underway since the economic recession of the later fourteenth and fifteenth centuries, saw a decline in the numbers and wealth of small proprietors, and the increasing consolidation of land in the hands of large estates, the owners of which asserted ever greater seigniorial authority over agrarian practices (Allison 1957; Bailey 1989; 1990). By the later fifteenth century, specialised sheep farming had become a viable commercial enterprise, leading landowners to consolidate their demesne lands into more efficient blocks, and to more closely regulate fold-course rights. They enlarged their sheep flocks and restricted the number of sheep kept by tenants in their 'cullet flock'. By c.1600 the classic system, as originally defined by Allison, emerged in villages located on the light soils, brought about by the standardisation and rationalisation of existing arrangements. Concomitantly, any loose fold-course arrangements that had existed on the claylands were eroded away by the process of piecemeal enclosure (Bailey 1990).

Bailey's argument is useful in that it emphasises the growing regional divergences as a result of agricultural specialisation and development of farming practices in both light soil and clayland regions: the more obvious physical changes relating to piecemeal enclosure occurring on the claylands were paralleled by the re-structuring of field systems in the Brecklands. It is important to note, however, that Bailey contrasts two unusually discrete and distinctive regions – the sandy Brecklands, and heavy clays of High Suffolk. Across much of Norfolk, the pattern of soil types was rather more complex and diffuse, giving rise to more subtle variations in the development of local farming systems. This is clearly evident for example, in the Northern Heathlands – a district of light soils, interspersed with heavier loams extending northwards from Norwich to the sea – where, as we shall see, the balance of interests between open field and enclosed land was particularly controversial. Indeed, it appears that in some places well outside the classic fold-course districts landlords attempted to emulate what was happening there, by replacing loose folding arrangements with a more standardised fold-course system.

One significant indication of the growing struggle over access rights to both arable and common grazing land is the rise in number of law suits brought before the central courts from the mid sixteenth century (Bailey 1990, 53). But to some extent the utilisation of the central law courts may also have provided a further standardising influence on the development of fold-course systems. A further sign of this is evident in the cartographic preoccupations of the landowning elite. From the late sixteenth century depictions of the landscape carved up into great blocks of open field, heathland and in some cases marshland, to accommodate large sheep flocks became popular as a means of representing manorial territories. A 1590 map of Holkham is a particularly good example and was probably drawn up in association with a dispute concerning the demarcation of four fold-course territories (NRO, MS 4535: Figure 34). Such maps represent, as they were intended to do, a clearly defined and ordered landscape. However, the deposition evidence, recorded for Holkham in 1592, relates the difficulties encountered by seigniorial lords in fixing the jurisdictions of their fold courses, both in relation to neighbouring fold courses and common rights claimed by local inhabitants. (TNA: PRO, DL4/155/9; TNA: PRO,

DL4/34/36). Of vital importance in revealing the complexities of fold-course arrangements, court depositions are also an invaluable source for revealing something of the social environment of sheep-corn villages.

Generally speaking, the transformation of light soil landscapes in the post-medieval landscape has been viewed from the perspective, and as the achievement, of a small minority of elite landowners. In areas dominated by sheep-corn economies the transition to a more rigid agricultural system is usually explained as the outcome of a number of inter-related economic and social factors, of which the decline of the smallholder, and subsequent consolidation of land in the hands of a small number of wealthy proprietors, was foremost. In consequence, the majority of local inhabitants have been relegated to the sidelines; they appear to be virtually non-existent in the landscape of power and lordship. It is an inescapable fact that the lower orders were beset by the unremitting and aggressive actions of local lords. Indeed, it was perhaps precisely during this phase of relentless change that popular knowledge of the landscape suffered its most severe battering, so that by the period of parliamentary enclosure in the late eighteenth century, their severance from the landscape had already been largely achieved. This aspect has been explored by Keith Allison who focused on the social consequences of the fold-course system as a cause of village depopulation (Allison 1957, 22–27). The deposition evidence used here sheds further light on the social dynamics that underpinned the development of farming practices and landscape change in the sixteenth and seventeenth centuries. Ordinary people had their part to play, at times forging alliances with their economic superiors, at other times standing against them. As a result, competing perceptions of the landscape existed, and the balance between 'open' and 'enclosed' was caught up in very local patterns of politics.

'Contrary to all the Order of Fowldcorses'

Lords, tenants and commoners each held clear views of how fold courses should operate. There was an acute awareness of the number of acres considered sufficient to support a certain number of sheep, and cases of over-stocking were hotly disputed. In one such case from Wighton in 1576, James Taverner was accused of 'over charging' the fold course by grazing six or seven hundred sheep on the shack lands over the winter months and on the commons during the summer. The number of animals deemed appropriate was judged on the amount of available pasture. Taverner's sheep had the grazing of seventy acres, which amounted to nine sheep for every acre. In contrast the number of sheep kept upon the neighbouring Crabbs Castle fold course did not exceed three sheep 'for every acre laid to pasture'. By today's standards this is a vast number of sheep: modern farmers on Lakenheath Warren graze one hundred sheep on 150 acres of heathland. Admittedly this is an area of particularly low grade Breckland soil, but the figure nevertheless gives some indication of the extent of overstocking (Bailey 1989, 80).

In conjunction with notions regarding the acceptable size of flocks in relation to available pasture, there was general agreement that the land should be kept open, and that any enclosures made in the open fields or outfield brecks, in order to protect crops from the sheep, should only be temporary structures. The land was to be re-opened during shack time – that is, after harvest when livestock were allowed to graze the stubbles. Under the 'developed' fold-course systems of the sixteenth and seventeenth centuries, such grazing primarily benefited the flocks of the lord or his lessee. In Elveden it was customary for the tenants to 'tie up their horses with cordes in their mouths in time of harvest' in acknowledgement that 'they had no liberty of feeding within the ... fold course but only the tilling of their lands and the crop when it was sown' (cited in Postgate 1973, 315). Grazing was an essential part of arable agriculture, ensuring that soils were replenished with nutrients, as well as providing an additional source of grazing to help maintain the balance of livestock to arable. Nevertheless, in an open landscape grazing required careful management. The incidence of sheep straying onto lands lying outside the fallows was a highly contentious issue. In seventeenth-century Roxham, for example, it was said that the land 'laye open and theire corne and grasse were often tymes spoyled' (NRO, PRA 469 380 x 5). The movement of stock to unsown land or fallows whilst avoiding land under crops was also a problem. As a result landowners had long attempted to control cropping arrangements by organising cropped land into continuous blocks or 'shifts', each under the same state of cultivation. But complaints made against trespassing indicate that such arrangements were not easily implemented. In Wighton former shepherd William Reader testified that it was impossible to move a flock of five or six hundred sheep, along the route way or 'stey' separating neighbouring fold courses, without trespassing on the lands of tenants lying within Crabbs Castle fold course (TNA: PRO, DL4/18/19).

The temporary enclosure of fallow land, providing that strict regulations were adhered to, was vital in preparing light soils for cropping and an accepted part of such arrangements. But temporary enclosures set up by farmers to protect growing crops were a different matter, as they denied feed to the manorial flocks and were considered to be 'things very mischeevous and will tend to ye overthrow of very manye foldcourses' (cited in Postgate 1973, 320). At Anmer in 1627 'the refusal of a few wilful persons to lett ye owners of foldcourses have their quilletts of land (lying intermixt in the places where ye sheep pasture is layd) upon indiffrent exchange or other recompense' was deemed to threaten the very foundations of the fold-course institution (cited in Postgate 1973, 320). In Tottenhill accusations were made against the tenants who had sown their strips with corn 'circlewise' in one of the open fields, presumably using temporary enclosures, thus disrupting the run of the manorial flock (Allison 1957). The threat of enclosure was employed elsewhere, in some cases to prevent the institution of the fold course from becoming established (Cornford 1986). But due to the nature of the poor, easily-leached soils it was not within the interests of farmers to attempt the permanent enclosure of their arable.

Allegations regarding the illegal setting up of hurdles were also made against lords. In one such case from Wighton, altercation arose between neighbouring fold-course owners regarding the boundary separating their two territories, part of which cut across a furlong aptly referred to as 'the partable furlong': it was suggested that 'the word partable may growe some ambiguitye and doubte', as indeed it did (TNA: PRO, DL4/18/19). The dispute is worthy of recounting in some detail. James Taverner, owner of Wighton manor and the fold course pertaining to it, was accused of entering the Queen's fold course belonging to Crabbs Castle, because the amount of grazing available within his own fold course was insufficient for the number of sheep within his flock. According to one deponent, he raised hurdles for the tathing of his sheep immediately after harvest and continued to do so when the land should have been re-opened for shack, until the feast of All Saints. According to seventy-two-year-old John Smith the elder, this was to the:

> Great preiudice of the Quene Maties right of shack and overthrowe of the flocke as also to the utter undoinge of her Graces tenants and contrary to all order of fowldcowrses if ever I have seene or hard tyme of my remembrance.

As well as infringing the shack rights belonging to Crabbs Castle fold course Taverner was also accused of entering the land of the Queen's tenants in the summer, as well as feeding his sheep on her demesne land. This Smith denounced with a stab at Tavernor's reputation, accusing him of being an upstart lord:

> Which he does as though he wer lorde beinge as rare a thing as ever I harde or saw that a meanne tenant sholde drive, feede and tathe within the somer pasture of the lorde.

In his defence, deponents maintained that Taverner raised hurdles on the 'partable foldcourse' during 'severall time', but took them down after harvest during 'shack time'. Attention was paid to substantiating these claims by calling on earlier precedents. Thomas Thorne, husbandman, deposed that six years previously, he heard eighty-two-year-old Robert Jackson say that he had kept the flock belonging to Taverner's predecessor Mr Giggs seventy-five years ago, and that the sheep had been kept on the fold course in question without interruption. But according to Christopher Cleres 'Old Gyggs and Russel never came in shacke tyme over Brusselmere northwards' until twenty-eight years ago.

A moral distinction was made between old manorial lords – the purveyors of custom and prescribed practices – and a new generation of landowners whose rapacious activities were deemed to threaten established farming customs. Taverner was accused of taking aggressive measures against his tenants. Witnesses spoke of his intimidating behaviour, of how he had threatened to kill their cattle, swine, sheep and horses found grazing on his sheep course. In Wighton, the elderly inhabitants of the area had a clear sense of the differences between the farming system under Taverner and that functioning in the first half of the sixteenth century: they had 'not knowne such trubles and suytes' in

Wighton before the arrival of James Taverner (TNA: PRO, DL4/18/19). These allegations illustrate well the basic problem encountered in sheep-corn districts – an increase in the numbers of sheep grazed on the arable threatened, in a variety of ways, the viability of cereal farming. In Allison's words, 'by abusing the fold-course system, landlords were able to enlarge their flocks without recourse to the large-scale enclosure and conversion of open field arable land to pasture that took place in certain parts of England' (Allison 1957, 24).

In contrast to the Good Sands region, the Northern Heathlands was characterised by a different pattern of change. Here areas of acid heath were interspersed with patches of more fertile soils, giving rise to a certain degree of flexibility and choice with regards to farming practices and specialisation (Wade Martins and Williamson 1999, 13–16). By the turn of the seventeenth century the landscape was already being transformed by piecemeal enclosure. It is usually assumed that this was due to the presence of less rigorous fold-course arrangements, as in the case of Cawston, or their absence altogether (Wade Martins and Williamson 1999, 16; Campbell 1986). However, the transformation from 'open' to 'closed' did not follow an uncontroversial linear trajectory. In some villages piecemeal enclosure was in fact slowed down by the attempts of wealthy landowners to impose fold-course arrangements – presumably motivated by the visible achievements of their neighbours a few miles away to the west. The tenants and inhabitants of Gimingham Manor living in Southrepps, Northrepps and 'other towns' complained that in the past they had liberty to enclose their freehold and copyhold lands until 'Peter Reade late fearmor denyed them so to doe' (TNA: PRO, DL4/24/6). As was the case in the Good Sands and Brecklands the process of 'rationalisation' saw a clear clash of interests between manorial lords and their lessees wanting to enforce and to extend fold-course arrangements, and their tenants wanting to maintain or enhance control over their land by enclosing it for more efficient production. Similarly, in Gimingham the late sixteenth century saw the tightening of seigniorial control and attempts to extend fold-course rights: 'it is not Lawfull nor standeth with the custome of the mannor of Gymyngham that any Tenant within the soken of Gimingham shold inclose any grownd wthin the libties to the preiudice of the foldcourse ... withowt lycence' (TNA: PRO, DL4/24/6).

Comparable developments were taking place in the cluster of 'Heathland' parishes around Cawston. Campbell's detailed analysis of the manorial structure of neighbouring Hevingham confirms that in the medieval period 'commonfield arrangements were altogether less systematized, not least because the hallmark of the latter system – the fold course – was effectively absent' (Campbell 1986, 249). In contrast to Breckland and the Good Sands region, manorialism was comparatively weak in this area, thus leading historians to suggest that seigniorial lords lacked the power and authority to achieve such extensive changes as a fold-course regime required. Indeed, in Campbell's words 'not even the Bishop of Norwich ... seems to have been prepared to attempt such far-reaching change' (Campbell 1986, 249). In nearby Marsham, according to contemporary witnesses, earlier folding agreements had been dissolved by the mid-sixteenth century. John Brown recalled that during the reign of Henry VIII an agreement was made between the Bishop of Norwich, then lord of the manor, and his tenants to discontinue folding arrangements in the village. This included fifteen acres of common, referred to as 'foldcourse land', which was granted by copy of court roll to thirty tenants at a yearly rent of eight pence per half an acre. The land was subsequently doled out in accordance with each tenement, which entitled the tenants to take ling and furze for fuel and to graze their sheep across the land (TNA: PRO, E178/4251). In contrast to the medieval period, it seems that in the late sixteenth century, landowners mustered a greater degree of authority and motivation in manipulating existing agrarian systems to their advantage.

In 1605 a dispute was brought before the Court of Exchequer by the inhabitants of Marsham against Thomas Thetford, owner of the manor, and regarding the imposition of a fold course. John Keymer a yeoman from Hevingham deposed that thirty years previously Clement Paston had gained 'by action at the comon lawe' the several land and fold course from the tenants of Marsham, previously granted to them by the Bishop of Norwich. Since then Thomas Wright grazed four hundred sheep within the fold course, and it was claimed that during that time, no inhabitants of Marsham pastured their sheep on the several doles. Another witness, John Brown, told the court how Thomas Thetford had kept three hundred sheep on the common, and kept them 'many and often tymes in wyntertyme in the fields and corne of the tenants of Marsham'. He went on to say that 'in his conscience' this was of great hindrance to the tenants, and when his servants attempted to drive Thetford's sheep from his crop of corn the servants of Thetford 'did beate and miseuse' him. William Sedney's deposition is particularly revealing of the strength of the motivation to enforce a 'fully-fledged' fold-course system. A former servant to the father of James Brampton, farmer of Hevingham Manor, Sedney claimed that thirty years previously, Brampton the elder had in his custody the records of the manor and 'made searche amongst them what records might in any wayes be for the tenants good and finding those rolls and evidence which might have done them good'. Gathering the records together Brampton allegedly handed them to Sedney and told him 'to burne them which he ... did accordingly' (TNA: PRO, E178/4251). Like the physical evidence of the landscape, written documents too were subject to manipulation, and in some cases destruction and forgery.

Campbell's emphasis on the complex, fragmented nature of the manorial system, which for him precluded the ability of manorial lords 'to change the status quo', had taken a very different course by the turn of the seventeenth century. In Marsham issues of access and control over local resources had shifted. Thomas Wright claimed that, as under-farmer, he had had the right of shack within the fields of the fold course from the feast of Saint Faiths until Christmas, and maintained that his sheep were fed on both the sown and unsown land without restraint. Similar processes can be observed in nearby

Felmingham where the owner of the manor was accused of claiming liberty of fold course when he had no right, and of employing a 'special keeper' for his sheep for 'the mayntenance of his pretended foldcourse' (TNA: PRO, E134/26Eliz/East13). In Cawston too, manorial grazing rights intensified. In 1601 Thomas Easton, a sixty-year-old yeoman, described the movement of the manorial sheep flock along prescribed routeways and through a number of open fields including Baywood Field, Windmill Field, Southawe and Woodgate Field:

> Hath herd by credible report that the flocke or shepe of the ... foldcorse of Cawston in anncient tyme did yerely use to come in the tyme of shacke vidz from myches till the puryficacon of our Lady from Cawston heath to the said field ... at the place named ... Jollycock lane or leches lane and the said flocke take ther feede through Baywood feld to a place called crabbes gapp into wyndmyll feld and so fedd the same feld together wth sowthawe and woodgate feld and so to passe feding to the heath agayne by a place called Perryes lane and he hath knowne and herd it credibly reported that the said foldcorse did fed in Lound feld as pcell of the same foldcorse as in the rest (TNA: PRO, E134/43&44Eliz/Mich7).

Easton emphasized the antiquity of the right but, in view of Cambell's research, it is likely that the fold course in question was a re-interpretation of an older system of loose folding arrangements exercised by both tenants and manor (TNA: PRO, E134/43&44Eliz/Mich7; TNA: PRO, E133/1/108).

In some places manors claimed grazing rights across several villages. In Gimingham in north-east Norfolk, since the early Middle Ages a group of neighbouring villages had been bound together as members of a single jurisdictional unit, Gimingham Soke (Hoare 1918; Williamson 1993, 94–95). Deposition evidence refers to the tenants and inhabitants of each town keeping their cullet sheep and cattle during the time of shack in the open fields and heaths. But the farmer of Gimingham Manor, Mr Gryme, had disrupted their 'quiet feeding'. John Bright, a seventy-year-old yeoman, deposed that Gryme had recently started bringing his sheep beyond Potters Head into Willisons Close. When he was challenged as to the legitimacy of his actions, Gryme allegedly responded by saying that he expected to be dealt with 'like a neighbor' for when the 'cattel of the men of Southrepps came or did feede within his libtie in Gimingham' he did not 'dryve the cattell or otherwise trouble them in shack tyme but did suffer them quietly to feede there'. Said with accommodating words perhaps, but Gryme's activities were causing great consternation among neighbouring villages, particularly his assertion to graze his sheep on lands outside the jurisdiction of Gimingham Manor (TNA: PRO, DL4/24/6).

The evidence from these Heathland villages points to a clear transitional phase in agricultural practice and the meaning of custom and right. The Dissolution and subsequent break up of monastic estates marked a significant juncture, as new owners set about organising and profiting from their acquisitions. Sheep were both lucrative, valued for their meat and wool, and a symbol of wealth and status among the landowning elite. In the later decades of the sixteenth century, manorial interest in large-scale sheep farming, usually associated with the light lands in the west of the county, was accompanied by an increased awareness of the authority of custom and right and how they might be used to gain greater control and authority over the land.

Further east, on the more fertile soils of the Flegg district fold courses remained rare, although the main bulk of the open fields here were not enclosed until the parliamentary movement of the late eighteenth century (Wade Martins and Williamson 1999, 46). This is largely attributed to the inherent quality of the soils, being amongst the most high yielding and most expensive land to be found in the county. In contrast to the western light soils districts, where large estates predominated, the social structure here was more variegated, consisting of large numbers of small freeholders, yeomen and minor gentry farmers. As a result of these social and environmental factors, farming systems tended to be less communally organised, with farmers exercising a marked degree of freedom and flexibility in their cropping arrangements (Wade Martins and Williamson 1999, 48). The period of shack, for example, was comparatively short taking place immediately after harvest when the tenants were permitted to graze their livestock over the arable fields (Cornford 1986).

There are signs, however, that even in Flegg some landlords attempted to assert fold-course arrangements. In the village of Clippesby, for example, an attempt was made by Randolph Crewe, owner of the manor, to impose a fold course in the first half of the seventeenth century. Andrew Green, a wealthy yeoman, refuted this claim maintaining that a fold course had never existed but only the right of shack, which was common to all tenants. Green threatened to enclose his freehold land to prevent 'the evil beginning of a fold course creeping on' (Cornford 1986, 15–17). At neighbouring Ormesby by the late sixteenth century an estimated one hundred acres of open field land had been enclosed with the lord's licence, a process that had effectively dissolved communal shack rights. But in the 1580s the owner of the manor refused to accept these earlier agreements and demanded that the enclosures were laid opened again, in order to increase the availability of grazing and thus enlarge his sheep flock. As in Clippesby, the local inhabitants were probably well aware of the development of fold courses elsewhere in the county, William Esto stated his concern: 'if the inclosures shold be layd open agayne and the lorde to feede the same with his sheepe ... he doe thinke it wold be a discomoditie to the tenants' (TNA: PRO, E134/29&30Eliz/Mich8). Similarly in nearby Hickling the once flexible field system was threatened by the development of a more clearly defined fold-course. According to Robert Skeet, who had known the village for forty years, the owner of the manor (the plaintiff in the case) had no right to feed his sheep on the common arable fields and 'hath such sheepe as he hath fedd heretofore or shall hereafter feed in the same fieldes in (his) opinion an Innovacon or new pretence which the plt wold beginn or introduce' (TNA: PRO, E134/7Chas1/Mich18).

In some villages the rate of piecemeal enclosure was slowed down, if not halted, by the attempts of wealthy landowners to impose fold-course arrangements, often based on rather spurious claims to past precedent. As was the case in Ormesby and Clippesby, piecemeal enclosure in Hickling had been carried out without question until the closing decades of the sixteenth century when attempts were made not just to halt the process but to reverse existing agreements also. Even when land had been physically enclosed with fences and hedges, its status was by no means fixed and could be redefined at a later date. Evidently landlords and their tenants had different ideas regarding their route to economic success, sometimes involving enclosure, at other times not.

Piecemeal Enclosure: A Private Landscape?

Piecemeal enclosure is usually considered to be a less contentious form of enclosure than the wholesale reorganisation of landscapes resulting from the various forms of general enclosure. But this was only true up to a point. Extinguishing manorial, and in some instances tenant, grazing rights over arable land was not easily achieved, in many cases having to await an act of parliament in the eighteenth or nineteenth centuries. Indeed, throughout the sixteenth and seventeenth centuries the extent to which newly created closes were considered to be the exclusive property of the individual is questionable. The physical enclosure of land did not automatically mean the elimination of the established customs and land use rights attached to it and lords, and sometimes tenants, continued to insist upon exercising their shack rights.

Johnson has suggested that enclosure 'create[d] very new forms of boundaries ... boundaries that cut across old lines and redeployed power over the land in new ways' (Johnson 1996, 75). It is worth noting, however, that the boundaries represented as continuous features on maps did not necessarily form impassable barriers to movement. At certain times of the year they might be permeable, in the sense that livestock could move through an enclosed landscape supposedly unhindered. Indeed, it was often a condition of enclosure that owners allowed access for grazing during shack time. In Cawston, shack time fell between 'the feast of St Michaell tharchangell' and 'the puryficacon of Our Lady'. During this period the owner of the fold course claimed liberty and common of shack on the unsown lands, which included the arable fields mentioned above. It also included former parcels of open field land, since enclosed and converted to pasture:

> [The sheep] goinge and fedinge in ther said foldcourse in myllfeld and other feilds in Cawston and that diverse grounds that were inclosed in Cawston were yerely layd open by the owners of the same for the walke and feede of the shepe in the tyme of shacke (TNA: PRO, E134/43&44Eliz/Mich7).

In order to give the manorial flock access, the owners of the enclosed lands were obliged to 'leaveth the gate open and diverse gapps in the same'. In connection with this dispute a map was made of Cawston in 1599 (NRO, MS 4521; Figure 23). It shows approximately half of the area of arable lying in open fields and the rest enclosed piecemeal from the arable strips. The map also distinguishes between land 'anciently' enclosed, more than forty years ago, and land more recently enclosed: a distinction which was to have a profound impact on the enclosure history of the parish. The more recent enclosures continued to have shack rights attached to them, whereas the ancient enclosures were exempt from additional access rights. Here as elsewhere, there was a clear clash of interests between seigniorial lords wanting to extend and reinforce fold-course arrangements including shack rights – to keep the land open – and their tenants wanting to gain or maintain control over their land, to protect and enclose in order to specialise in cattle farming.

The claim of manorial lords to have the right to enter their tenants' pasture closes was deeply divisive in many villages. In Wighton, for example, James Taverner claimed the rights of shack on enclosed parcels of land. George Feecke complained that Taverner impounded his cattle when they were being driven to his own pasture closes after harvest. To their 'greate distresse' Taverner kept them for a day and a night. The issue was resolved through the arbitration of Mr Bedingfield, who advised that Feecke should accept payment of two pence for each close for the forbearance of the shack rights (TNA: PRO, DL4/18/19). When such formal, or informal, agreement about access had not been reached, or were intentionally breached, fold-course owners and others might resort to direct action. In Cawston witnesses described the destruction of enclosures, not by disenfranchised tenants and commoners as historians more usually refer, but under the directives of the owner of the manor. Apparently two gates in a close in Alvington Field were broken open and the bars, which presumably were used to block up the gaps, were 'sawen in peces' and the sheep belonging to the alleged fold course 'forciblie' grazed there (TNA: PRO, E134/43&44Eliz/Mich7).

Landlords were accused of enclosing their demesne land, disregarding their tenants' shack rights, while continuing to graze their own stock over the open fields. In Marsham, for example, diverse portions of the open fields had been enclosed by the defendant Thomas Thetford Esquire and his father, yet Thetford 'doth still withstandinge the same contynewe his feede wth his sheepe in the wynter tyme in the feilds and upon the corne of the inhabitants' (TNA: PRO, E178/4251). Shack rights usually belonged to the farmers of the arable strips, and controversy arose in Felmingham when the owner of the manor, Mr Crofts, had let out 'for the most part' his forty acres within the open fields but continued nevertheless to graze his sheep and cattle during shack time (TNA: PRO, E134/26Eliz/East13). In Cawston the tenants complained that their shack rights pertaining to newly enclosed land lying adjacent to Haveringland Park, and to eighty acres lying near 'makerell pond', had been lost: 'the tenants and inhabitants of Cawston and other townes adioyninge ... when they came thither of ther owne accord out of Cawston Heath or comon and that they cannot nowe have the same comon of pasture since the inclosure as in tymes past they have had' (TNA: PRO, E134/43&44Eliz/Mich7).

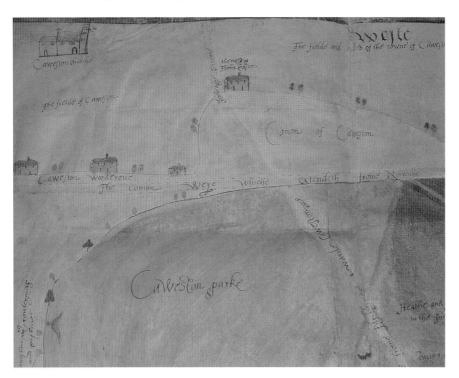

FIGURE 24. The houses of 'Woodrowe', Cawston in 1580. The adjacent common and enclosed lands became the scene of controversy between the residents and warreners over the right to trap and kill rabbits (NRO, MC 341/12, 706 x 4a).

For villages located on the poorer soils of the Good Sands and Breckland regions, there were rather different issues and complexities regarding the nature of enclosure and common access rights. In particular, the practice of temporary ploughing outfield 'brecks' gave rise to frequent disputes over shack rights. Between phases of ploughing the land reverted to heathland, during which time the soils would be replenished with nutrients. When possible, sheep would be tathed on the land for more efficient manuring, a procedure that required the setting up of hurdles: when under the plough, outfield brecks were also sometimes fenced, in order to protect crops from roaming livestock. The evidence suggests that increasingly such parcels of land were being more permanently enclosed. In Snettisham for example 'More Close' and 'Downe Close' were described as 'two closes inclosed yerely and everye yeare', although they were meant to have been 'layed open' after harvest. John Barnard, a labourer from Snettisham deposed that More Close had been enclosed some thirty years previously yet:

> He verely beleveth that betwene the feast of St Michaell and Thannuncacon of our blessed lady mary the vyrgyn the defdt hath not at any tyme by the space of seaven yeres last past layd open ye said cloase called morecloase so as the tennts and Inhitants of the said Towne might have their shacke with their great cattell there And this he knoweth the rather to be true for that he hath sene the gate of the said cloase usually kept locked during the sayd tyme (TNA: PRO, DL4/43/4).

Common shack rights were also claimed by the tenants on 'Down Close', which ran into direct conflict with the manorial right to incorporate the close within the grazing grounds of Southcote fold course. The rights of tenants and lord to pasture their livestock on the close were just one aspect giving rise to dispute. There were other ways in which land enclosed piecemeal from the open fields might fall short of full private property, free from rights of use or access. As we have seen in Snettisham, the warreners also claimed access to 'Down Close' in order to trap and kill conies.

Rabbit warrens were a prominent feature of light and heathy soils since the medieval period. In Snettisham the warren had long been a focus of disagreement and resentment among the tenants and farmers of arable lands in the village. Elderly witnesses recalled when the warrener's lodge was pulled down during the 'commotion time' in 1549, a time synonymous with the uprising of the commons against the enclosing activities of seigniorial lords (TNA: PRO, DL4/43/12; Fletcher and MacCulloch 1997; Wood 2002, 62–71; Wood 2007). Difficult to contain within their allotted space, the rabbits spread onto neighbouring arable land, not only within Snettisham but the land of neighbouring manors including that owned by the Le'Strange family who, together with the tenants and farmers, became incensed enough to destroy the warren. Fifty years later the boundaries of the warren, proliferation of rabbits and devastation caused to arable land, continued to fuel local tensions. However, little agreement could be reached regarding the legal jurisdiction of the warren. In the mid-sixteenth century it reputedly contained only five acres bounded by an old ditch, though the warreners maintained their burrows outside the enclosure as far as Heacham market way named 'Holgate Way' (TNA: PRO, DL4/43/12). According to John Wraske when, some twenty years after the lodge had been demolished by the rebels, the lord of the manor considered erecting it again and creating a new warren. But John remembered his father Thomas saying that there would be no profit in it for conies could not be kept beyond 'marketsede way' (TNA: PRO, DL4/43/12). By 1602 the lodge had been 'reedyfied' again by Wymond Cary, farmer of the Duchy manor, and the perimeter of the warren was once again a matter of controversy. On behalf of Cary a number of deponents set out the extent of the bounds, which encompassed a much wider area than its opponents maintained. According to Robert Bunting who had known Snettisham all the time of his memory, since he was six, the warren extended from Spittle House to Southgate Moor, to a place called the 'Lock' to Hardwick Gate, to the Fens End, to Dunstall Ditch, along the highway to Steynhill before returning to Spittle House (TNA: PRO, DL4/42/41).

The right of warreners to kill rabbits on neighbouring areas of enclosed land was a long-running point of contention in many villages. In Cawston, the warreners claimed to have the right to enter and to fetch out the 'coneys with ther lynes to tend to have taken them with ther hayes and netts' in the grounds known as Larwoods, and in other lands adjoining the heath. Liberty of warren was also claimed on the closes and grounds that lay within 'Woodrowe', the owners of which had been punished for killing conies on their lands (Figure 24). Despite the fact that the closes were physically enclosed and held in severalty, the owners were not permitted to trap rabbits. Indeed if caught with hays and nets on their own land their presence was viewed as trespass. In Cawston John Vyntor, a servant to Edward Hamond, deposed that a fortnight after Michelmas, whilst he and Thomas Gerrard were out trapping rabbits on enclosed grounds belonging to Hamond, the warreners arrived and, accusing them of trespass, entered the enclosure 'with ther swords drawne' and 'did stryke and beat' Vyntor and Gerrard, and cut into pieces their nets (TNA: PRO, E134/43&44Eliz/Mich7).

Divided Landscapes: the Commons

Commons, even those on the poorest land, provided a range of resources for local inhabitants. In Hargham the commoners had at all times of the year the right to keep 'all manner of beasts' including neat cattle, sheep, swine, geese and other fowl' on Hargham Common. They were also permitted to fell, dig up and carry away for their messuages and tenements furze (gorse), brakes (bracken), and clay, and to use pools of water to rett their hemp (TNA: PRO, E134/42&43Eliz/Mich28). The right to use such resources was granted for the benefit and subsistence of the tenants – a pool of resources that should remain within the boundaries of the village. Specialised industrial production – such as the making of bricks, which became a major activity on Mousehold (Lucas 1997) – was often frowned upon, as it involved not only the removal of resources which should, by custom, have remained within the manor, but also impinged on the other resources the common offered (TNA: PRO, E178/7153). For common land was a carefully managed resource. It had to be, for the same area was often used in diverse ways. In Kilverston the inhabitants claimed common rights on the heath and 'low grounds' over which they had the right to take underwood 'to burne or expande in or aboute ther howses'. The Lowes was also used to make hay, and at other times to feed their cattle (TNA: PRO, E134/35Eliz/East24). Over the course of the sixteenth and seventeenth centuries, though remaining physically open, the commons became increasingly bounded spaces. Stints were imposed to regulate the number of animals kept, and sometimes the gathering of fuel was restricted – in Cawston, for instance, to the period between Lady Day and Lammas (TNA: PRO, E134/43&44Eliz/Mich7).

In part two, I referred to the argument put forward by social historians that the poor were, in fact, granted access rights to common land as part of informal relief systems (Birtles 1999; Hindle 2004; Wales 1984). Local ratepayers tolerated this kind of use, rather than meet the expense and inconvenience of fulfilling the obligations set out in government Statutes (Birtles 1999, 78). As Thompson has argued: 'custom as praxis – village usages – generally afforded greater latitude for the exercise of minor rights than will be found in a formal view of the law' (Thompson 1993, 150). Yet, while these arguments are persuasive, the poor were not *always* permitted to use commons in this way, and even where they were there was no doubt that the *rights* to use, at least in strict legal terms, usually remained with a more limited group, those in possession of the ancient commonable tenements of a manor. Indeed, the importance of such tenements in the allocation of common rights is clear from the attempts made by manorial lords in villages such as Felmingham and Hargham to buy up common edge tenements in order to claim exclusive rights over the land (TNA: PRO, E134/26Eliz/East13; TNA: PRO, E134/42&43Eliz/Mich28); and, more commonly, by the way in which both manorial lords, and their tenants, undertook careful and detailed analysis of written records, and compiled numerous oral accounts from local inhabitants, in order to ascertain who had rights to use particular areas of land, and in what manner.

During periods of economic instability and increasing poverty, especially in the late sixteenth century, lords and their wealthy tenants made particularly strenuous attempts to tighten their control over the commons, often leaving the poor in a precarious position. In 1601 Henry Yonge deposed that:

> For the space of twelve or sixteene yeres or thereabouts diverse pore people inhabitants of Cawston have yerelie used to gett the most part of their lyvinge by graving flaggs and cutting of lyng for diverse other inhabitants from and after the Anunciacon of our Ladie until the first daie of August in everie yere upon the comons of Cawston and he saith that he doth thinke that the poore people aforesaid have ther cheifest lyving and mayntenance by graving of flags and cutting of lynge for wthout that he thinketh that some of them might begg ther bread (TNA: PRO, E134/43&44Eliz/Mich7).

Tim Wales has used this same source to illustrate the 'blending of use-rights, by-employments and informal relief in the livelihoods of the town's poor' (Wales 1984, 369). But further reading of this document reveals that the tenants and 'all other inhabitants' of the village were entitled to fuel from the commons on condition that they paid each year a customary 'stickpenny' to the manor which, at eight shillings and four pence, made this a more exclusive right than might at first appear. Yonge's concern for the 'cheifest lyving' of the poor indicates his growing anxiety regarding the extra burden it would bring to the poor rates (see also Amussen 1988, 19–20). But these kinds of uses of the commons by the poor – whether sanctioned by the 'middling sorts' as a form of poor-relief, or exercised as a right – were also threatened by environmental changes in the character of the commons themselves, changes brought about by: over-population and pressure on resources; overstocking by manorial sheep flocks; the extension of warrens; and ploughing up outfield brecks.

While increasing pressure on resources encouraged both manorial lords, and wealthier tenants and commoners to attempt a more rigorous definition of those who had legitimate rights to use the commons, it was easier to exclude some claimants than others. In 1589 Richard Lathe of Thorpe remembered how the 'poor folks' of Norwich and Pockthorpe, under licence of the owner of Thorpe manor, used to take furze and brakes from Mousehold Heath except upon the doles, until recently 'they have bene Restrayned and not suffered to take any brakes or other fewell in and uppon the sayd places' (TNA: PRO, E178/7153).

Similarly in Holkham in north-west Norfolk, the poor inhabitants of the town at all times of the year used to fell and carry away the whines growing on the heaths and several grounds, for their firing, in recent years they had:

> bene distourbed and ther hockes and ther ropes have bene taken away from them ... diverse tymes by Mr Wheatly and his servants and shepards at any tyme when they were sene takinge any the said firrs (TNA: PRO, DL4/35/4).

Despite being accused of carrying away fuel 'by stealth', it seems that in the past the activities of the poor inhabitants of Holkham had been tolerated. The traditional method of carriage by 'back burdens' indicates a quantity of fuel sufficient for personal consumption. In the years preceding the court case, however, fuel had been taken away in carts, suggesting that more was being carried away than was needed for the individual household, and the likelihood that it was being sold. The depletion of fuel and timber stocks was a particularly critical issue in these light soil areas, and perhaps led to the development of illicit trade networks that worked against local customs. Certainly, the deposition evidence implies that in Holkham at least this was an organised activity, creating local affiliations that cut across social divides. In this case a local gentleman Richard Mansner encouraged the digging up of furze, an opportunity he evidently seized as executor of the will of Lady Gresham's husband and former owner of the manor. Robert Empson a labourer, described how:

> Ther was not any firrs carred away by carte by any the inhitnnts of Holcham that ever he heard or knewe untill about iiij or five years last past at wch tyme Mr Richard Mansner did aponte this depont to dygge firrs upon the sd pece of ground sayinge unto him that it was my Ladie Gresshams grounde and that she wolde enter at michelmas then next followinge and therfor ... Mr Mansner let us take them while we may have them. (TNA: PRO, DL4/35/4)

Mansner encouraged the digging up of furze evidently to sell, and also to convert the parcel of heath to arable: a moment of opportunism on the part of Mansner and collusion on the part of Robert Empson, which further reduced the quantity of fuel available in the village.

There were other potential conflicts over underwood. Furze and whines provided the sheep flocks with much needed shelter and feed in these exposed heathland landscapes. In Kilverston 'two or three places of furres usually preserved for the layer and succar of the shepe' were kept on the heath (TNA: PRO, E134/35Eliz/East24); while in Wighton an enclosure made in Crabbs Castle fold course, to shelter the sheep of the fold course, was considered to be 'rather beneficial than hurtfull' for it provided protection in winter, in stormy weather and during the lambing season (TNA: PRO, DL4/40/49). The physical enclosure of heath for the benefit of manorial flocks was a controversial issue in many villages. In Snettisham a case was brought before the Duchy Court in 1622 concerning Jeffrey Cremer, the owner of the East Field fold course. He was accused of grubbing up decent cover for his sheep: a covert of 'very high firres' amounting to approximately sixteen acres, which was apparently 'much better for the harburrence of the sheepe in hard wether' than 'Shorte Whinnes'. The clearance of ground for cultivation placed pressure on the availability and quality of grazing, especially over the winter months: 'in the tyme of hard frostes and snowe so covered with ysses as sheepe cannot feed there', as well as in times of 'extraordinarye great snowes' for protection from the weather and feed the sheep were kept on 'the upp grounds' and 'Shorte Whinnes', situated 'betwixt the great downes and the howses in Snettesham'. The implementation of this new grazing regime was described as a 'hindrance to the tenants', who had the right to graze their cattle on the ground, 'by reason thereof the said grounds are surchardged' (TNA: PRO, DL4/71/29).

In some cases, conflicts over the various different uses to which the commons were put, and disputes over the fair allocation of resources, were resolved by enclosing portions, usually on a temporary basis, so that they could be used for particular purposes or allocated to particular families or individuals. Areas of heath or fen were often 'doled' – assigned to individual use – even while the common itself remained open. Indeed, the apparent physical openness of common land often masks a system of internal divisions, marked out using posts, stones or cross shapes cut into the soil. Such division was apparently the outcome of negotiation between the manorial lord and tenants, the number of doles generally corresponding to the number of tenements (such as Marsham TNA: PRO, E178/4251). The tenants retained the right to graze over the common; but the extraction of fuel and other resources now took place within the framework of individual doles: Robert Marshall, a husbandman from Salhouse, described how he had worked for the owners of the doles on Mousehold Heath, digging flags and felling ling and brakes (TNA: PRO, E178/7153). Permanent, physical enclosure was, however, a matter of controversy. In the Flegg village of Ormesby the poor also cut fuel from a number of doles but their access was threatened by enclosure. In the words of eighty-five-year-old Thomas Ilbert 'it wolde be a great discomoditie to the poore inhabitants if the sayd dolles sholde be severallie layd together and enclosed' (TNA: PRO, E134/29&30Eliz/Mich8). Enclosure was accompanied by an attempt to rationalise use rights, which in a landscape increasingly denuded of resources, especially fuel, prompted rising consternation among ratepayers and the poor.

Pressure on common land came, however, less from competition for resources within local communities as from the aggressive actions of manorial lords and demesne farmers, and in particular from their desire to maximise their incomes from the grazing such areas offered to sheep and rabbits. Indeed, the over-stocking of commons seems to have been more of an issue, initially anyway, than enclosure. Such resentment was expressed in the articles drawn up by Robert Kett in 1549, particularly the allegedly spurious rights of lords to take the profits of the commons (Fletcher and MacCulloch 1997, 144). A Star Chamber case from the clayland parish of Hingham (TNA: PRO, STAC2/29/140; STAC2/27/55) in the 1540's reveals the extent of animosity towards the manorial lord, Sir Henry Parker, who was accused of having 'no respect to the decay and utter dystrucon of the comen welthe of the said towne of Hyngham'. The inhabitants maintained that they had 'tyme wherof the mynde of man' the right to graze their cattle on the common. But in recent years Parker had let the commons out to 'certeyn covetous psons', who were accused of over-stocking the common and thus reducing the pasture available for the commoners' cattle. Parker claimed the land as part of his manorial demesne, and accused the inhabitants of forcibly entering the grounds 'in most riotous maner' and pasturing their sheep there. The sheep were subsequently impounded but the owners broke into the pound to retrieve them accusing Parker of having no right to detain them. Parker maintained the exclusive right to run a 'fold course' over the commons, presumably a misrepresentation of inherited folding rights claimed by tenants and lord collectively. Clearly this was not recognised by the inhabitants who threatened to kill his livestock 'withot delaye' if they should find them grazing there (TNA: PRO, STAC2/29/140). The inhabitants complained that because their area of grazing had been depleted, the productivity of their arable lands was also threatened due to a reduction of livestock and consequent lack of manure: being 'not able to occupie ther tyllage as they were want to do' (TNA: PRO, STAC2/27/55).

One of the major sources of problems, as this case makes clear, was that in many parts of Norfolk manorial lords had particularly strong rights over commons. In many heathland villages common land was often absorbed within fold-course territories, across which lords might attempt to claim almost exclusive rights of grazing. Fold-course commons might, for this reason, have been subject to unilateral, if partial, enclosure. In the dispute over Mousehold Heath (referred to as 'Free Mussold' on account of the common belief that it was outside manorial jurisdiction) deponents complained of encroachment, and exclusion from local resources (TNA: PRO, E178/7153). Apparently in the past the lord of the manors of Woodbastwick and Laviles had kept their sheep flocks on the demesne and 'several grounds then lying open'. But since the manors had passed into the ownership of John Corbet and his son Miles, large amounts of land had been enclosed and, whereas in the past the flocks had been kept on the demesne 'as hath in anncient tyme bene used and accustomed', the sheep flock was now kept on Mousehold. As a result, the inhabitants of Woodbastwick were forced to reduce their cullet flock as the heath was: 'overlaide with the lordes flock' and consequently they were 'dryven to keepe their grete cattell onlie uppon the said heathe that before did pasture and feede in the ground now inclosed (TNA: PRO, E178/7153). In his testimony William Cubitt, a husbandman of sixty-three, referred to the 'commotion time' in a noticeably inflammatory comment on Corbett's activities. He reminded the court that since 1549 the tenants had grazed their sheep on the heath:

> Till of late tyme since the comoccon cullets of sheep upon the parcell of Mussold where flocks were kept But … he hathe harde that the said Tenants were inforced to leave keepinge of the said cullets because Mr Corbets shepard did chase their shepe that they colde not keep them quietlie as of ancient tyme they had done.

William went on to accuse Miles Corbet of encroaching on Mousehold by 'fetching in' part of it during the perambulation of Woodbastwick and making new boundary markers by digging crosses into the earth of 'free Mousehold' where there were none before. Once again we return to the economic interests of those taking part in perambulations, and the consolidation of manor and parish in the contest over common land.

In the second half of the sixteenth century in Cawston there was a measured campaign to restrict areas subject to common grazing, in order to give precedence to the five hundred or so sheep belonging to the fold course (TNA: PRO, E133/1/108; E134/23&24Eliz/Mich14; E134/43&44Eliz/Mich7). The lord attempted to limit the rights of tenants to graze their cullet sheep to 'Eastgate Green', a comparatively small parcel of land separated from the Great Common by the 'Norwich Way'. The shepherd of the fold course patrolled the boundary between commons and frequently used his dogs to chase strays back to Eastgate Green. Recourse to the Exchequer Courts came at the end of protracted attempts by the owner, or lessee of the manor, to prevent others using the grounds. Clement Neadwell, a labourer, recalled in 1601, when he was farmer to a Mr Hopkins in the 1570's he had been permitted to keep fifty cullet sheep. But his landlord Hopkins warned him that they should not feed over Norwich Way, 'for if they did then his landlord did bid him stand at his owne perill'. He admitted that the sheep sometimes escaped and yet he 'was never punished nor trobled for the same' (TNA: PRO, E134/43&44Eliz/Mich7). In the same set of depositions William Larwood of nearby Saxthorpe insisted that as well as feeding upon Eastgate Green the tenants always had access to the great common 'without restraint'. This was further supported by George Jenkinson who remembered when he was ten-years-old his father, then shepherd of the fold course, ordered him to bring the manorial flock as far as 'dryncklemere pytte' located about two furlongs north from 'stonegateway'. The tenants of Cawston, however, held a different view of the course of the bounds and instructed Jenkinson to feed the sheep only as far as Stonegate Way assuring him that this was the correct boundary of the fold course (TNA: PRO, E134/43&44Eliz/Mich7).

In order to substantiate their claims the tenants of Cawston produced a plan of the common, which conveyed the spatial relationship between their ancient tenements and the commons (see below, Figure 25 p. 119). William Larwood gave an account of those inhabitants (past and present) who occupied tenements adjoining the commons. Edward Smyth, for example, lived in a tenement 'nere adoyninge to the great common ... by the right of which tenement ... Smyth did use to fede and depasture upon the ... common ... viij xx shepe in all tymes of the yere'. The tenement near to Smyth's once occupied by 'Old Warnes', and now Edward Easton held the right to graze thirty sheep on the great heath. Robert Easton lived near a common known as 'old marketsted'. While John Weg, William Ellison, John Reve, Edmond Bulman and Edmond Johnson dwelling near Eastgate Green 'did likewise' feed their sheep there, 'and also upon the great comon when they wold go over unto the same' (TNA: PRO, E134/43&44Eliz/Mich7). The tenants of Cawston presented a powerful statement of claims through their memories of the past, and in relation to the organisation of settlement. Their detailed plan of the commons consolidated the tenants' knowledge and experience as commoners. Custom and right was fixed in terms of space, and in terms of genealogical time. Cawston common provided a point of contact across which the boundaries of belonging were drawn.

The Environmental Impact

The tenants of Cawston managed to retain their right to graze their cattle on the Great Common. But over-stocking by the owner of the fold course together with the extension of the rabbit warren, presented a grave threat to their livelihoods. The dispute over the warren was one of many that occurred in the county at this time. The warreners argued that the tenants had 'sufficient comon for the feede of ther great cattell ... notwithstandinge the number of conyes there'. John Buller considered this to be clear because the cattle were 'in good lyking'. Indeed, along with the other warreners he blamed the tenants for the lack of grazing accusing them of 'excessive graving of flaggs' which 'they let ly and rott' upon the common. The commoners replied that the holes in the surface of the heath were the consequence of the warreners 'setting falls' – digging of holes which were then covered with brushwood – in order to trap rabbits. It was alleged that Edward Hamond, a large landowner and one of the defendants in the case, had encouraged 'one Bishopp' (possibly Raynold Byshope, a poor man owning neither 'cow nor cottage' listed in the Overseer's Accounts; Wales 1984, 392), should he 'want any wood for fewell', to 'pull upp the complainants fales for vermyn' – that is, wooden vermin traps (TNA: PRO, E134/43&44Eliz/Mich7).

By the turn of the seventeenth century the growth of the rabbit population was causing great concern. Seventy-four-year-old John Blome considered 'the game of coneys in the said comon is very greatly increased within this thre yeres more than ever that was before in his memory' and was hugely detrimental to the provision of grazing:

> The tenants and inhabitants ... have susteyned great losse in ther grasse for ther fede of ther cattell and shepe upon the comon of Cawston by the multitude of conyes ... and have susteyned very great losse in their corne and grasse springs and fences in ther severall grounds ... the damage thereof is so great and conserne to so many that he ... dare not take upon him to value the same (TNA: PRO, E134/43&44Eliz/ Mich7).

The extension of Cawston warren was the focus of a long-running dispute. Some deponents remembered that in the mid-sixteenth century objections were made by the 'cheife tenants' of Cawston Manor dwelling near to the common regarding the damage to their corn. At this time the warren was maintained within the boundaries of the park, but gradually the warreners had been encroaching upon the common. The right to take coneys from the common became a matter of contention, with the warreners claiming that they held the exclusive right to do this.

The expansion of the warren, beyond the old boundary ditches of the park, was visible on the ground, not just in the number of rabbits that could be seen but also in the construction of earthwork 'burrows' – the earthwork mounds that archaeologists usually refer to as 'pillow mounds' (Aston and Bettey 1998). John Masham, a seventy-five-year-old thatcher and tenant of Cawston Manor, deposed that 'he hath sene of late certen newe borrowes for coneys newly made upon the comon of Cawston nere Drincklemere and Brandston dooles where ... [50] yeres past he knewe none'. Not only was the grazing potential of the commons jeopardized, yet more damage was caused by the activity of digging for rabbits. To Henry Younge's mind there was never such digging on Cawston Common by the warreners until recently:

> The sand and gravell is cast upp in such great heapes upon the playne grownd by reason of the digging therof that ther will noe grasse growe upon the said grownde in a verie long tyme and ... the ... digging now lately used is a great hindrance to the inhabitants of Cawston as well in the fede of the cattell as in dangering ther said cattell (TNA: PRO, E134/43&44Eliz/Mich7).

The proliferation and expansion of warrens caused tensions elsewhere. In a court case dating to 1592 concerning the jurisdiction of warren rights belonging to Castle Rising Chase, the local inhabitants judged that an unprecedented increase in the rabbit population had occurred within their lifetimes (TNA: PRO, E134/34&35Eliz/Mich7). William Swanton deposed that forty years previously few burrows had existed on the West Heath of Congham yet within the last five years it had become 'almost wholly burrowed with conies'. He also mentioned that several parcels of ground 'stored with coneys' were being maintained in the west part of Congham where there had been none before. In the late sixteenth century eighty-five-year-old Thomas Ilbert reported that the number of rabbits in Ormesby was far greater than in his father's or grandfather's time: 'the enlardgment of the coneys is very hurtfull unto the tenants there in respecte of there comonage' (TNA: PRO, E134/29&30Eliz/Mich8). In some places the impact of rabbits was so great that the value of fold courses was threatened. The run of court case records from Cawston reveals that the manorial flock amounted to eight or nine hundred sheep in 1571 but by the turn of the seventeenth century had been reduced to four or five hundred (TNA: PRO, E134/43&44Eliz/Mich7). Enclosure was partly to blame of course. In Congham, similarly, the sheep flock belonging to Sir Henry Spelman in right of his Manor of Rustens had to be reduced by 1599:

> By reason of the great increasinge of coneys ther have been so small feede lefte for the feede of the sheepe as they could not tarry ther so that by the space of this xxxti yeares the said Henry ... hathe not kept annie sheepe ther but onely for the preservinge of the right and interest in the same (TNA: PRO, E134/41Eliz/East5).

As this statement implies, land use rights and customs required continual observance, otherwise there was the threat that new precedents would be set, and old ones called into question and 'forgotten'.

Breckland was particularly badly affected by the environmental deterioration caused by overgrazing of sheep and rabbits. By the end of the seventeenth century the region was noted for its sand blows, described by John Salmon as 'blowing days', when fields drifted 'like the billows of the sea' (Kent 1910, 5). In 1668 Thomas Wright described 'A Curious and Eaxact Relation of a Sand-Floud', which he attempted to prevent by planting furze hedges 'set upon one another as fast as the Sand levell'd them' and creating banks twenty feet high (Sussams 1996, 180–182). The deterioration of resources seems to have accelerated in the seventeenth century. Deponents remembered that in the past the inhabitants of Hockwold and Wilton had kept large numbers of livestock on the extensive heaths here, but by the mid-seventeenth century grazing had been entirely discontinued, due to the destruction caused by rabbits (TNA: PRO, DL4/104/1658/5). Indeed, it seems that at times there was little vegetation to sustain even the rabbits: during bouts of severe weather the warreners were accused of allowing them to encroach upon the open fields. In 1578, Edward Russell estimated that over the course of two winters the rabbits of Methwold Warren had eaten what amounted to 300 acres of corn (TNA: PRO, DL4/20/7). The great heath had apparently supported two flocks each containing 1700 sheep at the turn of the seventeenth century, yet by 1658 the number in each flock had been reduced to 800 (TNA: PRO, DL4/104/1658/5).

While the customs and rights of local inhabitants were threatened, and in many places gradually eroded away by the determination of landowners and their wealthy tenants farmers, it is important to note that the commons engendered powerful emotional sentiment within local societies (Hindle 2004, 27). In particular overstocking was a divisive issue throughout this period. A matter that continued to be a cause of contention well into the eighteenth century: the commoners of Tottington, for example, accused their landlord of overstocking the commons in a deliberate attempt to diminish the value of the commons in order to reduce the compensation due at enclosure (Neeson 1993, 88). The case of Tottington brings us to the connected question of management. Jeanette Neeson has argued that the commons were carefully regulated, usually by imposing stints, to ensure ongoing productivity and sustainability (Neeson 1993). Woodward has also surmised that in the seventeenth century the widespread implementation of by-laws restricted exploitation by stipulating, for instance, quantities and season in which resources could be taken: without these regulations 'many of the commons and wastes of early modern England would have been quickly denuded' (Woodward 1998, 54). Yet, the contemporary accounts mentioned here convey a striking image of the deterioration of resources on the commons and heaths of many Norfolk villages. Deponents often contrasted their present landscape with that of the past. Perhaps to some extent their memories were mistakenly optimistic their judgements having

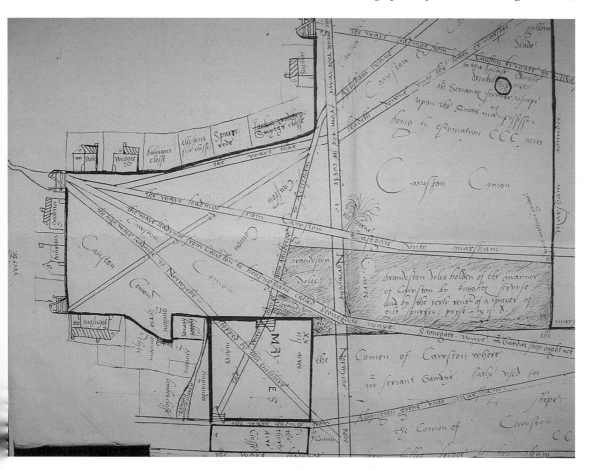

FIGURE 25. Detail of a sketch map drawn up in relation to the commons dispute in Cawston in 1571. It gives details of the names of the occupants of tenements adjoining the common and various landmark features including 'the thorne' and 'drynkel myre' (TNA: PRO, E133/1/108).

been clouded by the passage of time. But there is landscape and archaeological evidence to confirm that the desire for profit and status, among sixteenth- and seventeenth-century landowners in light soil areas, had a profound impact on local environments (Aston and Bettey 1998). The extension of livestock numbers, whether for wool or fur, was both hugely detrimental to the commons and heaths and was potentially in opposition to grain production.

Enclosure: Landscapes of Inclusion/Exclusion

Enclosure was a divisive issue in the sixteenth and seventeenth centuries, but one that cannot be easily categorised according to the social status of those involved: people supported enclosure or accepted it, when it did not directly impinge upon their livelihoods. Moreover, there were a number of different forms of enclosure, as we have seen. Piecemeal enclosure might be acceptable to neighbours, and to manorial lords, if rights of access for shack grazing were maintained. Even the enclosure of common land for specific purposes, at least on a temporary basis, might be condoned. But the more general enclosure of common land, and unilateral and complete enclosure of arable, was strongly resented. Deposition evidence for Norfolk points to an undercurrent of everyday protest expressed in terms of the material environment: newly set hedges were pulled up, banks knocked down, and boundary marks defaced.

The enclosure of common shared by Worstead and Tunstead by Cuthbert Leverington caused disquiet among the villagers. John Pestle of Westwick recalled that one of the enclosers, Leverington, had said that he understood that his enclosures were unlawful but threatened that if 'any man would ioyne in lawe with him he sholde be compelled to throwe downe the same again But if that were throwne downe fyve hundred acres sboulde be throwne downe allso' (TNA: PRO, DL4/49/3). Another serious dispute arose in Congham over the enclosure of the half-year meadow lands. The inhabitants claimed to have common of pasture from after the hay harvest until Candlemas, a strongly held conviction which led them to destroy the fences and quick-set hedge of 'young ashes' and to break up the bank and ditch surrounding it. One witness related the events from the time the agreement was made, to the setting out of the boundary before the enclosure was made, when a 'marke was made right againste acerteyne ashe tree in the hedge of a certeyne close ... the tre remaineth but the said marke is defaced' (TNA: PRO, E134/40&41Eliz/Mich21).

The problem with such small-scale enclosures was that were accretive. The inhabitants of Snettisham, for example, described the gradual impact of enclosure on the heaths. William Chamberlain a labourer from Sedgeford recounted his involvement, some thirty-six years previously, in enclosing a ten-acre close lying in 'Westgate': 'at which tyme ... [he] did dike and fence all the west side ... thirty two yeres sithence one Thomas Crispe of Sedgeford did dike and enclose the south head therof before which tyme the east and north parts therof were aunciently enclosed sithence which tyme ... more close hath bene and contynewed enclosed' (TNA: PRO, DL4/43/4). In Cawston an area of heath adjoining the common called Mayes, had already been extensively enclosed by 1571, a process that continued over the following years. In 1601 many of the deponents could still remember the tenants and inhabitants grazing their cattle there (TNA: PRO, E133/1/108; Figure 25).

The enclosure of common land was a complicated matter, however: as we have seen, temporary enclosures were tolerated, providing there was some continuity of access to at least demonstrate that common rights were still attached to the land, and that the enclosures were defined by patently temporary barriers. Even permanent encroachments were sometimes acceptable in the immediate vicinity of commonable tenements, as in the case of Widow Andrews in Felmingham, or for the building of tenements for the poor (Birtles 1999). The preoccupations of manorial lords and tenants in defining their rights to common land adds to an already complex picture of the ways people identified with their landscape, and the networks of affiliation which often cut obliquely across socio-economic divides. There was, at times an intense, friction between manorial and parochial interests – tensions that do not fall into neat territorial and social categories.

Conclusion

I began this chapter with the dispute of Snettisham warren where, for seventeen years, sixty-year-old John Doughty was warrener in the right of Wymond Cary, farmer of the Duchy manor. While Doughty strove to maintain his right to trap conies on the warren, and endured at least two aggressive assaults as a result, it was the activities of Cary that lay at the heart of local tensions. Cary caused concern within the village when he removed the court rolls of the manor from a chest in the church – locked with two locks one key kept by the steward of the manor, the other key by the churchwardens – and kept them to himself 'contrary to the said anncient order and custome' (TNA: PRO, DL4/34/46). He engaged in a sustained campaign against the customs and rights of the tenants and inhabitants of Snettisham, grazing his sheep flocks over the open fields and enclosures of outfield, including More Close, Down Close and Horsewell Furlong discussed earlier, and denying others the same rights (TNA: PRO, DL4/42/41). His administration of the manor was aggressive, John Walker described as being 'a very poore olde man' was beaten and abused by Cary's servant, 'his face was very pore scratcht and disFigured and received a black Iiey' for being on Snettisham common (TNA: PRO, DL4/34/46).

Cary's alleged mistreatment did not end with agrarian matters. He was also accused of taking profits due to the churchwardens and was blamed for the impoverishment of the town and parish. In the words of Richard Greene, a fifty-six-year-old husbandman, who was born in Snettisham: 'the churchwardens of the towne of Snetisham ... have accustomed to receive of the owners of every shippe that dried their fishe upon a certeine place in Snetisham ... called the comen stone certeine money or fishe which was imployed and bestowed aboute the maintennce and repacon of the Church of Snetisham'. Ever since he could remember this custom had been respected until, that is, Cary came to the town. Green accused Cary of taking the money for 'his owne private use ... all such benefitt and profitt as they before so received for the drying of the said fish and will not suffer the said churchwardens to take the same any more to the great decay of the said church (the pishioners of the towne being very poore people)' (TNA: PRO, DL4/34/46). The consolidation of manorial and parochial interests was a common theme in the post-medieval development of territorial structures in Norfolk, particularly in the setting out of ambiguous boundaries across commons and heaths. In Snettisham, a relatively large village situated on the coastal fringe of the Good Sands region, the consolidation of jurisdictions was used to bolster the control of the manor.

This chapter has examined the principal changes affecting the landscape of sixteenth- and seventeenth-century Norfolk – enclosure, the changing use and management of common pasture and arable fields – at a very local level, using in particular the evidence of court depositions. Such an approach reveals, perhaps not surprisingly, the complexity both of landscape change and of the social and economic forces driving it, but it also indicates something about the character of contemporary experience of, and understanding of, the physical environment.

Social historians have emphasised the role of perambulation ceremonies in forging senses of collective identity, and mutual systems of knowledge within parish communities (Bushaway 1982; Thomas 1971; Underdown 1985; Fletcher; Hindle 2000). Others have looked at the ordering of space in parish churches as evidence for contemporary notions of hierarchy and order at the political and social centre of the 'little commonwealth'. Recent research has revealed how the organisation of seating in parish churches, for example, points to a complex articulation of social standing, reputation and belonging (Marsh 2005). Moreover, church seating arrangements were often attached to ancient tenements, which suggests a far more extensive articulation of social space (Hey 1981). Indeed, the plan drawn up by the tenants of Cawston reveals a further extension based on common rights and the geography of habitation. At the core of these studies is the notion of boundedness and the premise that identities were forged through the collective articulation and negotiation of boundaries (Cohen 1985; Withington and Shepard 2000).

While interesting research has been carried out on the ways local societies defined and mediated the social and moral boundaries of their neighbourhood, this chapter has attempted to understand local identities formed through the physical knowledge and experience of the landscape. The oral testimonies presented before the law courts gives voice to a wide range of people who possessed a great depth of understanding of the farming landscape: of the boundary features used to demarcate internal agrarian divisions relating to open field and common land; the varying status of old and new enclosures; and the layers of customs and rights pertaining to particular tracts of land.

In his study of the medieval manor of Hevingham, Bruce Campbell concluded that the complex and fragmented charcater of manorial and landholding structures must have precluded any sense of community solidarity. He suggested that a collective sense of identity must have been generated through the shared obligation to pay tithes. (Campbell 1986). Social historians have shown how social solidarity among non-elite groups was created through the collective recognition, agreement and articulation of local customs and common rights (Neeson 1993; Thompson 1991 ch. 1 and 3; Wood 1996; 1997; 1999). The evidence for Hevingham, and surrounding villages, has revealed that here, as elsewhere in Norfolk, local identities were forged, or re-forged, through the need to protect local resources and land use rights from the encroachments of the wealthy. This is most evident for instance in the court cases where, as at Marsham the 'inhabitants' took their lord to court over abuses of fold-course rights. Research carried out for this book also illustrates that alliances often cut obliquely across hierarchical structures with those of middle rank siding with their poorer neighbours. At other times knowledge of local customs was contradictory, dividing social relations rather than binding them. The evidence presented here reveals that at a micro-level the history of the landscape was shaped by complex claims and diverse interests in the land. This is revealed most notably in the attitudes towards, and meaning of, enclosure.

Piecemeal enclosure, as an agreement between individuals, has been considered a form of enclosure 'with less overtly divisive social implications' (Johnson 1996, 50; Williamson 2000). This assumes that the process of enclosure was consensual and straightforward, and that when a piece of ground was 'enclosed' its private status was both recognised and respected. As we have seen recent models of enclosure portray a sense of cohesiveness from a social and geographical perspective and fail to take on board the underlying social dynamics and conflict that propelled change at a local level. Old enclosures, for instance, were considered very differently to those of more recent origin. Furthermore, the nature and geography of pre-parliamentary enclosure cannot be understood without understanding the interrelated significance of custom. For individual perspectives were bound up with the collective obligations and rights set by the 'community': responsibilities and expectations manifest in the meaning of custom and right (Wood 1999; Wrightson 1996). In early modern Norfolk, the concept of custom exerted a powerful place within local societies among elite landowners, yeomen farmers, husbandmen, labourers and the resident poor.

Johnson has argued that the demise of the central role of manorial courts in the continuation and re-negotiation of agrarian practices was part of the process of 'closure', the break down of communal knowledge and emergence of individualism (Johnson 1996). Perhaps: but the legal and organisational changes of the period also involved the increasing competence of the central law courts. The role of the Equity courts in stipulating the collection of oral testimonies from within communities suggests that knowledge of the landscape and customary practices were still firmly rooted in the common experiences of the land. Rather than disconnecting local societies from the landscape, the activities of the central law courts served to forge new links both within and between village communities and the land (Wood 1999). On the other hand, in their role as the mediators in local disputes, the central law courts encouraged a degree of standardisation of inherited medieval agrarian systems, practices and customs. As we have seen, in light soil districts, large landowners not only used the courts to protect their fold-course interests, but also to create new fold courses where none had been before. This, in a sense, amounted to the use of new legal institutions to create new institutional arrangements, which were themselves modelled on what purported to be ancient, traditional rights. But the courts, and other instruments of the central state, were also used to create entirely new forms – landscapes of enclosure – and would continue to be so employed, with increasing success, during the following two centuries.

Examining the local context of nascent capitalism reveals the contentious, muddled and far from homogenous development of landscape history, especially regarding pre-parliamentary enclosure. Central to notions of territory, and the shifts underway in farming customs and practices, was the interpretation of a range of material and cognitive structures inherited from the past. In Gosden's and Lock's words: 'in daily life there is always a tension between the inheritance from the past, the intentions of the present and the possibilities held by the future' (Gosden and Lock, 1998, 4). As national courts intruded more and more into the field of local custom, the search for old and the creation of new written records became increasingly important for landlords, tenants and commoners alike. Andy Wood has argued that no longer the exclusive preserve of an elite minority the written word had become 'intertwined with popular senses of custom' and of the past (Wood 1999, 152). In the following chapter we will explore the ways popular conceptions of the past shaped the development of farming. At times the past was used as a provocative device and local memories became 'a clash between ... sets of values in the present' (Thomas 1984).

CHAPTER FIVE

Landscape and Memory

....

> However different the ways in which these landscapes were inhabited, each of them
> would only have been comprehensible in terms of a sequence that grew out of the
> ruins of the past (Bradley 2002, 81).

For the post-medieval period the historiographical emphasis on the march towards rational 'modern' modes of production and the transformation of the rural landscape into a field of utility overlooks the influence of the past in shaping 'capitalist' landscapes of production. The oral testimonies of witnesses gathered during litigation proceedings offer a valuable insight into the deep interrelationship between individuals, their social lives and their situated experience and knowledge of the landscape. Social relationships and identities were mediated through an understanding of a material 'language' of place. This language was by no means static: for each generation the inherited landscape became the focus of interrogation, reinvention and sometimes neglect, in keeping with the concerns and objectives of the present. It is widely noted that, in a court of law, the authenticity of customs and land use rights was based on popular conceptions of antiquity and the proof that such practices had existed before anyone could remember (Thompson 1993, chapter 3; Wood 1997; 1999; Fox 2000 chapter 5). This chapter examines the various ways in which early modern individuals and social groups assessed and disputed the authority of customs and rights by interpreting what was physically evident on the ground.

Social historians have tended to use the material environment as an illustrative device and a backdrop to their arguments. In such accounts the role of the landscape is a passive one – the scene where the dynamics of social interactions and change take place. Some have, however, indicated the importance of the landscape as a mnemonic tool in sustaining oral traditions (Rollison 1992). Popular perceptions of the landscape in this period are more usually assigned to the realms of folklore. The debate has been predominately focused on the development of an historical imagination traced in the shift from orality to literacy. During the 1980s scholars emphasised a dichotomy between learned elite and popular illiterate cultures (for example Thomas 1984; Woolf 1988). Historical knowledge was, for the most part, born from medieval literary tracts; the chronicles and stories contained within them becoming popularised and transmitted through oral traditions propagated by the growth of the print culture in the seventeenth century (summarised by Fox 2000, 242–258; Thomas

1984; Woolf 1991). For many historians such narratives illustrate the shallowness of the historical imagination (Fox 2000, 256; Woolf 1988). Woolf has argued that oral cultures have little sense of relative time. Chronological time is 'telescoped' the basis for this being that sense of the past in the early modern period were 'focused less on time than on space, less on dates than on locations' (Woolf 1988, 31). Keith Thomas has also suggested that 'episodes from different periods were not ranged in temporal order; they seem to have existed alongside each other in a single conflated past' (Thomas 1984, 6). This was to gradually change over the course of the sixteenth and seventeenth centuries when 'oral traditions transmuted into written words' (Fox 2000, 289). Rising literacy rates and the circulation of popular printed material propelled a conceptual shift, enabling people to appreciate more linear modes of thought (Thomas 1984, 6). In all these studies local landmarks appear as merely the objects on to which the latest fashionable legend was attached.

While it may not have been possible for people living in predominately oral societies to arrange the past into a chronological sequence of events, as we do today, this does not mean that popular notions of the past lacked order or authority. In the early modern period, there were times during the life-cycle of rural societies when the past took on powerful meaning; during such episodes conceptions of 'ancient time' became central to the mediation of access rights to local resources and customary practices. Social historians have carried out important research into the ways in which plebeian groups used the past as a political tool in their attempts to defend their rights to the land, and to sustain their livelihoods (Fox 1996, 2000; Wood 1998, 1999). In his study of the early modern Peak Country Andy Wood (1999) has demonstrated how contemporary notions of the past had an important role in solidifying a sense of collective consciousness among the free-miners of the region. Furthermore, recourse to the law courts had an important effect in homogenizing versions of the past; the political standpoint of the miners was reinforced through outward displays of unity articulated through a shared memory of custom and land use rights. In rural Norfolk the evidence of the past was also vital in substantiating the claims of tenants and farmers in their attempts to secure access rights to the land. But in contrast to the Peak Country, where the free-miners asserted strong political autonomy into the late seventeenth century, in Norfolk the wealthy minority generally triumphed in disputes brought before the central equity courts. As historians are well aware the period was marked by the demise of the small landowner and steady acquisition of land, and access rights, in the hands of a small minority. Power over the land in the present, and in the future, was vested in knowledge of the past. In court it was a prerequisite for wealthy landowners and tenants alike to articulate through their 'genealogical' and social memories their comprehension of past land use and long established custom.

Some landscape historians and archaeologists have recognised that there was an underlying stratum of landscape history, still evident in the material world that helped shape future social, economic and cultural relationships

(Hooke 2000; Williamson 2003). Tom Williamson has argued that in order to understand post-medieval landscape change, we must first acknowledge the influence of antecedent structures inherited from the medieval past (Williamson 2003, 192–193). In the sixteenth and seventeenth centuries specialisation in agrarian production, or the continuation of traditional practices, required the ongoing mediation of the past in terms of, for example, tenurial arrangements, patterns of landholding, the layout of settlements and field systems, all of which played a crucial part in structuring farming practices in the post-medieval period. In clayland districts, farmers encouraged by an expanding market economy, negotiated the conversion of their arable land to pasture; and those within sheep-corn areas extended their warrens, fold courses and cultivated acreage by ploughing up portions of heathland as 'outfield brecks'. The achievements of these farmers often rested upon their assertion of conflicting ideas about how the landscape should be organised and exploited, notions based on an understanding of the past.

Recent research carried out by prehistorians and early medievalists is particularly useful here for our understanding of how people living in the past perceived the past (see for example, Bradley 1993, 2002; Williams and Holtorf 2006; Williams 1998; Holtorf 1998). The proponents of this field of study have demonstrated that despite lacking our modern methods of dating, people interpreted the relative historical sequence of various earthwork features and indeed entire landscapes. The visible evidence of antiquity became a powerful tool in the mediation of authority and control of land and society. This has been shown, for instance, in the evidence for the reuse of Bronze Age burial mounds by Anglo Saxon elites as a symbolic appropriation of the material past to demonstrate ancestral longevity and to legitimise power and authority (Bradley 1993; Williams 1998). In order to understand the significance of such features – the reasons why they were chosen and preserved – it is important to consider that archaeological and natural features had, to use Holtorf's term, 'life-histories' of their own: as old landmarks were given new meanings – earlier uses were gradually forgotten, but the significance of the feature endures long after its original creation (Holtorf 1998).

The Relics of the Catholic Past

The majority of studies regarding changing attitudes towards the landscape have focused on folklore traditions and impact of printed material in accelerating the shift from Catholic inspired beliefs to Protestant ones (Thomas 1984; Fox 2000; Simpson 1986). Acts of iconoclasm have, for example, been employed by some historians to suggest that 'once the visual representations disappeared so the legends which they had evoked faded from memory' (Fox 2000, 253). However, the attack on superstitious images and monuments did not produce a blank canvas, but rather left a palimpsest of references to the pre-Reformation past. Thomas has interpreted these redundant remains as representing an 'unassimilated, unfunctional past (that) could not so easily be shrugged off' (Thomas 1984, 3). It will be argued here that it was precisely because of the re-assimilation and renewed functions of relic features in later landscapes that help explain aspects of their survival.

There is a strong degree of ambiguity regarding the extent of destruction and continuing significance of religious artefacts and holy sites (Tarlow 2004). Of the evidence for wayside crosses, discussed in chapter two, the great majority of references date from the late sixteenth and seventeenth centuries – clearly crosses were not all simply torn down and disregarded. A search of early cartographic material enhances the picture further by revealing yet more traces of the late medieval religious landscape. As we have seen 'holy wells', such as those of Appleton and Sedgeford continued to be a feature of local topographies in the seventeenth century (NRO, BRA 2524/6; NRO, LEST/OC1): as did the remains of small wayside and pilgrims chapels for example, St Edmund's Chapel in Hunstanton and St James' in Hillington (NRO, LEST/1C 68; NRO, NRS 21381). Of course it is possible that the cartographic depiction of such landmarks reflects the religious conservatism of those who commissioned the maps. Among the wider population too, the spiritual associations and material remains of late medieval religious life were not easily ignored, nor were they merely assigned to folk memory, but continued to structure peoples' spatial topographies.

When Cozens-Hardy made his inventory of Norfolk crosses in the 1930s, he found that none of the structures survived intact, unless there had been an attempt to restore them in the nineteenth century (Cozens-Hardy 1934). The extent of damage varied, with some such as that of North Walsham (TG277283; Figure 26) standing almost to its original height, with only the top broken, others were merely broken stumps, such as that of Southrepps (TG26223641), and Aylmerton (Figure 27, TG18103880). Not all of the damage can be blamed on the religious fervour of the late sixteenth and mid seventeenth century. The HER records the 'unintentional' destruction of some of these monuments in recent years, such as that of Marham (HER11391). There is insufficient evidence to suggest when crosses started to be referred to as 'stumps'. An early example comes from a map of Sedgeford dating to 1634 (NRO, LEST/OC). Of the other crosses for which we have map evidence the majority were presumably referred to by their pre-Reformation names either in descriptive terms, with reference to the parish, or some personal name. The 'Stump Cross' indicated on the modern Ordnance Survey map of Cawston, for example, was known as 'Stantling Cross' throughout the sixteenth and seventeenth centuries (NRO, MS 4521; NRO, MC 341/13; NRO, NRS 21404). The longevity of the name is noteworthy, indicating an ongoing interest in maintaining links with the past; as are the various ways it was depicted. The stylistic difference between the late sixteenth-century drawings of this cross and that of the late seventeenth century is particularly striking (compare Figures 22, 28 and 29).

Other crosses were depicted as similarly elaborate structures, apparently left unscathed by iconoclasm such as 'Fringe Cross' depicted on the seventeenth-

FIGURE 26. The medieval cross in North Walsham (TG277283) stands at the point where the parish boundary crosses the Norwich Road.

century map of Sedgeford (NRO, LEST/OC); 'Coldham Cross' included on a map of Holkham dating to 1590 (NRO, MS 4535); and the two crosses standing on 'Walsingham Way' in Hillington in the seventeenth century (NRO, NRS 21381; NRS 21383). In Babingley 'Butlers Cross' appears to have survived in its pre-Reformation condition, judging from its depiction on a map of Castle Rising Chase dating to c.1580, yet at some point was knocked down leaving just its base stone, the remains of which are still extant. The cartographic evidence suggests the cross was broken at some time after the map was made, which implies as with the other examples mentioned above, a strand of continuity linking the late sixteenth and seventeenth-century landscape to the pre-Reformation past. On the other hand landowners and cartographers were probably depicting fairly standardised cross motifs that, in many cases, bore little resemblance to what was on the ground.

Cozens-Hardy discussed the reuse of many in purely secular, often domestic, contexts, as mounting blocks, doorsteps and as pillars, for example (Cozens-

FIGURE 27. Aylmerton cross. Though restored in the nineteenth century, its medieval origins, and partial destruction during the Reformation, are clearly visible in the remains of the base stone. Despite the diminishing of its overt spiritual associations, the location of the cross on a parish boundary and crossroads ensured its continuing importance in the post-medieval landscape.

Hardy 1935). Some landscape archaeologists have considered these new uses to reveal the persistence of pre-Reformation beliefs and rituals, and the idea that incorporating potent religious artefacts within new structures would lend power to the user (Tarlow 2004, 116). But as Duffy points out, the mutilation and deliberate reuse of the relics of Catholicism in profane contexts signifies a 'desacralizing effect of such actions' (Duffy 1992, 586). This is most obviously the case in the conversion of religious buildings into barns, such as St Andrew's church in New Buckenham (NRO, MC22/11). In the case of wayside crosses it seems that their multiple meanings in the late medieval landscape, as commemorative monuments and as places where travellers might pause to pray, as well as their spiritual role during ritual events such as Rogationtide, were gradually stripped away so that they became mainly functional objects, most notably as territorial markers.

The depiction of crosses on maps appears to contradict the principles of religious reformers, but if we consider the reasons for commissioning maps to show landownership, and the practical functions of crosses as 'ancient' monuments, a somewhat different story emerges. 'Stantling Cross' in Cawston for example had a significant function in marking the parish boundary of Cawston, which spanned the medieval and post-medieval periods. Elsewhere, the continuing post-Reformation importance of 'Butler's Cross', as a boundary marker of Castle Rising Chase, was expressed with pictorial flourish and elaboration. The territorial jurisdiction of the chase had become a matter of controversy in the late sixteenth century and thus precedence was given to the

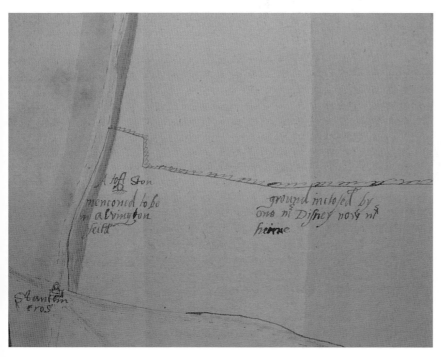

FIGURE 28 *(left)*. 'Stantlin Cross' as shown on a late sixteenth-century sketch map of Cawston (NRO, MC 341/13) contrasts strikingly with its later depiction of 1674 (Figure 22).

FIGURE 29 *(right)*. The remains of 'Stantling Cross' today. It is worth remembering that the redundant relics of apparently little note in modern times were in the past valued landmarks and their preservation a matter of social and economic consequence and concern.

setting out of its bounds: 'Begynning at Rysinge towne and soe from there to a bridge called great stonn bridge and soe from there to a lane in Babingley called Rattellmans lane and soe from thence to a lane in Babingley called Butlers lane and soe over Butlers greene to Butlers cross' (TNA: PRO, E134/35&36Eliz/ Mich16).

As relics of the past, crosses became potent symbols of the struggle over local territories and access rights to resources. For the inhabitants of Hindringham, for example, a cross that once stood on common land shared by the adjacent parish of Binham had been, before the mid-sixteenth century, part of the spiritual fabric of local life. Incorporated in the annual ritual of beating the bounds local inhabitants recalled saying prayers and hearing gospels read at the cross. In the late sixteenth century the structure remained, and while there were those who could remember and perhaps lamented its pre-Reformation significance, for others it had become a vital landmark in the demarcation of local resources. It signified to the inhabitants of Hindringham their rights to graze stock on the common, as far as the cross. Emma Cley told the court how during Rogation week the inhabitants of Hindringham were accustomed to walk up to a wooden cross standing upon the common 'about the mydest of the ende thereof' and from there 'went downe by the same crosse in procession nighe a certen brydg called woodbrydg leavinge the greater part of the comon on hindringham side' (TNA: PRO, DL4/18/37). In this respect the cross stood as a powerful memorial to the past, and as such was used to provide physical proof of the boundary of custom and right. The physical presence of old monuments and the continuing use of place names, provided tangible links with the past, which could explain the depiction of other boundary crosses on maps, such as that of South Creake (TNA: PRO, DL3/16/T2; Figure 30).

Historians might examine the distribution of wayside crosses as evidence for late medieval spiritual topographies, but monuments were not simply discarded as the vestiges of a redundant past and forgotten. Rather, the physical apparatus of late medieval religious life continued to provide a frame of reference for local societies. Recent writers have pointed out that while the religious changes of the period were dramatic so as to undermine the beliefs and practices of the Catholic Church, in equal measure, it is important to observe elements of continuity with the past (Marsh 1998, 210). It is possible, likely even, that to certain individuals and recusant groups, crosses held deeper spiritual meanings. But the remains of them were preserved (either *in situ*, or re-located) because they held important connotations in the historical imagination, other than their overt Catholic associations. The Dissolution, and subsequent religious statutes, imposed a material break from the past. Thus crosses were deliberately preserved precisely because of their associations with the remote past: a sense of the past that did not just reside in the memories of old people, but was projected by the physical form of the monument itself. Their apparent physical dilapidation belies a range of secular and 'economic' contexts, which created strands of continuity linking the present with the landscape of the pre-Reformation past. As emblems of that past, the significance of the cross was re-invented and reinforced rather than diminished.

Remembering the Saints

Interesting parallels can be drawn between the shifts in meaning and relevance of the material relics of the pre-Reformation past, and the increasingly secular contexts of festive customs. It is well attested that a range of old rituals and ceremonies survived the sixteenth century but in non-ecclesiastical contexts. Cressy has highlighted the role of the state in simplifying the ritual year by abolishing many of the old feast days, and moving others to alternative dates more in keeping with modern national events and Protestant sensibilities (Cressy 1989). Interested in the impact of the Reformation at a local level, Ronald Hutton has recovered evidence for a revival of festivity in the late sixteenth and early seventeenth centuries, with the authorities generally tolerating popular rituals and practices providing they did not violate the church and its precincts (Hutton 1994, 237; Marsh 1998, 106). There was also the added benefit of raising parochial funds: 'opportunities for local fund-raising and redistribution, bounty and largesse, rooted traditional holidays in the soil of the local economy' (Cressy 1989, 15). Though reliance on festivals for fund-raising was steadily superseded by a more dependable compulsory rate system (Marsh 1998, 107).

Enclosure has been cited as a major cause of the demise of popular festivities: in its guise as the physical manifestation of individualism the enclosure of

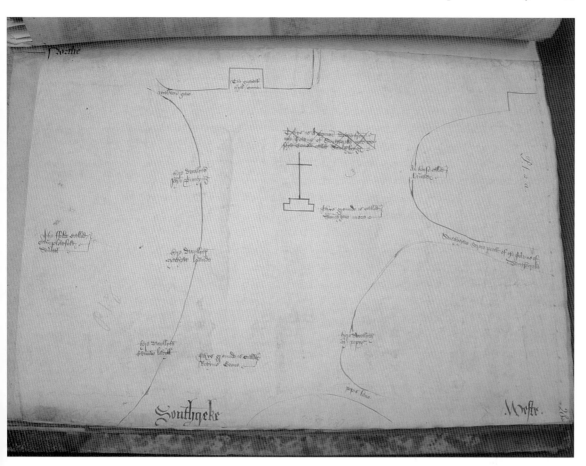

FIGURE 30. South Creake cross stood on the common in the sixteenth century. As the visible relics of the pre-Reformation past, freestanding crosses continued to serve important functions in later landscapes, especially in demarcating socio-economic territories (TNA: PRO, DL3/16/ T2).

common land generated tensions within local communities between those in support of popular traditions and those against them (Underdown 1985). N.J.G. Pounds, for example, has argued that 'a calendar of celebration had been adjusted to a common agricultural regime; it was ill suited to the growing individualism of early modern times' (Pounds 2000, 332). It is clear from the foregoing discussion that the relationship between enclosure and the decline of Rogationtide perambulations was far from straightforward. Similar lines of reasoning can be applied to other calendar dates. Rather than seeing them as necessarily a time for 'jollity, idleness and superfluity' – which for Cressy was the reason 'why so many people looked forward to them' (Cressy 1989, 5) – they also had a contemporary and logical function in structuring the farming year. Bob Bushaway has considered the function of popular customary calendars in the eighteenth and nineteenth centuries, in blending together seasonal events in the labouring year with various festivities. In Bushaway's period of study there seems little left of an earlier religious calendar, the rituals and customs had by then assumed a predominately secular significance (Bushaway 1982).

The observance of customary dates was essential for the organisation of agricultural activities and customs, including common grazing, fold-course, shack rights, haymaking, and the gathering of fuel. But of crucial importance, in order to substantiate their claims, deponents of all social standing used these 'ancient' dates as common reference points. In the late sixteenth century for example, it was the custom for the tenants of Mildenhall on 'Trinite mondaie' to enter the fens and take sedge and thatch (TNA: PRO, DL4/24/64). In the same parish the land known as the Breach was grazed between the Feast of St Peter and the Feast of the Purification of Our Lady, commonly called Candlemas (TNA: PRO, DL4/33/38). Customary dates were often contentious. In the same set of depositions Robert Croft asserted that there should be no sheep on the Breach before Holy Rood Day. However, when there was a shortage of grazing, the sheep were permitted to graze over the winter months on Caliestreet Green and Homestreet Green from the Nativity until the Feast of the Annunciation (TNA: PRO, DL4/30/27).

Some dates were ubiquitous in local agricultural calendars, usually those which had been the most important in the late medieval period. With government sanction their value continued after the Reformation as part of the revised Protestant calendar (Cressy 1989). Michaelmas, the feast day of St Michael the Archangel (29th September) was one such date, celebrated with harvest suppers, fairs and feasts devoted to church dedications (Hutton 1996, 349). Henry VIII attempted to curtail these September revels by moving them to the first Sunday in the month of October though, as Ronald Hutton has found, there is little evidence of compliance. The Elizabethan government, who saw the sanction of Sunday revels as deeply troublesome, took up the issue again. Viewed as a desecration of the Sabbath they attempted to ban them entirely, provoking a controversy that was to span the seventeenth century (Hutton 1996, 350). It was probably the importance of Michaelmas in the farming calendar, especially with regards to common grazing rights, that preserved its importance as a day of celebration and as a collective statement of customary rights to the land. In 1584 Thomas Wood insisted that the inhabitants of Wells 'used to have theire feade with theire mylche neate from the feast of St Mychell Tharchangell untill the Feast of St Martyn in winter', and sixty-eight-year-old Edmund Burden asserted that they had done so 'longe before his tyme' (TNA: PRO, DL4/26/37). Martinmas fell on 11th November, and as the date when animals were slaughtered before the winter was an important juncture in the farming year (Hutton 1996, 386).

Lammas Day, the feast day of St Peter celebrated on August 1st, provided another key date in the agricultural calendar. Throughout the Middle Ages Lammas was a significant time for holding fairs, electing officers, collecting rents and, after the hay had been cut and carted away, opening up meadow grounds for grazing (Hutton 1996, 331). It was also the date at which livestock were moved off other commons, to allow them to recover from the impact of summer grazing, the cut meadows providing alternative sustenance. In 1609 Adam Mason, a seventy-two-year-old yeoman, deposed that both he and his father had the right to graze their sheep on Hindringham common until the Feast of St Peter 'commonly called Lammas day' (TNA: PRO, DL4/55/10).

Again the date was used to clarify knowledge of the landscape, and to support claims to customary rights that had existed since 'time out of mind'.

Other old feast days had a more limited importance in the Protestant calendar (Cressy 1989, 29) and yet continued to mark stages in the farming year. In Shernborne the inhabitants turned out their horses on the common called the Ling 'yerely from the feast of St Michall Tharcheangell untill the feaste of all Saynts' (TNA: PRO, DL4/18/6); at Congham the 'Castell Flock' grazed the West Field from the Feast of St Michael to All Saints (TNA: PRO, E134/40Eliz/East3); in Flitcham the lord of the manor had liberty of fold course upon the common every year from St Luke to the Annunciation of Our Lady (TNA: PRO, E178/1587); while in Marsham, the lord laid claim to shack rights in the common field between the 'feast of Sct Fayth until the feast of Sct Agnes' over his tenants lands (TNA: PRO, E134/43Eliz/East17) as part of his attempt to impose a fold course. Here, as in a number of other places, claims to new rights were bolstered by reference to established, ancient calendar dates. While, for some time after the Reformation, many inhabitants could clearly remember the religious significance of these dates, saints' days had always been as much about the mundane 'economic' aspects of everyday life, but the balance had decisively shifted.

Understanding Place-Names

Scholars interested in the history of minor place-names have mainly been concerned to catalogue names without any real consideration of their significance in a local context (Field 1993). Yet, names can provide powerful clues about the ways past societies viewed their landscape: 'messages ... encoded in a name, messages which bear invaluable information about the name-givers and their world' (Taylor, 1996 1). But little attention has, in fact, been paid to precisely *why* names continued to be considered 'appropriate'.

Eighteenth-century estate maps often reveal the colonial and imperial perspectives of landowners, with names such as 'Botany Bay', 'Waterloo' and 'Trafalgar' given to fields and plantations, perhaps metaphors for the colonisation and transformation of the dry heathland 'wastes' of Breckland and Good Sands district. But it was not until enclosure and the privatisation of land in the middle decades of the eighteenth century that large landowners in these areas could indulge in the comprehensive re-naming of landscapes. In earlier periods the boundaries across the open heaths and commons were, as we have seen, highly contested. Disputes over access rights and customary land use often involved the broader base of local society including small farmers and cottagers. In this context the names given to common arable and grazing land, and internal divisions and boundary features, were a vital means of validating claims to access resources. Quite simply, the very act of naming the land and landmark features grounded them in local histories as commonly recognisable reference points. To use Tilley's phrase, 'in a fundamental way names create landscapes'

(Tilley 1994, 19). Indeed, the act of naming itself served to perpetuate the importance of certain monuments, such as freestanding crosses, highlighting the fact that they were as much to do with the present, everyday 'inhabitation' of the landscape as with some redundant past (Barrett 1999).

The relevance of the late medieval religious landscape is indicated in local place names. In his description of the boundary of Thorpe as it crossed Mousehold Heath, Edmund Cosen recalled a number of religious reference points. He presented his knowledge of the territory as a 'moving tour' remembered through a sequence of historic landmarks (Rollison 1999). He began by recounting his route westwards from Thorpe Wood which ran past 'St Leonards to Bishopps Gates' from there northwards past 'Lathes Stone' and another 'dole stoone' at the south east end of 'Magdalen Chappell yard' and from there 'assendinge upp to a hill in Ravengate waie' proceeding eastward in another green way on the north side of 'St Willms in the Woode' where 'sometime stood a chappell' and then to the bound called the 'White Stake'. Within his perambulation of the heath, Edmund included a number of other historic landmarks including 'St Michells chappell on the hill' and 'St James Hill', and the boundary cross of Little Plumstead and Rackheath – the controversial landmark where Richard Marker's body was conveyed between parishes (p. 85). In Thorpe local place-names and the presence of pre-Reformation landmarks gave credibility to the layout of the jurisdiction of the manor and parish.

It was commonplace in the lists of interrogatories compiled during court proceedings, for people to be asked to confirm local place names, and for how long they had known them. The tenants of Binham, for example, knew the parcel of common land shared by Hindringham, as Le Holmes alias Southmore, but their neighbours knew it as Northmore or Lunshurne (TNA: PRO, DL4/20/8). The use of alternative names did not indicate a lack of communication between neighbouring villages, but were instead part of the process of laying claim to local resources. In the same dispute Thomas Applegate of Hindringham testified that he had never heard 'Derbyes Well', one of the boundary marks separating the commons, called by any other name 'until nowe of late'. Two years previously octogenarian William Cooper of Binham, husbandman, testified that he had known the common for sixty years and that 'a certen place or lymytt which was and is comonly called Dereberies well which place is on the southe part of woodbrydge as it hath bene reported unto hym devidinge the comon called sowthmore als le Holmes'. The deponents stressed that the common known as 'South Moor' alias 'le Holmes' had always been known as such, and that the inhabitants of Binham had always fetched it in during their perambulation, and 'tyed and staked their cattell in somer tyme' upon the ground there. A sketch map drawn up in relation to the dispute shows two 'wells', 'Darbys Well' and 'Dapur Well' the latter marking the boundary of Northmore in Hindringham, and the former in the midst of common land. The evidence suggests that there may have been a deliberate conflation of names and landmarks (TNA: PRO, DL4/18/37).

Place-names survived in the landscape because they continued to have a practical role in the organisation of farming activities. But in addition to this, the proven antiquity of names was key to legitimating customs and rights. Robert Buxton of Tibenham knew that 'in oulder tyme' the fields in Westwick were called by the name of 'Fauerton field or Bowds flock' and the Lodge Flock was part of Westwick Manor. According to Buxton, the grounds had 'reteyned those names very long tyme by these hundred yeares at the lest' (TNA: PRO, E134/1Jas1/Trin7). Old names were as important for seigniorial lords as they were for tenants and commoners. Fold-course owners, for example, sought to confirm their rights by establishing that the names given to their flocks had existed since time out of mind. During a protracted dispute of the 1580s and 1590s concerning Holkham's complex division of fold courses, Thomas Gunthorpe of Wells remembered that his father had informed him that the name of the fold course in question was Caldoe and that he had 'not hard it called by any other name' (TNA: PRO, DL4/30/28).

In Wighton dispute festered between the Manor of Wighton held by the Duchy of Lancaster and Boroughhall Manor, owner of the Caldoe and Boroughall fold courses. Both manors claimed to hold the right to graze their sheep flocks on a tract of common heath located within South Field. The deponents' memories, together with written evidence taken from 'a verye faire auncient Booke', were used to demonstrate that the Prior of Peterston formerly owned the Caldoe Flock as part of his manor. The dividing up of monastic estates following the Dissolution resulted in enormous complexity regarding the layout of boundaries and fold-course rights. Reputedly there was a designated area within the common of South Field where the sheep of Caldoe fold course were entitled to graze, appropriately named 'Caldoe'. In 1593 Edmund Newgate of Holkham recalled that four years previously a survey had been made of the lands in question, but the precise location of 'Caldoe' was never resolved (see TNA: PRO, DL4/30/28; TNA: PRO, DL4/34/36; TNA: PRO, DL4/35/8). The attempt to set down in tangible terms, both in writing and on the ground, a parcel of common belonging to the Caldoe flock had obvious implications for the commoners whose area of common grazing was under threat from encroachment and over-stocking by fold-course owners (TNA: PRO, DL4/155/9). Knowledge of local place-names demonstrated familiarity with the landscape and proved longevity of customs and rights attached to the land. At the same time, names could also be used to dispute such claims.

The act of naming inevitably involved an associated act of re-naming and forgetting: giving a feature or field a new name over-wrote and obliterated past connotations. In the early modern period landowners quarried written documents for the evidence of former place-names. In Wighton, the boundary across the 'Four Gongs' or the 'partable furlong', which (as we have seen) was the focus of dispute concerning fold-course rights in the sixteenth century, was again called into question in the first decade of the seventeenth century, this time concerning the allocation of tithes. The field-name evidence was used in an attempt to dispute the right of the lessee of the rectory, belonging to the Dean and Chapter of Norwich, to take the tithe corn; a right that had been exercised for at least the previous fifty years. A chapel dedicated to Saint Botolph had once stood in the parish to which, it was claimed the 'Botolph tithe' pertained (TNA: PRO, DL4/55/47; TNA: PRO, DL4/57/67). Since destroyed, the existence of the chapel was hotly disputed. Roger Brightmer, for example, deposed that he had heard John Angell say that the chapel had stood in a close adjacent to a house he remembered as belonging to 'one West'. Brightmer's statement was emphatically denied by seventy-three-year-old husbandman John Angell (presumably the same) As an inhabitant of Wighton for fifty years, Angell maintained that there was never a chapel dedicated to Buttolph in the town. According to Brightmer, Henry Bedingfield owner of the manor possessed 'three fayre and auncyent feild books' which confirmed that the 'Buttolph' tithe extended onto the land called the Four Gongs. Again this was refuted by Angell who, as a long-standing tenant of the manor, recalled hearing the field books read and the word 'Buttolph' was never mentioned (TNA: PRO, DL4/57/67).

Minor place-names were far more than simply a matter of practical agrarian convenience: they were a central concern in the allocation of rights and dues for manorial lords and commoners. The attempt of some landscape historians to trace the origins of names negates the deep undercurrent of controversy and meaning given to the preservation of old names, or introduction of new ones, in the past. Such names were part of intricate agrarian systems reliant on collective knowledge, the durability of some, and disappearance of others, was linked to the struggle over local memory.

Interpreting the Landscape

At a purely practical level the organisation of manorial territories, communal field systems and grazing rights, which continued to operate in many places well into the eighteenth century, were enormously complex (Figure 31). In view of this, written accounts were of little worth unless commonly recognised place names and the physical evidence on the ground could be used to corroborate their contents. In 1631, seventy-two-year-old Francis Holmes told the court commissioners that he had heard the court rolls and field books of Netherhall Manor in Hickling 'read in his hearinge distinguishinge and setting forth the said lands' however, without seeing the physical proof on the ground he considered such documents were insubstantial evidence for the layout of boundaries. In his opinion the towns and fields of Hickling, Ingham, Sutton and other towns adjoining ought to be physically demarcated by 'meeres bounds or divisions for the setting out knowinge and discerninge aswell of the tythable places belonging to the complt said Rectory ... from the tythable places of other Rectories there as for the discerning and knowledge of the demeanse free and copihold lands' and to distinguish 'from one parcell of copyhold land from another parcell therof within the said mannor' (TNA: PRO, E134/7Chas1/Mich18).

The credibility of supposedly ancient documents was frequently a matter of controversy. In Roughton one such field book of land belonging to the manor had been made 'withoute the pryvitie or knowledge of the tenantes' and as such 'the saide boke never was of any credyte' (TNA: PRO, DL4/12/6). Accusations and rumours of forgery proliferated in other villages including New Buckenham where the parson's wife admitted that her husband had made 'a writing' in order to falsify the bounds of Carleton common. In order to make the document look old he apparently hung it in the smoke above the fire (TNA: PRO, E178/1538; TNA: PRO, E134/38/Hil24). In other places documents were deliberately destroyed. As mentioned earlier, in Marsham the owner of the manor burnt old documents found to be favourable to the tenants (TNA: PRO, E178/4251). Whilst old documents were searched for during court proceedings, so was the tangible evidence of the past in the landscape.

Just as Rogationtide was intrinsic to the ongoing recognition and maintenance of parochial bounds, manorial boundaries were similarly perambulated. Richard Manser, a sixty-year-old husbandman, related how all his life he had known the 'olde bounds' separating the arable fields of Stanhoe and North Creake 'made of stoone heapys and so of old tyme knowen'. As tenant of the manor of North Creak he was responsible for the upkeep of the bounds: 'on a leet held at North Creake on Saint Johns day in Eastmasse he and others were charged to enginer the bounds and to renew them which they did and cast stones to the said heaps of old time for bounds' (TNA: PRO, DL3/16/T2). There are references to manorial perambulations taking place in other villages including the manors of Suffield and Gimingham (TNA: PRO, E134/26Eliz/East13), Castle Rising Chase (TNA: PRO, E134/34&35Eliz/Mich7) and Cawston (TNA: PRO, E134/43&44Eliz/Mich7).

The influence of these internal divisions of villages on the physical and social structures of local life has been overlooked, with precedence being given to the parish. A map of Cawston dating to 1599, for example, reveals a number of boundary stones distributed about the open and enclosed fields of the parish. Figure 32 shows the bound stone of the seventh toft situated within an area of 'ancient' enclosures, which indicates a further layer of territorial complexity attached to enclosed land (see also Figure 28). In 1449 Cawston manor was divided into nineteen tofts each containing forty acres of free and copyhold lands and a number of cottages (NRO, NRS 2604). The bounds of the tofts were set out on the ground and, for their continual preservation, each year they were perambulated by the hayward 'chosen by the moore voyse' of the cottagers, who would view them with the rest of the jury of the manor court. In the late sixteenth century these internal divisions of the manor were still perambulated on the first day of August, when lists of offences were drawn up by the 'headboroughs', these mainly concerned the neglect and destruction of boundary features, obstruction of common paths and ways, and mistreatment of the commons. Intricate, often over-lapping networks of boundaries defined the landscape. Over the course of the post-medieval period their function

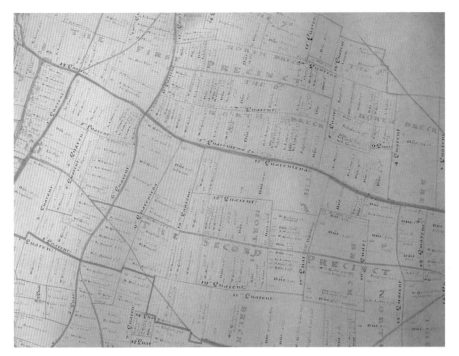

FIGURE 31. A section
of a map of Sedgeford
revealing the complexity
of open field systems
operating in north-
west Norfolk in the
seventeenth century.
Various internal divisions
are marked: precincts,
brecks, quarentena
(furlongs), and individual
strips (NRO, LEST/
OC1).

and status was subject to change as manorial and parochial territories were
gradually consolidated and simplified, and hitherto ambiguous jurisdictions
were tightened.

Agricultural historians often note that fold courses and common grazing
rights were meticulously defined but little is said about precisely how. Nor,
perhaps, is enough emphasis placed on the extent to which such boundaries
were the subject of disputes. Landowners, not surprisingly, justified and defined
their fold courses in relation to long-established features of the landscape. In
his description of the bounds of a fold course in Thetford, for example, Robert
Munnings included a number of elements from the pre-Reformation past:

> Twoe peeces of medowe lyinge neere St Edmund pole [probably the remains of
> a cross] towards Santone buttinge upon Jackes hill towards the common ryver of
> Thettforde and the butts upon great Norwicke sheepes pasture and within an arrowe
> shott of St Ellins chappell (TNA: PRO, E134/33&34Eliz/Mich29).

'Frances Cross' is also mentioned – 'the sheepe did feede also in Barnham lowes
neare Frannces crose'. In Holkham, similarly, 'Anngell Crosse' marked the
boundary of Crabbs Castle fold course and in Gimingham the 'White Cross'
reputedly marked the limits of the fold course belonging to the manor (TNA:
PRO, DL4/18/19; TNA: PRO, DL4/24/6). The material evidence of antiquity
was used to bolster often spurious claims to fold-course rights.

One of the most distinctive things about fold-course territories was the
way in which they were poorly related to the arrangement of open fields,
furlongs and strips, often cutting obliquely across the pattern of boundaries
– a clear enough indication of their relative youth, as well as of the way in

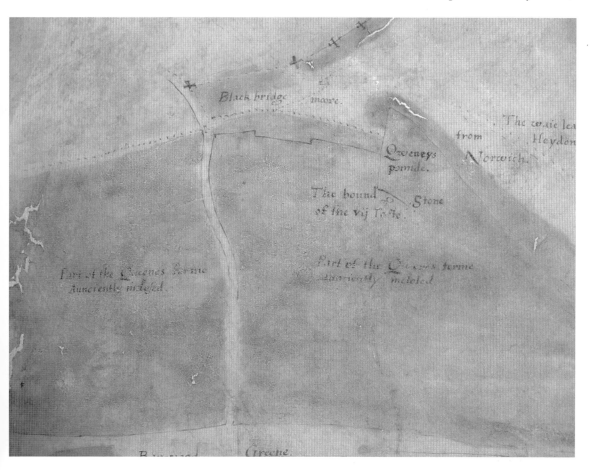

FIGURE 32. The bound stone of the seventh 'toft' in Cawston, 1599. The internal divisions of manors are not always immediately apparent. Cawston Manor was divided into nineteen 'tofts', the boundaries of each were marked by a series of stones (NRO, MS 4521).

which the balance of economic interests was weighted in favour of the lord's sheep flock rather than the arable cultivation of local farmers. One reason why boundaries were laid out in this way was that they frequently followed roads (referred to as gateways or sties), features which – while old – were often later than, or at least stratigraphically at variance with, furlong boundaries. James Taverner was accused of encroaching on the Queen's foldcourse by grazing his flock on one hundred acres of land lying between 'Brushmer and Brushmer stie', 'Creakgateway' and westward to 'Wyllitstie' (TNA: PRO, DL4/18/19). Stonegateway in Cawston provided one of a number of contentious boundaries separating the tenants grazing rights from the fold course (TNA, PRO, E133/1/108). Roads provided conspicuous, continuous and established features, and for many manors an obvious template for the organisation of grazing for sheep as well as rabbits. In Snettisham at the turn of the sixteenth century, John Wraske recalled how forty years previously a commission, devised to ascertain the boundaries of the warren, found that the bounds should extend no further than 'Marketsted Way' (TNA: PRO, DL4/43/12).

Antiquity gave boundaries legitimacy: and where open commons existed *manorial* fold-course boundaries might be surreptitiously extended by changing the course of *parish* bounds – part, of the more general convergence in the definition of the two kinds of jurisdiction which, as we have seen, occurred in this period. Miles Corbett, for example, owner of the manors of Woodbastwick and Laviles, was accused of extending the perambulation of Woodbastwick by 'fetching in' part of Mousehold Heath and digging crosses as 'dooles' to mark the boundary. This, it was claimed, he did in order to keep more sheep within his manorial flock, John Monforth describing how the heath was 'overlaide with the lordes flock of Bastwick'. To oppose the encroachment, some deponents recalled that when the Abbot of St Benet's had been lord of the manor there had been no crosses dug on the heath, and the sheep flock had been restricted to grazing the demesne, and not the heath (TNA: PRO, E178/7153).

Natural features, such as trees, hills, glacial erratics, water courses, pits and meres all provided obvious landmarks. Their incorporation within boundaries seemed, once again, to proclaim the antiquity and longevity of arrangements that were, in many cases, only just being brought into existence. In Breckland 'Ringmere', widely noted for marking the point where nine parishes converged thereby giving each access to water variously found within this mere (Winchester 1990): in the sixteenth century it was also used to mark the boundary of 'Black Downe' fold course (TNA: PRO, E134/33&34Eliz/Mich29). Veteran trees, such as the 'Parsonage Thorn' in Stirston, were also employed to delimit fold courses (TNA: PRO, E134/38&30Eliz/Mich9). In some places tenants and commoners conducted their own perambulations, which contradicted the layout of boundaries claimed by manorial lords (TNA: PRO, E133/1/108; Figure 25). In Cawston George Jenkinson remembered grazing the sheep belonging to the manor as far as 'Dryncklemere Pytte':

> until such tyme as the tenants of Cawston beinge ther purrelynge willed him to kepe his shepe upp to Stonegate tellynge him that the bounds of the foldcorse went so farr and willed this depot in ther presents to drive the shepe thither which he did and he and those shepherds that followed his father in the kepinge of the foldcorse ever since have contynued the same course (TNA: PRO, E134/43&44Eliz/Mich7).

In a multiplicity of ways minor landmarks thus conveyed meaning and defined rights in a way – and to an extent – that are often hard to recover from the evidence of maps alone. More than this: particular features in the landscape had 'life histories' of their own. Crosses were re-invented as fold-course boundaries; natural topographical features came to be regarded as disputed territories; place names needed to be confirmed. All these aspects associated with delineating local resources were based on judgements of authenticity, and antiquity, in the landscape.

Deciphering the Past: Evidence in the Field

So far I have discussed the role, in dividing the landscape and allotting rights and obligations, of features that were described simply as 'ancient' by contemporaries. But as noted at the start of this chapter, local populations had a more subtle and precise understanding of landscape chronology, and of relative chronology, at least when it came to the comparatively recent past. In the dispute over Downe Close in Snettisham seventy-eight-year-old William Baxter testified that:

> Downe Cloase was within the said eight yeres twice or thrice sowen wth Rye together And this he knoweth the better to be true for that he ... was then farmor of the said ground to the said Sr Nicholas Lestrange and reaped the croppe therof to his owne use and that the said grounde wthin the said cloase before the same were by hym so sowne wth corne were aunciently rigged and furrowed (TNA: PRO, DL4/43/12).

In a number of other villages plough marks were used as evidence of land use history. In the dispute over the encroachment of Castle Rising warren into surrounding villages, William Swanton described how land in Congham had been ploughed 'right unto a place called the Shorte trees and ... the furrowes and rigge of the said lands are yet to be seen' (TNA: PRO, E134/35&36Eliz/Mich16). Robert Rydde described 'the greatest part' of the grounds in South Wootton, claimed as warren 'hath bene heretofore in anncient tyme used in tylth as doth appeare by the rigges and furrowes'. Rydde's use of the term 'ancient' is interesting as it did not mean that the ploughing had taken place in remote antiquity. He recalled that he had heard his father, along with 'one Jeffery Kydd and one Allen Glover and one Mawde Nann a very old woman all which be nowe deceassed' say that corn used to grow in sundry places 'where the warren is nowe pretended to be' (TNA: PRO, E134/35&36Eliz/Mich16). By confirming that the land had been cultivated its more recent use, as part of the manorial warren, was called into question. Clearly the land had not been parcel of the warren since time out of mind.

Signs of ploughing were used as evidence in court cases elsewhere – in disputes concerning Brandon Warren in 1612 (TNA: PRO, E134/10Jas1/East27) and Roxham (NRO, PRA 469), again using the term 'rigge and furrow'. For the landscape historian these references are intriguing. There is general agreement that ridging was normally carried out to improve drainage, and yet all of these instances come from areas of light, free-draining soils. The distinctive corrugated pattern was formed by ploughing with a mouldboard plough in the same direction over a number of consecutive years, though the direction of the plough might be reversed in order to prevent the ridge from becoming too high (Hall 1999). Rain water falling onto the ridges would run off into the furrows, thus leaving the ridges less prone to the detrimental affects of waterlogging, and more conducive to crop growth. Ridge and furrow is, indeed, mainly found today – in relic form – in clayland districts, mainly in the Midlands where a shift to livestock farming in the post-medieval period produced a landscape dominated by permanent pasture (Williamson 2003, 153). In Norfolk, ridge and furrow is rare, the few recorded examples come from the strip of heavy clay soils on the edge of the Fens. Whether, outside this district, arable land was seldom ridged; or whether the present pattern is the consequence of later land use, with the intensity of arable cultivation over most of the county having served to remove all traces of these earthworks, remains a matter for debate (Liddiard 1999; Williamson 2003, 152–3). But either way, the presence of ridging on this light land remains difficult to understand.

In such areas, however, while drainage posed no problem to farmers, the land presented other difficulties, most notably the rapid leaching of nutrients – hence the need for systematic folding. But some land was so poor that it could only be cultivated as outfield 'brecks', on a long rotation, and for only a short period before returning once more to heath or rough grazing: a practice which, it has been suggested, became more common and more systematic in the course of the post-medieval period (Bailey 1989). Such 'outfield' land was, like the permanent arable, often divided into strips. It is possible therefore that farmers employed 'rigge and furrow' as a means of identifying the divisions within outfield brecks, abandoned to long restorative fallows, thus making it easier to identify the allotments of particular farmers when the land was brought back into cultivation. Such a practice would also serve to identify the land as specifically part of the outfields, rather than permanent heath. Kerridge refers to a similar practice in other parts of the country – the uplands of the West Country, in Devon and Cornwall – where periodic cultivation of outfields was also a part of the agricultural regime:

> Ridge-and-furrow ploughing was not confined to fields of permanent tillage. The temporary tillage plots of shifting cultivation were often ploughed ridge-and-furrow, and this enabled men to know for certain that some plots had been ploughed at some time in the past (Kerridge 1973, 35).

Such land often came to be permanently abandoned, absorbed into private heaths or warrens, but former evidence of cultivation would be hard to erase, and provided a useful way of identifying its former use and status on the part of local inhabitants.

During local land disputes the physical evidence of ploughing held particular and important connotations for local people, especially regarding the apparent association of ridge and furrow with communal farming regimes, on which their livelihoods depended. Eighty-year-old Nicholas Tilborough remembered his ancestors telling him the layout of the 'auncient shiftfields' of Brandon, which he confirmed with reference to the physical evidence: as 'it doth appeare by Ridge and furrowe that itt hath bene shiftfield, though now used as warren'. Describing the village as standing 'chiefly upon tillage' he condemned the encroachment of the warren on the arable fields for, in 'short time', it will 'be to the utter decay of tillage and the impoverishinge of the most part of the town' (TNA: PRO, E134/10Jas1/East27). The evidence of ploughing was also used to reinforce claims to customary grazing rights. In the dispute over Down Close, Snettisham where, as mentioned earlier ancient 'ridge and furrow' was identified, the tenants claimed to hold common access rights to the close and surrounding heaths. They complained bitterly that in recent times the gate was kept locked which prevented them from exercising their accustomed shack rights. The physical evidence and memory of earlier ploughing served to bolster the claims of local inhabitants that common grazing rights were attached to this parcel of outfield.

A similar set of circumstances gave rise to dispute in Cawston (TNA: PRO, E134/23&24Eliz/Mich14). Here disagreement concerned the extent of Jerbridge Park or Wood the boundary of which, by the late sixteenth century, was decayed and uncertain. Controversy arose when Roger Townshend, sought to enclose the park from the common. The farmers of Cawston manor leased from the crown, together with the warreners, tenants and inhabitants of Cawston, claimed access rights to the ground they referred to as Jerbridge Wood. During litigation proceedings in 1581 eighty-year-old Edward Howchins, who was born in Cawston, confirmed that the inhabitants had 'tyme owte of mynde' the right of common pasture within the wood. Within the previous decade however, part of the wood had been enclosed and ploughed, according to Howchins the grounds were 'never inclosed nor plowed before to his remembrance'. The defence produced a rather different version of the land use history of the grounds in question. John Fuller clarified the antiquity of the boundary saying that he knew an 'old ditche which went rounde abowte Jerbridge Woode' and 'uppon the dyke of the northe side of the said Jerbridge ther wer anncient oks growynge'. Furthermore, a number of deponents contested the longevity of common shack rights by referring to the evidence of ridge and furrow within the park. According to Thomas Crotche, 'ther be diverse furrowes and Riggs in the said Jerbridge Woode playnly to be seen where the lynge and ffurres nowe grow whereby it appeareth that it hath ben plowed'.

In the absence of written documentation, and in order to substantiate oral memories, contemporaries employed the visible traces of land use history as a means of proving their rights and ancestral inheritance, however distorted, or disconnected this link with the past had become. As a result the furrows etched into the soils of heathland villages were the focus of deep conflict, as an earlier system of agricultural practice was gradually and persistently eroded by the activities of a wealthy minority of landowners. The inhabitants of sixteenth- and seventeenth-century Norfolk thus had complex, multi-layered attitudes to, and appreciations of, the past in the landscape. Antiquity was used to bolster claims to property, rights and privileges, and could be employed – somewhat paradoxically – to justify unprecedented encroachments on established custom. But knowledge of the past could also be used to challenge and resist the established order, and in particular the novel claims asserted by the landed elite to hold fold-course or warren rights. Sometimes the documentary evidence suggests only a vague awareness of landscape chronology; at other times a clearer knowledge of the order of events and processes, at least in the recent past, is revealed. The evidence of court depositions and maps shows how the use and function of features in the landscape could change dramatically over time, as they were appropriated for new ends by successive generations.

But there is an added level to this complexity. Some of the meanings attached to particular sites, or places, had been evolving over very long periods of time – they were not simply forged in the period under consideration here. Given all this, it is useful to consider, in some detail, the *long-term* histories of such features in the landscape – prehistoric barrows (Figure 33).

FIGURE 33. Bronze Age burial mound in Harpley, north-west Norfolk.

Time Out of Mind of Man: Attitudes towards Prehistory

Traditionally the distribution of prehistoric monuments has been used as an aid to understanding the changing social and economic character of prehistoric societies, although it is generally accepted that the present distribution is a function both of original locational patterns, and of subsequent patterns of land use (Lawson *et al.* 1981). A higher proportion of earthworks have survived on lighter soils, such as the heathlands of Breckland, where they have been inadvertently protected by a long history of pastoral farming. In contrast, in areas of heavier or more fertile land intensive cultivation in the medieval and post-medieval periods has obliterated a substantial proportion of upstanding prehistoric archaeology (Williamson 1998). At a more local level a correlation between soil type and agricultural land use can also be made; common grazing land, in both clayland and light soil regions, usually occupied the poorest or least tractable soils and it was here that prehistoric earthworks were most likely to be preserved. In this explanatory model the destruction of barrows and other early monuments is considered the outcome of rational, economic processes, and by implication any that survive do so by accident. Old earthworks were generally an irrelevance in an era of progress and improvement, except as the subject of local folklore narratives (Lawson *et al.* 1981).

It will be argued here that the relics of antiquity had other important functions in later societies which may help to explain their survival in post-medieval landscapes, as neither the chance outcome of land use patterns, and nor as the backdrop to popular myths and legends. It goes without saying that people did not have the conceptual frameworks that we do today: they could not assign barrows to a *prehistoric* past. Yet across the centuries everyone perceived barrows to be 'old', existing beyond the boundaries of imaginable time. Popular attitudes towards the past presented themselves as enduring strands of continuity and barrows, as visible reminders of an assumed past, could be essential to the mediation of contemporary landscapes. In order to contextualise the preservation of prehistoric monuments in medieval and post-medieval landscapes, it is important to take a long view, acknowledging that strands of continuity can be discerned from the Anglo-Saxon period, if not earlier, in the ways that barrows, as visible reminders of an inherited past, were assimilated within contemporary landscapes.

The subject of the 'afterlife' of barrows, in the later prehistoric and early Anglo-Saxon periods has received considerable attention, with a number of writers arguing that their recurrent use and reuse was integral to the ways past individuals and societies structured and perceived their physical surroundings (Barrett 1998; Bradley 1993; Williams 1997, 1998; Holtorf). A consideration of the landscape context of barrows in all periods can tell us something about attitudes towards the past and in equal measure how, as symbols of the past, barrows were appropriated or re-negotiated to fit in with changing perspectives and ideologies. Recent research has shown that, as the physical manifestations of an unknown and in that sense powerful past, prehistoric burial mounds were appropriated by Anglo-Saxon elites in order to create an ancestral lineage, to lend authority to their political objectives (Bradley 1993). Following conversion to Christianity a dichotomy emerged between the treatment of Christian deaths and deviant or heathen burials. Criminals were denied burial in hallowed soil and were interred in marginal locations, frequently at barrows, where judgement and execution would also be carried out (Reynolds 1997, 37). The association of barrows, boundaries and execution continued into the medieval and post-medieval periods. Cartographic and place-name evidence has revealed a strong correlation between boundaries and unchristian deaths (Whyte 2003b; below p. 155).

The location of Anglo-Saxon execution sites was paralleled in the choice of meeting places, which were also frequently sited on barrows located on, or close to, significant boundaries in particular hundred boundaries (Reynolds 1997; 1999). In both cases, neutrality was defined in terms of geographical marginality and the perceived permanence of the chosen location, existing since time immemorial. These spatial associations, between barrows, boundaries and meeting places, continued to structure territorial jurisdictions into the post-medieval period. In the late sixteenth century, for example, the inhabitants of New Buckenham encompassed a grass knoll known as the 'Haugh Head' in their annual procession of the bounds. Deponents recalled that the mound had served as the meeting place of the court of Shropham half hundred where, as sixty-eight-year-old Thomas Rutland remembered, 'the hundreders had performed their suites and paid their duties' (NRO, PD 254/171). Court cases from other villages offer further evidence of the use of earthwork mounds as places of assembly. The annual court leet of Great Fransham manor was held at a place called Mills-on-the-Moor; a mill mound – possibly a barrow – close to the parish boundary of three parishes, those of Great Dunham, Kempstone and Beeston (Rogerson 1995, 345–346). 'Frettenham Hill' was the meeting of the manorial leet court in the sixteenth-century (TNA: PRO, DL4/59/32). Excavation of this feature, in the nineteenth century, revealed that it had been deliberately constructed (Rye 1920, 21), presumably to serve as the meeting place of the manorial court, though it may have had its origins as the assembly place of Taverham Hundred (Williamson 1993, 129). The deliberate construction of such earthworks as meeting places suggests that barrows were deemed to be particularly appropriate for such purposes: the material relics of the past were re-invented to fit in with contemporary needs

There are wider, more general associations between barrows and boundaries, which endured into much later periods. Late Anglo-Saxon charters show that ancient monuments were prominent among the topographic features used to delimit estate and parish boundaries (Bonney, 1976; Goodier 1984; Lawson *et al* 1981; Winchester 1990). As we have seen, early modern communities were deeply aware of their social and geographical boundaries expressed in parochial, and manorial, perambulations (Bushaway 1982, 81–83; Hutton 1996, 278–287; Thomas 1971, 71–75). As ancient elements of the landscape, barrows provided key focal points along customary routes. One such probable barrow described in a seventeenth-century document as the 'hyll in East Field of Hunstanton', marked the boundary separating Hunstanton from Holme (NRO, LEST/NR). 'Gospel Hill', is depicted on a map showing the lands subject to the perambulation of Little Cressingham and Great Cressingham in 1779 (NRO, WLSLXI/I): it has since been levelled but aerial photography has detected a probable ring-ditch at this location (HER39714).

As highly visible features, barrows had long been employed to demarcate contentious spaces within otherwise open landscapes, and they thus played a key role during boundary disputes, especially across tracts of open heath. In an attempt to strengthen and legitimate their fold-course territories, seigniorial lords often incorporated barrows into their boundaries. A late sixteenth-century map depicting Marham fold course includes three mounds: 'Anker Hill', 'Tuts Hill', and 'Great Hill', all of which defined the fold-course boundary (NRO, HARE6811). Court evidence from Thetford explicitly states that 'Barrowe Hill' was 'a Bounderie' of the bottom flock – namely the fold course in the Southfield of Thetford (TNA: PRO, E134/33&34Eliz/Mich29). Another likely barrow, the 'hille called the Brente hille or Burnt hille' depicted on a map of Holkham in c.1590 was also referred to as a boundary mark dividing the south and north parts of Holkham common and fold course (Figure 34; TNA: PRO, DL4/35/8; NRO, MS 4535). To some extent landowners and communities were merely using convenient and visible landmarks: but the prevailing knowledge that

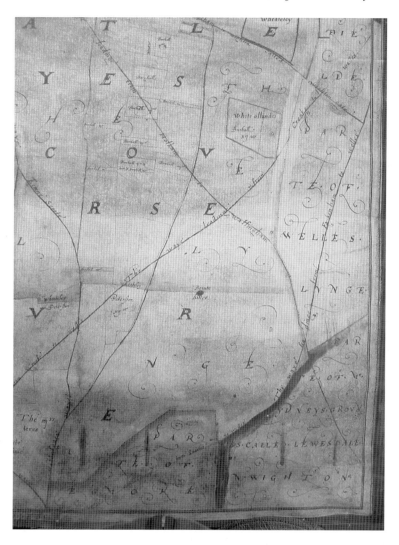

FIGURE 34. As highly conspicuous, ancient, and 'permanent' landmarks barrows were frequently employed to demarcate manorial and parochial territories. The 'hille called the Brente hille or Burnt hille', shown on a late seventeenth-century map of Holkham, provided a boundary mark dividing the south and north parts of Holkham Common and manorial fold course (NRO, MS 4535).

barrows were ancient and 'permanent' features lent greater authority to their role as boundary markers.

The integration of barrows within fold-course boundaries was paralleled in their use to demarcate warrens. A map of Methwold Warren drawn up in 1580, in connection with a long-running boundary dispute, depicts a number of mounds marking the perimeter of the warren, which extended into the surrounding parishes of Feltwell, Cranwich, Weeting, and Mundford (NRO, MC 556/2; see Whyte 2003a). In celebration of this lucrative commodity the map depicts a number of rabbits, apparently enjoying the freedom of the heaths, while the inclusion of the barrows suggests the antiquity and permanence of the warren. In reality this was a highly contested landscape over which contemporaries held conflicting ideas about the past. In Weeting, for example, the tenants claimed that the rabbits of Methwold Warren had consumed

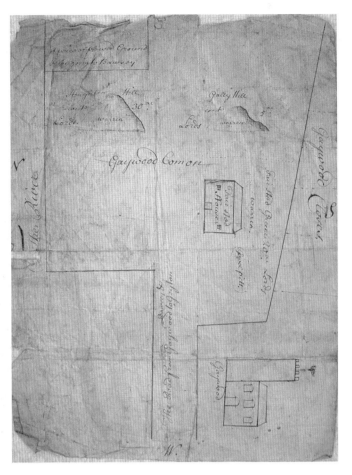

FIGURE 35. In Gaywood, the lord's warren was defined by two probable barrows, Houghton Hill and Gally Hill, shown on an eighteenth-century plan (NRO, BLIXa/35)

one hundred acres of ancient arable. Local inhabitants employed notions of 'antiquity' in their discourses of custom and right, in this case laying claim to an ancient division and order of the farming landscape in opposition to the encroachment of the warren (TNA: PRO, DL4/58/19).

Other maps also reveal the significance of barrows. An eighteenth-century plan of Gaywood shows the lord's warren defined by two probable barrows, Houghton Hill and Gally Hill, both depicted at a greatly enlarged scale (Figure 35, NRO, BLIXa/35). The maps of Gaywood and Methwold convey a sense of the ways elite landowners perceived barrows. Clearly conspicuous in open terrain and the subject of speculation regarding their origins – as indicated by the names many of them carried such as 'Robin Hoodes Butts' (NRO, MC 556/2) – the distribution of barrows on open heaths and commons also helped to structure manorial territories and the development of farming regimes.

During litigation proceedings barrows were also adopted as symbols of contention, and of common identity and purpose in the defence of customary rights. For example, the historic functions and antiquity of 'Haugh Head', the meeting place of Shropham Half Hundred, were invoked in order to give

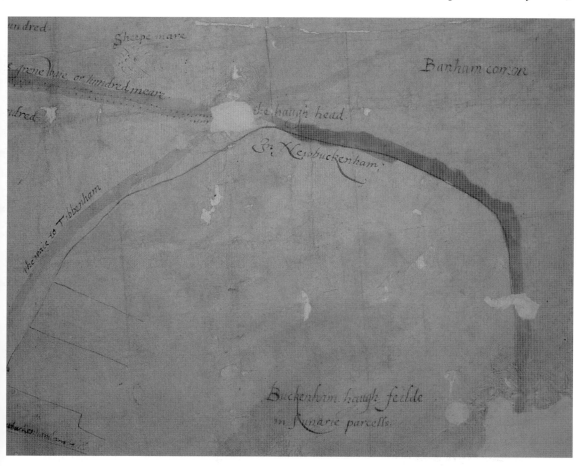

FIGURE 36. During a long-running dispute between the inhabitants of New Buckenham and Carleton, witnesses on both sides employed the material evidence of the past in order to substantiate their claims to access the common. In 1580, the 'Haugh Head' (the place-name element 'haugh' indicates a barrow), was confirmed to be the ancient meeting place of Shropham half hundred, was also employed by the inhabitants of New Buckenham as visible proof of their common rights.

material substantiation to the division of common land shared by the parishes of New Buckenham and Carleton (Figure 36, NRO, PD 254/171). Elsewhere in Flitcham a clear distinction was made between a number of false boundary marks, allegedly made by the inhabitants of West Newton, and ancient landmarks, which included a probable barrow named 'Sweete Hilles' and other topographical features including 'Purles Well', a mere called 'Broad Water', and 'Wheston Pit' (NRO, MS 4291). Because they existed since time immemorial, these ancient boundary features were more difficult to contest than the more recently erected dooles. As a result of the knowledge passed on to successive generations of inhabitants, barrows occupying important and potentially contentious spaces were thus actively preserved in the landscape.

It is possible that the key role of barrows as boundary markers may, indeed, explain aspects of their survival, and recorded distributions may thus reflect something more complex, and more subtle, than original locations modified by subsequent patterns of land use. While it is certainly the case that earthworks are most likely to survive on agriculturally marginal soils, safe from the plough, there are a number of examples of the deliberate preservation of barrows on arable land. 'Gospel Hill', in Little Cressingham; and 'the hyll in Eastfield', between Hunstanton and Holme have already been discussed; but other examples include 'Threw Hill', marked on a map of Northwold which evidently had been preserved within the arable open fields of the parish, probably as a fold-course boundary, as late as c.1765 when the map was made (NRO, MC 62/64). Its name may derive from O.E. *pruh*, meaning 'a coffin' (Smith 1956, vol.ii. 217) and was transferred to a number of neighbouring features in the landscape – 'Threw Field', 'Threw Fen Road' and 'Threw Piece'. Elsewhere, on the dissected claylands to the east of Norwich – an area noted for the relatively low survival rate of earthwork features due to intensive cultivation throughout the medieval period and again in the nineteenth century – an early seventeenth-century map of Langley depicts a mound referred to as 'Garlock Hill' situated within the open fields of the parish. The significance of the feature is again further suggested by the fact that its name was given to the surrounding area, including 'Garlock hill way' and a furlong called 'Garlock hill went' (NRO, NRS 21407, Figure 37).

Given the long-term significance of barrows and their use as boundary markers, it is possible that more recently constructed features were deliberately formed in imitation of ancient barrows. In 1953 Grinsell noted how circular mounds were 'thrown up in order to mark a boundary between two or more parishes or estates', though they tended to be smaller and less regularly formed than barrows (Grinsell 1953, 101). An early sixteenth-century document from Thetford thus refers to the construction of 'certain hills formerly erected for dooles, as partition of the foldcourse' (quoted in Martin 1779, 192–3; Lawson *et al* 1981, 27; Sussams 1996, 117). A court case from Elveden, dating to 1539, saw the plaintiff taking issue with local inhabitants, accusing them of encroaching on his fold course by moving: 'certain Hills erected and made for Metes and Bounds and Dools for the partition of the Foldcourse of the said late Priory of Chanons and the Feedinges and furlongs of the Inhabitants' (Postgate 1973, 315). More strikingly, a survey of the 'Grounds known as Congham Severalls or the Galles' concerning 'the pece in contoversie betwene Congham and Hillington' shows 'proper dooles' and 'supposed dooles' used to demarcate open field strips – evidently mounds, to judge from their cartographic representation (NRO, NRS 21377).

This raises the question of how dooles were made; whether earth was thrown up from a circular ditch dug around a mound or from a nearby pit. Evidence for the former would have clear implications for our interpretations of ring ditches. So far the scant evidence that there is relating to the construction of these features suggests the latter method. An Exchequer case involving manorial boundaries across the downlands of Dorset included details of how these boundary marks were made. Although holes had apparently been dug for this purpose, it was decided that they were not substantial enough and that:

> the said holes shoulde be digged and made bigger into barrowes for the better distinguishing of the said heaths (as it seemeth) was done accordingly, for that the barrowes are nowe in the same places they agreed on to bee soe made (TNA: PRO, E134/11&12Chas1/Hil9; see also Aston and Bettey 1998, 127).

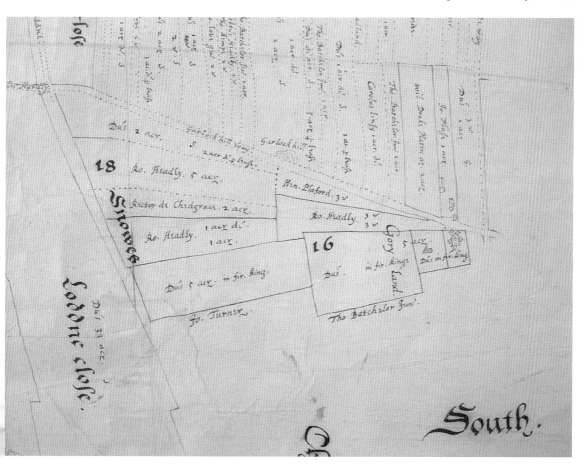

FIGURE 37. 'Garlock Hill', a possible barrow depicted on an undated early seventeenth-century map of Langley, evidently survived within the arable open fields of the parish (NRO, NRS 21407).

In the 1970s an archaeological survey conducted by the Royal Commission in this area of Dorset found twenty-nine round barrows, at least five of them in a straight line (Aston and Bettey 1998, 127). Map evidence for Marham, in Norfolk, shows a clear relation between 'Tuts Hill' and 'Tuts Pit' suggested by their names and also their spatial proximity (NRO, HARE 6811). If some dooles were intentionally constructed to resemble barrows, there are parallels with the much earlier building of mounds resembling barrows in Anglo-Saxon times to serve as hundred meeting places (Adkins and Petchey 1984). Certainly, some (possible) barrows were described as 'dooles' on early maps, which points to a measure of interchangeability in the popular mind. Sussams has thus suggested that a mound depicted on a map showing Methwold Warren in 1699 named 'High Dole' was probably a round barrow (NRO, MC 556/1; Sussams 1996, 117). An earlier map of Methwold Warren, surveyed in c.1580, shows two named mounds drawn in perspective, one of which ('Halmere's Doule') is today represented by a ring ditch (NF32252) not obviously different from those representing accepted round barrows (NRO, MC 556/2; see Whyte 2003a, 14). This in turn raises the possibility that some large earthwork dooles – or the crop marks indicating where they once stood – might be mistaken for barrows, as others have suggested (Lawson *et al* 1981; Sussams 1996). The fact that some dooles were named at all indicates that they were established landmarks existing since time out of mind, and were in this sense at least indistinguishable from prehistoric barrows; both being defined as ancient and permanent elements of the landscape.

It has long been recognised that in the early Anglo-Saxon period barrows were used to define boundaries, but this association of barrows with boundaries continued to be recognised into much later periods. Their liminal location, perceived antiquity and permanence, as well as their supernatural associations, all ensured a wider and more long-lived role as places of meeting and execution, as well as boundary markers, and invited emulation when new boundary markers or meeting places were being created. By recognizing the continuing practical functions of barrows, and other relic features such as freestanding crosses, in structuring post-medieval landscapes and their ongoing interpretation, not just as the subject of folklore, offers new insights into understanding the processes of destruction and preservation in the landscape. Rather than being the straightforward result of patterns of later land use, the recorded distribution of upstanding barrows may, in part, be a function of the new uses assigned to them over time by successive medieval and post-medieval societies. These ideas will be developed in the following section, which further investigates the long-term association of boundaries as places of execution and burial.

The Place of the Dead

The notion that certain elements of the landscape carried meanings and associations over several centuries has further relevance for our understanding of the geography of burial, or in some cases non-burial, of unchristian deaths in the post-medieval period. As mentioned earlier, archaeologists have discerned a strong correlation between execution sites (*cwealmstows*) and boundaries, especially hundred boundaries, in the late Anglo-Saxon period (Reynolds 1997). The *cwealmstow* at South Acre, for example, lies at the junction of three hundreds, those of Freebridge Lynn, South Greenhoe and Launditch (Wymer 1996). Further investigation has shown that the choice of location was frequently determined by existing associations with death and burial, in particular the presence of barrows. The barrow cemetery at Sutton Hoo provides an important example of the reuse of an existing site: well-known as the location of high status burials in the seventh century, recent excavation has revealed a much later phase of use, as a place of execution in the tenth and eleventh centuries (Carver 1998). As remnants of a distant past the re-assimilation of barrows reflects their obvious practical uses, as well as their enduring association in the popular imagination with death, burial and the supernatural (Semple 1998). While these studies have served to illustrate the prominence of such sites in the physical and cognitive landscapes of early medieval society, there has been much less consideration of the significance of old execution sites and patterns of reuse in later periods (Whyte 2003b).

The overwhelming majority of research dealing with the geography of burial and commemoration in the post-medieval period has focused, unsurprisingly, on churches and graveyards. A few studies have raised the problematic issue of 'bad' deaths and where to bury them (Daniell 1997, 103–9). In the fifteenth-century writers defined various categories of death considered to be polluting and unfit for interment in consecrated ground. One contemporary author included women who died in childbirth, thieves, 'lechers' and the 'cursed' and those who died suddenly 'unless they were good people, were drowned by mishap, or accidentally killed themselves by mischief against their will' (Daniell 1997, 103–4). Of those excluded from a Christian burial, suicides are the best attested group. Their treatment was a harsh one, and increasingly so from the late fifteenth century. Interred at crossroads the bodies of suicides were often staked down, thus keeping them physically and metaphorically in their place, the trees that allegedly grew from these stakes marked their graves (Daniell 1997, 106; MacDonald and Murphy 1990).

Denial of a proper burial was bound up with the early modern belief that even in death the body could receive further punishment (Gittings 1984, 74). Non-repenting criminals who were executed for their crimes were similarly cast out of the Christian community. Their bodies were often displayed and left to rot from gallows or gibbets, a terrible end consigning them to perpetual torment and misery of loneliness; their non-burial denying them reunion with family and friends on the Day of Judgement (Marshall 2002, 191). The boundary of the churchyard provided a clear symbolic and spatial separation of Christian and non-Christian deaths, but more than this, the choice of location for suicides and gibbets was to a great extent informed by the enduring material and conceptual presence of the dead in the wider landscape.

By taking a broad chronological perspective some important strands of continuity emerge regarding the ways the landscape was used to memorialise the 'deviant' dead. Throughout the medieval period gallows – the wooden structures on which criminals were executed, and where their bodies might be left to hang for some time afterwards (Hill 1976) – were frequently erected on parish boundaries (Whitelock 1954, 144). Recent surveys of minor-place names have served to corroborate this connection (Field 1993, 238; Whyte 2003b). As symbols of government and authority, the location of gallows was an important consideration: sites had to be chosen that were both visible across the surrounding area, and accessible to a large proportion of the local population. Certainly the remarkable longevity of many gallows sites must in part be a consequence of their original intention as permanent structures, as well as being a function of their particular landscape context. From the surviving place-name evidence it seems that most were located close to roads, often in close proximity to road junctions (Field 1993, 238). Indeed, it was following a change in the status of local routeways, that the gallows at Sutton Hoo was apparently moved to a new site in a neighbouring parish (Carver 1998, 144). In order to further accentuate their impact on the horizon, gallows were frequently constructed on purpose built mounds or pre-existing earthworks. It seems likely that the 'hill' referred to in many place-names was in fact a prehistoric barrow, in Norfolk, 'Gallow Hill' mounds in Kelling, Thorpe Market, East Walton, Buxton with Lammas and Thetford are all known barrows (Lawson *et al.* 1981, 12, 27).

Despite the clear association of gallows with parish boundaries, the parish was not a unit of criminal jurisdiction in the medieval period. Rather, manorial courts formed the most basic unit of local law enforcement, and many in the pre- and post-Conquest period retained the right to hang criminals (Briggs *et al.* 1996, 12). During the *Quo warranto* investigations under Edward I into the rights and privileges held by every manor, a total of eighty-five gallows were claimed in Norfolk (NRO, Clarke MS125). Criminal jurisdiction was granted to manorial leet courts and as fixed points in the landscape gallows reinforced their administrative authority over subsidiary manors. By the later medieval period, however, the functions of the manorial courts had greatly diminished, as the mechanics of royal justice came to be administered from county towns during the twice-yearly visitations of the assize judges (Briggs *et al.* 1996, 28). Yet the enduring recognition of rural gallows sites is striking. The ongoing interpretation and re-assimilation of gallows sites within later landscapes, is further testified by their depiction on estate maps produced between the late sixteenth and eighteenth centuries. One notable example is an eighteenth-century map of South Acre, which depicts a number of apparently extant barrows on 'Gallow Hill Heath', possibly the remains of the Anglo-Saxon *cwealmstow* (NRO, FX266/1).

Though more usually considered the inspiration for local folklore narratives (Lawson *et al* 1981), the longevity of gallows sites reflects the significance of their geographical contexts, especially in delimiting manorial and, increasingly from the late sixteenth and seventeenth centuries, parish boundaries across open commons and heaths. A late sixteenth-century terrier for Postedhall Manor in Burnham Westgate, for example, describes a piece of land abutting upon Lexham Manor and 'Gallowe hill' (NRO, ANW/5/2/15). 'Gally Hill', for example, was depicted on a map of Eccles made in 1733 at a significant junction on open heathland: situated at the point where the Norwich Way and Bury Way intersected, and where the parishes of Eccles, Snetterton and Hargham met (NRO, MC 168/4; NRO, CUL Buxton MSS Box 78; Davison 1980). 'Gally Hill' in Gaywood (Figure 35), is currently located 200 metres from the parish boundary, but in the eighteenth century was included in a description of the bounds (NRO, KL/C51/31). Though no longer in use, both the naming of gallows sites and, in many cases, the physical presence of the mounds on which they once stood, served to structure later social and economic topographies.

There is evidence to suggest that long after local gallows had disappeared from the landscape their sites might be re-appropriated as the locations for gibbets. Until the early nineteenth century, executed criminals were often returned to the scene of their crimes where their bodies were placed in iron cages and suspended high above the ground from a suitable tree or pole. Utilization of an existing mound gave added elevation, thus the tumulus known as 'Gallows Hill' in Thetford, which has its origins as a medieval execution site, was later reused for a gibbet (NRO, Clarke MS125). Another example comes from the Suffolk village of Flixton, where a man named Cesar, executed in 1594 for the murder of his wife and mother-in-law, was hung in a gibbet on 'Gallows Hill' (Lowestoft RO, HA12/E1/12/77). Even where we cannot show the reuse of medieval gallows sites – associated with barrows or otherwise – as locations for gibbets, it is sometimes evident that sites were used for the latter purpose on more that one occasion, often separated in time by a century or more. In 1790 the corpse of a thief was hung in chains on 'Denton Hill' (NRO, MS125), a barrow located on the Methwold/Feltwell parish boundary. A gibbet was recorded here on Faden's map of Norfolk published in 1797, but perhaps more interestingly a gibbet was also marked at this site on a map of 1607 (HER13114), clearly indicating that 'Denton Hill' had been used for this purpose more than once. At Quidenham in 1681 a gibbet was erected 'Gibbet Hill', again almost certainly a barrow (Lawson *et al.* 1981, 11).

Other categories of 'bad' deaths were similarly denied a Christian burial. As already mentioned in the early modern period, individuals who committed suicide were frequently interred in roads, especially at crossroads on parish boundaries, until the practice was abolished in 1823 (Daniell 1997, 106; Halliday 1994; 1995; MacDonald and Murphy 1990). Early maps offer evidence of the local context of this practice: one depicting Cockley Cley in 1579 thus includes reference to 'Dead mans grave in Lynn way' situated in the main road to Kings Lynn (NRO, MC 830/1 797 x 1); and a sixteenth-century sketch map of Banham shows 'Deade Mans Grave' located on a crossroads (NRO, WLS XXIV/5 414x5). As discussed in chapter two crossroads, particularly those on parish boundaries may also have been construed as liminal places thus adding to their suitability as places for the interment of the bodies of restless souls. Rather than necessarily denoting a much earlier prehistoric or Anglo-Saxon burial site (Lawson *et al* 1981), the occurrence of local place-names referring to 'dead man', or 'dead woman' surviving in many Norfolk parishes today are probably of more recent origins. It is interesting to note, for example, that the modern Ordnance Survey records 'Deadman's Plantation' in Cockley Cley abutting the parish boundary and a road leaving the village to the north-west, in the direction of Kings Lynn (TF77750505).

Evidence from other villages indicates that the practice of burying people on land outside the graveyard was not unusual, though at a local level noteworthy enough to provide conspicuous landmarks. In Gimingham the farmer of the manor was accused of grazing his flock of four or five hundred sheep over heathland 'to a place called the dead woman's grave in Cromer' (TNA: PRO, DL4/14/32); and 'a place called the deade man' in Elveden, provided a landmark feature for the inhabitants of villages around Thetford (TNA: PRO, E134/1Jas1/Trin7). Another 'Dead mans grave' was employed as a boundary in delimiting outfield 'brecks' in Syderstone (NRO, ANW/S 2/17). Minor place-names recorded on early maps also include such references: the map dating to 1599 of Cawston includes 'Dead Mans Grave' among the various landmarks separating the commons of Cawston and Haveringland (NRO, MS 4521, Figure 38); and in Ringstead 'Dead Mans Grave' marked the parish boundary adjoining Thornham Common on a seventeenth-century map (NRO, LEST/NR (box)).

The fact that manorial and parish boundaries were maintained by the collaborative efforts of local societies may have served to perpetuate this association. During ritual events, such as Rogationtide, ancient gallows mounds, gibbets and graves were acknowledged and reaffirmed as part of a sequence of mnemonics. Nan Saxby's grave, for example, was remembered in a perambulation of Barham Manor in Linton, Cambridgeshire (Halliday 1995, 114). Elsewhere, a written perambulation made by the rector of Newton Flotman in 1768 recorded the passage of parishioners along 'Dead Man's Lane' (NRO, Dun (c) 82, 499 x 6). In some places this connection was made more explicit in the apparent renaming of boundary features. For instance, it has been surmised that 'Mark's Grave', another boundary feature of Linton, was probably derived from OE *mearc*, meaning boundary mark (Halliday 1995, 114). In view of the long-term connections between boundaries and burials, the name may also reflect the intended, or appropriated functions of the grave as a territorial marker.

The landscape thus acted as a mnemonic device: both the tangible remains of the past and the names given to them, created and sustained popular perceptions of territory and community. The immediate geographical context of 'Pigg's Grave' in Swanton Novers, for example, suggests that this area carried a range of ominous connotations: the name – attached to a crossroads – implies the grave of a suicide victim but the place is also located at the end of 'Gallowhill Lane' and at the point where three parish boundaries converge. Contemporaries would have been well aware of the significance of these juxtapositions and associations: not only members of the communities responsible for marking and remembering boundaries but also outsiders, travelling through the area. The interment of suicides and gibbeting of executed criminals were events of wider social interest and significance attracting people from surrounding villages to view and remember the graves of suicides and gibbets. For those travellers passing across open heaths and commons, on seeing a gibbet or grave would have been well aware that they were crossing a township boundary. The social act of remembering and physically confirming the course of boundaries by singling out a series of landmarks helped to preserve the association of boundaries with death and burial.

While it is possible to trace threads of continuity linking unchristian deaths with boundaries it is important to stress that in all periods the choice of location reflects the particular concerns of the present. Recent analysis of Anglo-Saxon literary sources has suggested that, within the popular imagination, boundaries were construed as liminal places: existing on the threshold between life and

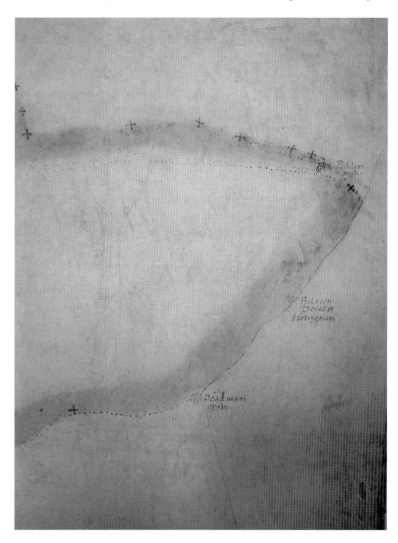

FIGURE 38. 'Deadmans Grave' in Cawston in 1599, was among the various landmarks used to define the boundary of commonland (NRO, MS 4521).

death, they were places steeped in the supernatural. The burial of 'deviants' at this metaphysical juncture would ensure eternal torment in the company of the Devil and his retinue (Reynolds 1997; Semple 1998). While it might be useful to equate boundary burial in the Anglo-Saxon period with concepts of liminality, it would, however, be misleading to apply such a concept directly to the later medieval and post-medieval periods (Halliday 1995, 113). It would seem unlikely, for instance, that boundaries in the eighteenth century were still thought of as representing the 'death boundary' of the village. More plausibly, the use of boundaries for the burial or display of the deviant dead was, by the later medieval period, intended not so much to convey territorial marginality, but rather to denote the eviction of the condemned from the spiritual heart of the community – the church and graveyard.

At the end of the eighteenth century William Faden recorded eight gibbets on his map of the county. Like earlier gallows sites, an examination of the landscape context of gibbets exhibits a remarkably consistent spatial pattern: on boundaries that once crossed open commons and heaths (Whyte 2003b). To some extent, practical considerations informed this choice, such as the desire to use grazing land rather than arable, where a gibbet might interfere with arable production. But the association of gibbets with boundaries is the point to emphasise; we are not merely seeing here the symbolic significance of lonely and peripheral spaces. Even in the desolate expanses of Breckland, dominated by extensive sheep-walks and warrens, gibbets were deliberately placed on boundaries. Evidently more complex factors were at play, factors that to a great extent tie in with the central themes of this book – the need to define ambiguous sections of boundary across open tracts of common and heath.

While, for the reasons outlined, crossroads provided suitable locations for the burial of suicide victims other sites were also deemed to be appropriate. During a dispute over grazing rights in Aylsham eighty-three-year-old Roger Comer, a labourer from neighbouring Blickling, remembered:

> Aboute threskore yeares paste that a prest which hadd drowned hym selfe in a well in Aylsham … and one Botte and one Palmer wch did hange them selves in the same towne aboute fyve or six yeares paste wer all buryed at severall tymes on the said pece of heathe or waste grounde lyeinge on the weste parte of the said comon waye leading from Aylsham to Cawston as in a pece of grounde then accompted and taken for the Kings comon grounde (TNA: PRO, DL4/25/43).

Judging from the number of interments carried out in the lifetime of Roger Comer, the parcel of common land in Aylsham was considered to be the customary place for the burial of suicides. That Roger Comer should have related his knowledge of the burials was not merely anecdotal, for this information was both crucial in verifying the common status of the land in question and also its location within the bounds of Aylsham. In another example from Cawston a map drawn up by the tenants of the manor, in defence of their common grazing rights, recorded two graves (see above p. 115). Both were located alongside route-ways suggesting their origins as suicide burials. However, of greater significance was the placement of both graves at prominent junctions in the landscape. 'Dead mans grave' was located on common land at the point where the boundaries of Cawston, Hevingham and Haveringland met. Similarly 'Jone Metton's grave' was situated on the section of boundary dividing the commons of Cawston and Marsham. Her grave was also employed to mark an internal division of the manor separating Cawston common from Brandeston doles – an area of common subdivided or doled into 'private' portions (TNA: PRO, E133/1/108; Figure 39). Of further interest is the possibility of a third burial, recorded on the modern Ordnance Survey, again on the parish boundary of Cawston common. Though referred to as 'Mickle Hill' in 1599, it is possible that this site was appropriated at a later date for burial.

Naming the dead in the landscape was in itself a powerful memorial statement. Obviously well known to their neighbours, the burials of Jone Metton and Nan

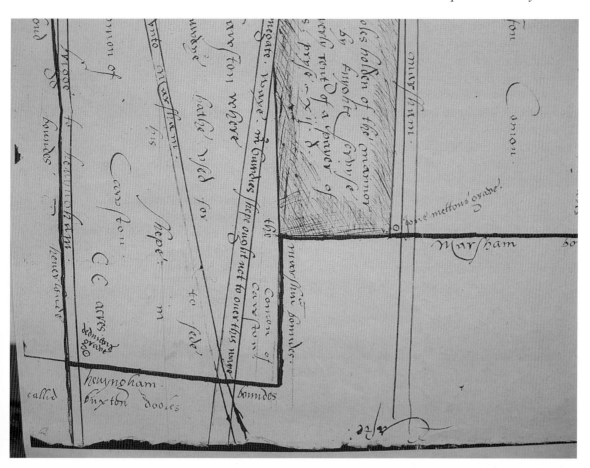

Saxby must have been events of great consequence for local residents. Bearing in mind the prevalent belief in the terrifying consequences of not receiving a proper burial in hallowed soil, the presence of such graves in highly conspicuous locations must have stirred dread and consternation in the minds of local people. Certainly in the nineteenth century, various stories regarding the restless ghosts of these unfortunate victims continued to be a source of fascination and terror (Halliday 1995). In other important ways the treatment of such deaths created a mnemonic event of practical significance: the decision to set up a gibbet or dig a grave for a suicide on a boundary was intended to provide a mnemonic spectacle to be remembered by future generations (Williams 2006, 90). As we have seen the placement of new boundary features, were occasions of broader social significance involving groups from neighbouring villages, their presence ensuring the correct identification of boundaries (Whyte 2007). Graves and gibbets attracted visitors from much further afield. In the late eighteenth century the gibbet set up on Badley Moor attracted visitors from outside the parish including Parson Woodforde who made an entry in his diary regarding his visit to see 'Cliffen's gibbet' on 4 April 1785: '... after breakfast, being fine Weather, I took a ride and Will with me, thro' Hockering, North-Tuddenham, to Baddeley Moor where Cliffen stands in Chains' (Beresford 1924, 182). Gibbets, grave mounds, the stakes that blossomed into trees, and the names attached to the landscape, were intended to preserve the correct course of boundaries in the future as well as the present.

It is possible that some of these burials were those of poor vagrants found dead outside their home parish and without sufficient funds for a churchyard burial. In Wymondham at the end of the eighteenth century, one such case concerned the burial of a dead man found on the common. The parish officers refused to bear the costs of his burial and, as a result, it was decided to bury him on the parish boundary of Wymondham and Hethersett, close to where he was found (White 1845, 694). The social and moral marginality of those individuals perceived to be standing outside the neighbourhood ideal founded on orderliness and good governance, was physically manifest in their treatment in death (Amussen 1988; Hindle 1996, 2000; Wrightson 1996). But, the creation of new boundary features was as much an economic phenomenon. Whoever they were, the use of the dead as quite literally territorial markers must be one of the most profound material expressions of the process of 'fixing' boundaries and delimiting access rights to resources.

People living in the sixteenth and seventeenth centuries were deeply aware of the distortions and fragility of memory, which threatened the boundaries of their customs and land use rights. As well as evoking the past in their present-day negotiations by appropriating and reusing relics of the past, they were also engaged in processes that served to create future memories (Bradley 2002, 82–111). While the details of their origins were slowly eroded from memory, monuments and place-names served as mnemonics for future generations who would in turn use them to their own ends, embellishing them and re-interpreting them in relation to the specific concerns of the present. It is in this sense that the landscape was an active component in peoples' everyday lives – it was embedded with meaning, of personal and common importance. The maintenance of the relics of the past, and creation of future pasts, was an active and ongoing social process in the post-medieval period as it was in earlier times.

Conclusion

The study of the 'life-histories' of monuments and topographical features has important implications for the workings of memory across an extensive chronological period. This chapter has demonstrated the profound affect that the material remains of the past had on the lives of future generations. Local memory, oral traditions, and the deliberate preservation of landmarks remained essential to the interpretation of landscapes. Daily encounters with the material relics of the past together with the continued recognition and use of local place names, provided the substance of human memory. This is seen most clearly by charting the long-term 'biographies' of ancient monuments (Bradley 2002;

Holtorf 1998) into the later historic period but can also be traced in the specific use of the landscape for the execution and display of the deviant dead. Certain places in the landscape evoked powerful sentiments over extensive periods of time. Even in the late eighteenth century boundaries were imbued with a range of meanings that fused together contemporary social, economic, spiritual and political perspectives with a deep-rooted knowledge of the past.

For generations barrows, and other less obvious features, especially those marking critical boundaries, were identified as communal landmarks, a process of recognition that promoted their survival into the post-medieval period. It was not capitalist modes of production *per se* which led to their destruction, but rather general enclosure, particularly by parliamentary act, and the subsequent large-scale reorganisation of the physical landscape which, in light soil parishes, occurred mainly in the eighteenth and nineteenth centuries. While the enclosure of open fields was a necessary precondition for market specialisation in livestock production, it was not the case for grain production, and in light soil arable districts the landscape usually remained open, agriculture operating within ostensibly medieval farming systems, until the adoption of new crops and rotations in the eighteenth century (Williamson 2000, 66–68). This development, however, made the heaths, and complicated folding arrangements, redundant: the heaths could be reclaimed and the splintered holdings of the open fields re-allotted as compact farms. But large-scale enclosure and reclamation imposed new ways of 'inhabiting' the landscape. Privatisation of the land and the extinction of common rights effectively dispelled old boundary disputes. As long-established causes of contention were resolved, and areas of common land allocated to individual proprietors, the familiar landmarks that had previously been integral to the organisation of landscapes became expendable. Large numbers of barrows preserved both on open heaths and within areas of arable land, were rapidly levelled. Numerous modest features – such as stones, posts, and crosses dug into the earth – that had once provoked strong emotion within local societies were no longer required. The saints' days that had served important functions in structuring the agricultural year were similarly rationalized, no longer required in the organisation of the customary terrain of local life.

Landscape historians and archaeologists frequently attribute the destruction of significant archaeological features, to enclosure and the subsequent cultivation of common pasture and heathland; yet ancient features were not the only ones destroyed in the aftermath of enclosure. The gibbets containing James Cliffen on Badley Moor, Stephen Watson on West Bradenham common, and William Suffolk on North Walsham common, were all taken down and presumably buried nearby, in the same year that the parishes were enclosed. The removal of landmarks, erected within the living memory of many local inhabitants, must have deepened the great sense of change that was taking place. Certainly the crowds that assembled to observe the removal of gibbets probably constituted some of the final displays of communal sentiment before the commons were enclosed. Stephen Watson's gibbet, for example, was taken down in 1801 to an audience of 'hundreds of people' from across Norfolk. It was reported that a starling's nest with young had to be removed from his breast; an event that was witnessed by the spectators 'as something singular and extraordinary' (Norfolk Annales 1801). A few years later a similar story was told in relation to Bennington's gibbet: it was reported that 'from his skull flew out a bluetit and her family of nine or ten' (NRO, Clarke MS125). There is archaeological evidence to confirm that gibbets were buried close to where they had stood before enclosure. In 1882 Mr Haggard, the owner of 'Gibbet Land' in West Bradenham uncovered Watson's gibbet whilst digging a ditch: the iron cage apparently still containing his bones and skull (Carthew 1883, 100).

It is clear that large-scale enclosure and the privatisation of common land effectively dislocated the material language through which oral memory operated: enclosure diminished the scope for communal systems of remembering; the course of parish boundaries and rights over common land were settled; landmarks both new and old were destroyed or, because the uses for them had been eradicated, their meanings were forgotten or perhaps re-invented. But it is worth stressing again that this process of 'forgetting' occurred at the end of a long, protracted period of enclosure and the rationalisation of local customs and land use rights. Whereas social historians have tended to highlight the consequences of piecemeal enclosure taking place in the seventeenth century as being significant in bringing an end to communal customs and traditions, in Norfolk at least the processes of social memory remained crucial in demarcating the landscape of numerous villages well into the eighteenth century. This was largely due to the fact that unlike an unequivocal act of parliament, achievable largely because the process was weighted against the minority of small landowners and occupiers, earlier piecemeal and general enclosures were susceptible to dispute both at the time and in later years. As we have seen in the case of Cawston, where piecemeal enclosure was taking place, the course of the parish boundary remained a source of bitter contention that simmered for well over a century.

CHAPTER SIX

Conclusion

....

Most studies of the post-medieval landscape have described a somewhat linear course of development, shaped by the growth of capitalism, 'individualism' and the comodification of agrarian practices. It is unquestionable that farmers were engaged in increasingly commercialised methods of production, and had been since the fourteenth century at least (Whittle 2000), but this development was in no way straightforward or linear. Some historians have conceptualised the post-medieval landscape as a backdrop analogous to a painting – a canvas manipulated and controlled by the individual – and thus a static image for surveillance. But, as I hope to have shown in this book, there are other ways of understanding the landscape by considering its development as part of a dynamic social process, based on a complex interaction of material and mental structures. By starting with the small-scale local conditions of change and continuity, we can begin to understand the landscape as a lived environment imbued with meaning and significance. The findings of micro-studies do not always accord with the over-arching regional models of landscape change, more familiar to landscape historians, but they can serve to nuance them. Our modern landscape was shaped by a number of overlapping and interconnected histories relating to a complex spectrum of religious, social, cultural and economic perspectives.

An attempt has been made to define some of the broad spatial changes underway in this period, of which the transformation of the religious landscape in the sixteenth century stands out as deeply significant. The Protestant reforms of this period had a major impact on religious topographies: a landscape imbued with 'holy' references was replaced by the consolidation of worship at a single place – the parish church. Yet the pre-Reformation connotations of the sites and monuments in the wider landscape were not entirely forgotten. Integrated within popular culture, many became the subject of folklore narratives; but of equal importance was the perpetuation and elaboration of their secular roles, often in new and much modified contexts. Important parallels can be drawn between the spatial re-configurations of late sixteenth-century religious practices and, under the directives of the Elizabethan government, the developing role of the parish as the basic unit for local governance. As social historians have demonstrated, the focus on the parish, rather than vill or manor, had a significant impact on senses of belonging and the ways in which people identified with their social environment. But it also had a major impact on the landscape history of many villages in Norfolk, as attempts were made to define and fix ambiguous sections of parish boundary – predominately those running across open heaths and commons. Indeed, the need to demarcate with greater clarity the areas of common land allocated to particular communities ensured the continuing observance of perambulation rituals.

Again, important parallels can be suggested with changes in the political and social spheres: in this case, with the advent of the Poor Laws. The impact of state legislation, in conjunction with localised initiatives in dealing with the growing problem of poverty, saw a hardening of attitudes among the wealthier 'middling' sorts of the parish towards the poor. Attempts were made to ensure that local resources were defined, and access retained for the 'deserving', resident poor. However, the motivations behind the concern to demarcate the physical boundaries were multi-layered. Relations within local 'communities' were fractured and re-forged in various ways and at various times – between manorial lords, tithe-owners, tenants, commoners, and the poor – over rights to access the commons. In light soil areas in particular, the desire to define parish boundaries was not so much part of an underlying social agenda but a much broader struggle over rights to the land between landowners and tenants.

The changing balance of interests between manor and parish constitutes another important strand of enquiry. It is widely considered that the demise of the manor as an institution can be traced in the decline of manorial courts in favour of outside arbitration. In some villages, however, the manor was superseded by a new generation of landowners, whose blatant disregard for the traditional organisational mechanisms of the manor, as in the case of Snettisham, engendered considerable discontent and bitterness among local inhabitants. Yet at other times parochial and manorial interests coincided, as in the disputes over the division of common land. Recourse to the central law courts was essential in the resolution of such disputes, but this in turn moved the emphasis away from the idiosyncrasies of 'local' customs and helped to facilitate greater consistency in practices between neighbouring villages and districts. This is particularly evident in the attempts of lords to enforce strict fold-course arrangements in villages where large areas of heathland existed, notably Breckland and North West Norfolk. The successful development of this system, from a set of loosely defined rights to a rigorous and inflexible manorial custom, encouraged landowners further east in the county, within Northern Heathland and Flegg villages, to attempt to follow suit. Their success in implementing such arrangements was variable, however, and largely dependent upon the strength of local tenants as a collective force.

An approach that views the development of agrarian landscapes in this period as the pursuit of rational, economic farmers in direct confrontation with the environment, produces a somewhat narrow picture of the ways people viewed their landscape. The decision and ability of individual farmers to develop the land was bound up with wider social and economic relations predicated on the concept of custom and right. Below the level of the elite minority, the ambitions of the individual were achievable through collaboration with those with broadly similar objectives. Tenants made a stand against their lords, and in so doing called upon the knowledge of the wider 'community' of inhabitants, stressing for instance the customary rights of the resident poor to use common land, or to glean across the arable fields. In most cases the concept of custom was bound up with sentiments that were not necessarily disinterested. Custom was used to substantiate the claims of tenants and inhabitants that the land held common status, to ensure their own continued access – as well, perhaps, to reduce their contributions to the poor rates, by allowing the indigent a measure of informal employment. In their concern to protect their rights individuals were engaged in the constant surveillance of their neighbours' activities, as they were in other social and economic networks formed in the alehouse, church, and home.

Once considered to be economically 'marginal' landscapes, the heaths were in fact a central focus in the lives of many Norfolk villages. Until relatively recently agricultural historians considered the heaths to be unproductive wastelands, the relics of a medieval system of farming which were waiting, in essence, to be turned into productive corn fields by eighteenth-century 'improvers' (Chambers and Mingay 1966). More recently, landscape historians have emphasised the value of heathland as an integral component of arable production – as part of the fold-course system. It was, however, precisely because of their more 'marginal' status in the medieval period – their function as open grazing grounds for sheep and rabbits – that they became sources of conflict in later centuries. Due to their ill-defined boundaries and the often ambiguous nature of the common rights attached to them, heaths became landscapes of contention, acting as focal points for various social groups, both internally and between neighbouring villages. The attempts to define and fix the network of boundaries belonging to manorial and parochial jurisdictions found social expression in the identification, preservation and construction of numerous landmarks. Of all the features employed to delimit these boundaries, it was the placement of the dead as quite *literally* boundary markers that more than anything encapsulates the depth of emotion – social, economic, political, moral – generated by these landscapes.

The past was a powerful concept in the mediation of capitalist landscapes of production. The sixteenth and seventeenth centuries are generally noted as a time of burgeoning literacy rates and increasing reliance on written documentation, which eventually displaced oral memory: a complex and protracted development. Written accounts of the landscape and maps were part of an integrated system of memory reliant on local knowledge and the physical evidence of the past in the landscape. In their defence of customs and access rights manorial lords, tenants and commoners alike integrated the landscape within a material language of memory. Customs and rights were structured through a series of collectively recognised place-names and landmarks. It was through the ongoing processes of recognition and interpretation of the material past that points of contact were forged between individuals and social groups and their physical surroundings.

Layers of function and meaning built up at specific places in the landscape. This is evident in the careful depictions of landmarks on early maps and in the manner in which contemporaries chose to explain aspects of their lives, and their genealogical histories, through their experiences and knowledge of the landmarks they encountered, which in turn were subsumed within collective narratives of

place. Whether during prescribed ritual events, such as Rogationtide, or the mundane episodes of daily life, the landscape was invested with meaning, and provided a mnemonic framework for the organisation of social and economic relations. This material language – founded on a common understanding of antiquity – was not static but open to re-interpretation, contradiction and outright hostility as individuals and social groups sought to protect their interests. It was through the manipulation of this material dialogue over time that people re-shaped their landscape and negotiated their terms of jurisdiction and right. By mapping the changing spatial contours of custom, and the process of consolidating and fixing territorial boundaries, a clearer understanding of the development of the post-medieval landscape can be attained.

FIGURE 40. Open heathlands in Breckland.

This book has hopefully achieved a more nuanced and subtle understanding of the post-medieval landscape than is often presented, by using highly localised accounts of the experiences and perceptions of the landscape, especially those provided by court cases, and by linking these to the evidence of early maps. It is through the small-scale moments of interaction illuminated by these documents that we can gain an invaluable insight into the complexities and contradictions inherent within local societies. In giving voices to local inhabitants the transformation of the post-medieval capitalist landscape emerges as a dynamic force that was as much about the collective re-interpretation and negotiation of the past as it was the achievement of individual farmers in direct confrontation with nature.

Bibliography of Secondary Literature

Adkins, R. and Petchey, M. (1984) 'Secklow hundred mound and other meeting mounds in England', *Archaeological Journal* 141, 243–51.

Airs, M. (1995) *The Tudor and Jacobean Country House: A Building History*, Sutton, Stroud.

Allen, R.C. (1992) *Enclosure and the Yeoman: The Agricultural Development of the South Midlands, 1450–1850*, Clarendon Press, Oxford.

Allison, K.J. (1957) 'The sheep-corn husbandry of Norfolk in the sixteenth and seventeenth centuries', *Agricultural History Review* 5, 12–30.

Amussen, S.D. (1988) *An Ordered Society: Gender and Class in Early Modern England*, Blackwell, Oxford.

Arnold, C.J. and Wardle P. (1981) 'Early medieval settlement patterns in England', *Medieval Archaeology* 25, 145–149.

Ashmore, W. and Knapp, A.B. eds (1999) *Archaeologies of Landscape: Contemporary Perspectives*, Blackwell, Oxford.

Aston, M. (1988) *England's Iconoclasts*, vol. I: *Laws Against Images*, Clarendon Press, Oxford.

Aston, M. (1989) 'Iconoclasm in England: official and clandestine' reprinted in P. Marshall ed. (1997) *The Impact of the English Reformation 1500–1640*, Arnold, London, 167–92.

Aston, M. (2003) 'Public worship and iconoclasm' eds D. Gaimster and R. Gilchrist, *The Archaeology of Reformation 1480–1580*, Maney 9–28.

Aston, M. (1985) *Interpreting the Landscape: Landscape Archaeology and Local History*, Routledge, London.

Aston, M. and Bettey, J. (1998) 'The post-medieval rural landscape c.1540–1700: the drive for profit and the desire for status' eds P. Everson and T. Williamson, *The Archaeology of Landscape*, Manchester University Press, Manchester.

Ault, W.O. ed. (1928) *Court Rolls of the Abbey of Ramsey and of the Honor of Clare*, Yale University Press, New Haven.

Bailey, M. (1989) *A Marginal Economy? East Anglian Breckland in the Later Middle Ages*, Cambridge University Press, Cambridge.

Bailey, M. (1990) 'Sand into gold: The evolution of the fold-course system in West Suffolk, 1200–1600, *Agricultural History Review* 38, 40–57.

Barrett, J.C. (1994) *Fragments from Antiquity*, Blackwell, Oxford.

Barrett, J.C. (1999) 'The mythical landscapes of the British Iron Age' eds W. Ashmore, and B. Knapp, *Archaeologies of Landscape: Contemporary Perspectives,* Blackwell, Oxford, 253–265.

Barrett, J.C. (1999) 'Chronologies of landscape' eds P. Ucko and R. Layton, *The Archaeology and Anthropology of Landscape*, Routledge, London.

Barrett, J.C. (2001) 'Agency, the duality of structure, and the problem of the archaeological record' ed. I. Hodder *Archaeological Theory Today*, Polity, Cambridge, 141–164.

Barringer, J.C. (1988) 'An introduction to commons', ed. M. Manning, *Commons in Norfolk: historical and ecological studies of selected commons*, Norfolk Research Committee, Norwich, 3–8.

Barringer, C. ed. (1989) *Faden's Map of Norfolk*, Larks Press, Dereham.

Barringer, C. (1993) 'Norfolk Hundreds' ed. P. Wade-Martins, *An Historical Atlas of Norfolk,* Norwich, 88–89.

Batcock, N. (1991) 'The ruined and disused churches of Norfolk' *East Anglian Archaeology* 51.

Bendall, A.S. (1992) *Maps, Land and Society: A History, with a Carto-Bibliography of Cambridgeshire Estate Maps c.1600–1836*, Cambridge.

Bender, B. ed. (1993) *Landscape: Politics and Perspectives*, Berg, Oxford.

Bender, B. (1993) 'Stonehenge – contested landscapes (medieval to present day)' ed. B. Bender, *Landscape: Politics and Perspectives*, Berg, Oxford, 245–279.

Beresford, M. (1984) *History on the Ground*, Sutton, Gloucester.

Birtles, S. (1999) 'Common land, poor relief and enclosure: the use of manorial resources in fulfilling parish obligations, 1601–1834', *Past and Present* 165, 74–106.

Blair, J. (1996) 'Churches in the early English landscape: social and economic contexts' eds J. Blair and C. Pyrah *Church Archaeology: Research Directions for the Future*, Council for British Archaeology, 6–19.

Blair, J. and Pyrah, C. eds (1996) *Church Archaeology: Research Directions for the Future*, Council for British Archaeology.

Blatchly, J. (2001) 'In search of bells: iconoclasm in Norfolk, 1644', ed. T. Cooper *The Journal of William Dowsing*, The Boydell Press, Woodbridge, 107–123.

Blomefield, F. (1805–10) *An Essay towards a Topographical History of Norfolk* (continued by the late Reverend Charles Parkin), 11 vols., Miller, London.

Bolingbroke, L.G. (1898) 'The Reformation in a Norfolk parish', *Norfolk Archaeology* 13, 199–216.

Bond, F. (1914) *Dedications and Patron Saints of English Churches: Ecclesiastical Symbolism, Saints and their Emblems,* Oxford University Press, London.

Bonney, D. (1979) 'Early boundaries and estates in Southern England', ed. P.H. Sawyer, *English Medieval Settlement,* Arnold, London, 41–52.

Brace, L. (1998) *The Idea of Property in Seventeenth-Century England: Tithes and the Individual*, Manchester University Press, Manchester.

Bradfer-Lawrence, H.L (1932) 'Gaywood Dragge', *Norfolk Archaeology* 24, 146–84.

Bradley, R. (1993) *Altering the Earth: The Origins of Monuments in Britain and Continental Europe*, Monograph Series, 8. Edinburgh: Society of Antiquaries of Scotland.

Bradley, R. (2000) 'Mental and material landscapes in prehistoric Britain' ed. D. Hooke, *Landscape the Richest Historical Record,* Society for Landscape Studies, supplementary series 1, 1–11.

Bradley, R. (2002) *The Past in Prehistoric Societies*, Routledge, London.

Bradley, R. (2003) 'The Translation of Time' eds R.M. Van Dyke and S.E Alcock, *Archaeologies of Memory*, Blackwell, 221–227.

Briggs, J., Harrison, C., McInnes, A. and Vincent, D. (1996) *Crime and Punishment in England: An introductory History,* University College, London.

Brown, A. (1996) 'Parish church building: the fabric', eds J. Blair, and C. Pyrah, *Church Archaeology: Research Directions for the Future*, Council for British Archaeology, 63–68.

Buchli, V. (2004) 'Material culture: current problems', eds L. Meskell and R.W. Preucel, *A Companion to Social Archaeology*, Blackwell, 179–194.

Bushaway, B. (1982) *By Rite: Custom, Ceremony and Community in England 1700–1880*, Junction Books, London.

Cam, H. (1930) *The Hundred and the Hundred Rolls: an Outline of Local Government in Medieval England*, Methuen, London.

Campbell, B.M.S. (1981) 'The regional uniqueness of English field systems? Some evidence from eastern Norfolk', *Agricultural History Review* 29, 16–28.

Campbell, B.M.S. (1986) 'The complexity of manorial structure in medieval Norfolk: A case study', *Norfolk Archaeology* 39, 225–61.

Campbell, B.M.S.; Overton, Mark (eds). *Land, labour and livestock : historical studies in European agricultural productivity*. Manchester: Manchester University Press, 1991.

Carmichael, D.L., Hubert, J., Reeves, B., and Schanche, A. eds (1994) *Sacred Sites, Sacred Places*, Routledge, London.

Carthew, G.A. (1883) *A History, Topographical, Archaeological, Genealogical, and Biographical, of the Parishes of West and East Bradenham, with those of Necton and Holme Hale, in the County of Norfolk*, Norwich.

Cartwright, A. (1988) 'The Legal Background' in M. Manning ed. *Commons in Norfolk: Historical and Ecological Studies of Selected Commons*, Norfolk Research Committee, Norwich, 9–13.

Carver, M. (1998) *Sutton Hoo: Burial Ground of Kings?*, British Museum Press, London.

Chambers, J.D. and Mingay, G.E. (1966) *The Agricultural Revolution, 1750–1880,* Batsford, London.

Chapman, J. (1987) 'The Extent and Nature of Parliamentary Enclosure', *Agricultural History Review* 35, 25–35.

Chapman, J. (1993) 'Enclosure Commissioners as Landscape Planners', *Landscape History* 15, 51–55.

Clarke, W. (1925) *In Breckland Wilds,* Cambridge.

Clay, R.M. (1914) *The Hermits and Anchorites of England*, Methuen, London.

Cohen, A. (1985) *The Symbolic Construction of Community*, Horwood, Chichester.

Cook, G.H. ed. (1965) *Letters to Cromwell on the Suppression of the Monasteries*, J. Baker, London.

Cooney, G. (1994) 'Sacred and secular neolithic landscapes in Ireland' eds D.L. Carmichael, J. Hubert, B. Reeves and A. Schanche, *Sacred Sites, Sacred Places*, Routledge, London, 32–43.

Cooper, T. ed. (2001) *The Journal of William Dowsing*, The Boydell Press, Woodbridge.

Cooper, T. (2001) 'Brass, glass and crosses: identifying iconoclasm outside the journal', ed. T. Cooper *The Journal of William Dowsing*, The Boydell Press, Woodbridge, 89–107.

Corbett, B. and Dent, D. (1994) 'The Soil Landscapes' ed. P. Wade-Martins, *An Historical Atlas of Norfolk*, 2nd edition, Norwich, 18–19.

Cornford, B. (1984) 'Hemsby in the later Middle Ages' *Bulletin of the Norfolk Research Committee*, 33, 22–27.

Cornford, B. (1986) 'The Enclosure of Clippesby Common and the Upstart Yeoman' *Bulletin of the Norfolk Research Committee* 35, 15–17.

Cornford, B. (1988) 'The Commons of Flegg' ed. M. Manning *Commons in Norfolk: Historical and Ecological Studies of Selected Commons,* Norfolk Research Committee, Norwich, 14–20.

Cosgrove, D. (1984) *Social Formation and Symbolic Landscape*, Croom Helm, London.

Cosgrove, D. and Daniels, S. eds, (1988) *The Iconography of Landscape: Essays on the Symbolic Representation, Design and Use of Past Environments,* Cambridge University Press, Cambridge.

Cozens-Hardy, B. (1935) 'Norfolk crosses', *Norfolk Archaeology* 25, 297–336

Cressy, D. (1989) *Bonfires and Bells: National Memory and the*

Protestant Calendar in Elizabethan and Stuart England, Berkeley, CA.

Cummings, B (2002) 'Iconoclasm and bibliophobia in the English Reformation', eds J. Dimmick, J. Simpson, and N. Zeeman *Images, Idolatry and Iconoclasm in late Medieval England*, Oxford University Press, Oxford, 185–214.

Daniell, C. (1997) *Death and Burial in Medieval England 1066–1550*, London.

Darvill, T. (1999) 'The Historic Environment, Historic Landscapes, and space-time-action models in landscape archaeology' eds P. Ucko and R. Layton, *The Archaeology and Anthropology of Landscape*, Routledge, London.

Davies, J.G. (1968) *The Secular Use of Church Buildings*, SCM Press, London.

Davison, A. (1980) 'Heaths, highwayman and gallows', *NARG News* 23, 4–6.

Davison, A. (1988) 'Six deserted villages in Norfolk', *East Anglian Archaeology* 44.

Davison, A. (1990) 'The evolution of settlement in three parishes in south-east Norfolk' *East Anglian Archaeology* 27, 145–57.

Doggett, N. (2001) 'The demolition and conversion of former monastic buildings in post-dissolution Hertfordshire' eds G. Keevill, M. Aston, and T.Hall *Papers on the Study of Medieval Monasteries*, Oxbow, Oxford.

Doggett, N. (2002) *Patterns of Re-Use: the transformation of Former Monastic Buildings in Post-Dissolution Hertfordshire 1540–1600*, BAR British Series 331.

Dominy, J. (1988) 'Commons of East and West Rudham' ed. M. Manning, *Commons in Norfolk: Historical and Ecological Studies of Selected Commons*, Norfolk Research Committee, Norwich, 29–33.

Duffy, E. (1992) *The Stripping of the Altars: Traditional Religion in England 1400–1580*, Yale University Press, New Haven and London.

Duffy, E. (1997) 'The Parish, Piety, and Patronage in Late Medieval East Anglia: the Evidence of Rood Screens' eds K. French, G.Gibbs and B. Kümin *The Parish in English Life, 1400–1600*, Manchester University Press, Manchester, 133–162.

Duffy, E. (2001) *The Voices of Morebath: Reformation and Rebellion in an English Village*, Yale University Press, London.

Dyke, R.M. and Alcock, S.E. eds (2003) *Archaeologies of Memory*, Blackwell.

Dymond, D. (1990) 'A lost institution: the camping close', *Rural History* 1:2, 165–192.

Dymond, D. (1990) *The Norfolk Landscape*, Bury St. Edmund's.

Dymond, D. (1999) 'God's Disputed Acre', *Journal of Ecclesiastical History* 50:3, 464–97.

Edwards N. (1996) 'Identifying the archaeology of the early church in Wales and Cornwall' eds J. Blair, and C. Pyrah, *Church Archaeology: Research Directions for the Future*, Council for British Archaeology 49–63.

Edwards, P. (2004) 'Competition for land, common rights and drainage in the Weald Moors (Shropshire): the Cherrington and Meeson disputes, 1576–1612', ed. R.W. Hoyle *People, Landscape and Alternative Agriculture: Essays for Joan Thirsk*, The Agricultural History Review Supplement Series 3, 39–74.

Ernle, Lord (R.E Prothero) (1912) *English Farming Past and Present*, London.

Evans, E.J. (1976) *The Contentious Tithe: The Tithe Problem and English Agriculture, 1750–1850*, Routledge and K. Paul, London.

Evans, E.J. (1984) 'Tithes' ed. Thirsk, J. *The Agrarian History of England and Wales V.II: 1640–1750 Agrarian Change*, Cambridge University Press, Cambridge, 389–406.

Everitt, A. (1977) 'River and wold', *Journal of Historical Geography* 3, 1–19.

Everitt, A. (2000) 'Common land' ed. J. Thirsk, *The English Rural Landscape*, Oxford, 210–35.

Everitt, A. (1979) 'Country, county and town: patterns of regional evolution in England', *Translations of the Royal Historical Society* 29.

Everson, P. and Williamson T. (1998) *The Archaeology of Landscape*, Manchester University Press, Manchester.

Falvey, H. (2001) 'Crown policy and local economic context in the Berkhampsted Common enclosure dispute, 1618–42', *Rural History* 12, 123–58.

Field, J. (1993) *A History of English Field-Names*, Harlow.

Finberg, H.P.R. (1967) *The Agrarian History of England and Wales V. IV: 1500–1640* Cambridge University Press, Cambridge.

Finch, J. (2003) 'A reformation of meaning: commemoration and remembering the dead in the parish church, 1450–1640' eds D. Gaimster and R. Gilchrist, (2003) *The Archaeology of Reformation 1480–1580*, Maney, 437–449.

Fletcher, D. (2003) 'The parish boundary: a social phenomenon in Hanoverian England' *Rural History* 14:2, 177–97.

Fletcher, A. and MacCulloch, D. (1997) *Tudor Rebellions*, fourth edition, Longman, Harlow.

Forby, R. (1830, reprinted 1970), *The Vocabulary of East Anglia*, two volumes London.

Fox, A. (1996) 'Custom, memory and the authority of writing' ed. P. Griffiths, A. Fox, and S. Hindle, *The Experience of Authority in Early Modern England*, Macmillan, London, 89–117.

Fox, A. (2000) *Oral and Literate Culture in England 1500–1700*, Oxford University Press, Oxford.

Frazer, Bill. (1999) 'Common recollections: resisting enclosure "by agreement" in seventeenth-century England'. *International Journal of Historical Archaeology*, 3:2, 75–100.

French, H.R. (2000) 'Social Status, Localism and the 'Middle Sort of People' in England 1620–1750' *Past and Present* 166, 67–99.

French, K., Gibbs, G. and Kumin, B. (eds) (1997) *The Parish in English Life 1400–1600*, Manchester.

Gaimster, D. and Gilchrist, R. (eds) (2003) *The Archaeology of Reformation 1480–1580*, Maney, Oxford.

Gaimster, D. and Stamper, P. (eds) (1997) *The Age of Transition. The Archaeology of English Culture 1400–1600*, Oxbow Monograph 98.

Gatrell, V.A.C. (1994) *The Hanging Tree: Execution and the English People 1770–1868*, Oxford University Press, Oxford.

Gelling, M. (1978) *Signposts to the Past: Place-names and the History of England* J.M. Dent, London.

Gibson, A. and Simpson, A. (1998) *Prehistoric Ritual and Religion*, Sutton Publishing, Stroud.

Gilchrist R. and Morris R. (1996) 'Continuity, reaction and revival: church archaeology in England c.1600–1880', in J. Blair and C. Pyrah, (eds) *Church Archaeology. Research Directions for the Future*, Council for British Archaeology, 112–26.

Gilchrist, R. (1995) *Contemplation and Action: The Other Monasticism*, Leicester University Press, London.

Gilchrist, R. (2003) 'Dust to dust: revealing the Reformation dead' in D. Gaimster and R. Gilchrist (eds) *The Archaeology of Reformation 1480–1580*, Maney, 399–413.

Giles, K. (2003) 'Reforming corporate charity: guilds and fraternities in pre- and post-Reformation York' in D. Gaimster and R. Gilchrist (eds) *The Archaeology of Reformation 1480–1580*, Maney, 325–340.

Gittings, C. (1984) *Death, Burial and the Individual in Early Modern England*, Routledge, London.

Glennie, P. (1988) 'Continuity and change in Hertfordshire agriculture, 1550–1700, 2 : trends in crop yields and their determinants', *Agricultural History Review*, 36.

Goodier, A. (1984) 'The formation of boundaries in Anglo-Saxon England: a statistical study', *Medieval Archaeology* 28, 1–22.

Gosden, C. and Lock, G. (1998) 'Prehistoric histories', *World Archaeology* 30: 2–12.

Gosden, C. (1999) *Anthropology and Archaeology: a Changing Relationship*, Routledge, London.

Grinsell, L.V. (1953) *The Ancient Burial Mounds of England*, London.

Grinsell, L.V. (1976) *Folklore of Prehistoric Sites in Britain*, London.

Haigh, C. (ed.) (1987) *The English Reformation Revised*, Cambridge.

Hall, D. (1999) 'The drainage of arable land in medieval England' in H. Cook and T. Williamson (eds) *Water Management in the English Landscape: Field, Marsh and Meadow*, Edinburgh, 28–40.

Halliday, R. (1994) 'Wayside graves and crossroad burials', *Norfolk Archaeology* XLII, 80–83.

Halliday, R. (1995) 'Wayside graves and crossroad burials', *Proceedings of the Cambridge Antiquarian Society* LXXXIV, 113–19.

Harding, V. (2003) 'Choices and changes: death, burial and the English Reformation' eds Gaimster, D. and Gilchrist, R. *The Archaeology of Reformation 1480–1580*, Maney, 386–397.

Harley, J.B. (1988) 'Maps, knowledge and power' ed. D. Cosgrove and S. Daniels, Cambridge University Press, Cambridge, 277–312.

Harris, T. (1995) *Popular Culture in England, c.1500–1850*, Macmillan, Hampshire and London.

Harrison, C. (1997) 'Manor courts and governance of Tudor England' eds C.W. Brooks and M. Lobban *Communities and Courts in Britain 1150–1900*, Hambledon, London.

Harvey, P.D.A. (1993) *Maps in Tudor England*, Public Record Office and British Library, London.

Hassall, W. and Beauroy, J. (1993) *Lordship and Landscape in Norfolk, 1250–1350*, Oxford University Press, Oxford.

Havinden, M. (1961) 'Agricultural progress in open-field Oxfordshire', *Agricultural History Review* 9, 73–83.

Hesse, M. (1998) 'Medieval field systems and land tenure in South Creake, Norfolk', *Norfolk Archaeology* 43, 79 – 98.

Hey, D. ed. (1981) *The History of Myddle*, Harmondsworth.

Higgins, D. (1988) 'West Winch Common' ed. M. Manning *Commons in Norfolk: Historical and Ecological Studies of Selected Commons*, Norfolk Research Committee, Norwich, 22–28.

Hill, C. (1969) *Society and Puritanism in Pre-Revolutionary England*, Panther, London.

Hill, D. (1976) 'Bran Ditch – the burials reconsidered', *Proceedings of the Cambridge Antiquarian Society* 66, 126–128.

Hindle, S. (1996) 'Exclusion crisis: poverty, migration and parochial responsibility in English rural communities, c.1560–1660', *Rural History* 7, 125–149.

Hindle, S. (1998) 'Power, poor relief and social relations in Holland Fen, c.1600–1800', *Historical Journal* 41, 67–96.

Hindle, S. (2000) 'A sense of place? Becoming and belonging in the rural parish, 1550–1650' eds P. Withington and A. Shepard *Communities in Early Modern England: Networks, Place, Rhetoric*, Manchester University Press, Manchester, 96–114.

Hindle, S. (2001) 'The political culture of the middling sort in English rural communities, c.1550–1700' ed. T. Harris *The Politics of the Excluded, c.1500–1850*, Palgrave, Basingstoke, 125–153.

Hindle, S. (2002) *The State and Social Change in Early Modern England, 1550–1640*, Palgrave, Basingstoke.

Hindle, S. (2004) *On the Parish? The Micro-Politics of Poor Relief in Rural England c.1550–1750*, Clarendon Press, Oxford.

Hipkin, S. (2000) '"Sitting on his penny rent": conflict and right of common in Faversham Blean, 1595–1610'. *Rural History*, 11, 1–35

Hoare, C.M. (1918) *The History of an East Anglian Soke*, Bedford.

Hodder, I. (2001) ed. *Archaeological Theory Today*, Polity, Cambridge

Hodder, I. (2001) 'Introduction: A review of contemporary theoretical debates in archaeology' ed. I. Hodder *Archaeological Theory Today*, Polity, Cambridge, 1–13.

Holmes, C. (1985) 'Drainers and Fenmen: the problem of popular political consciousness in the seventeenth century' eds Fletcher and Stevenson, *Order and Disorder in Early Modern England*, Cambridge, 166–95.

Holtorf, C. (1998) 'The life-histories of megaliths in Mecklenburg-Vorpommern (Germany)', *World Archaeology* 30, 23–38.

Holtorf, C. and Williams, H. (2006) 'Landscape and memory', in D. Hicks and Beaudry, M. (eds) *The Cambridge Companion to Historical Archaeology*, Cambridge.

Hooke, D. (1998) *The Landscape of Anglo-Saxon England*, Leicester University Press, London.

Hoskins, W.G. (1955) *The Making of the English Landscape*, Harmondsworth.

Hoskins, W.G. (1976) *The Age of Plunder; King Henry's England 1500–47*, Stanford, Cal.

Howard, M. (1987) *The Early Tudor Country House. Architecture and politics 1490–1550*, George Philip, London.

Hunt, J.M. (1996) *Garden and Grove: The Italian Renaissance Garden in the English Imagination 1600–1750*, University of Pennsylvania Press, Philadelphia.

Hutton, R. (1987) 'The local impact of the Tudor reformations' reprinted in ed. P. Marshall, *The Impact of the English Reformation 1500–1640*, Arnold, London.

Hutton, R. (1994) *The Rise and Fall of Merry England: The Ritual Year, 1400–1700*, Oxford University Press, Oxford.

Hutton, R. (1996) *The Stations of the Sun*, Oxford University Press, Oxford.

Ingram, M. (1995) 'From reformation to toleration: popular religious cultures in England, 1540–1690' ed. T. Harris *Popular Culture in England, c.1500–1850*, Macmillan, London.

Ingram, M. (1996) 'Reformation of manners in early modern England' eds P. Griffiths, A. Fox, and S. Hindle *The Experience of Authority in Early Modern England*, Macmillan, London.

Innes, M. (2000) 'Introduction: using the past, interpreting the present, influencing the future' eds Y. Hen, and M. Innes *The Uses of the Past in the Early Middle Ages*, Cambridge University Press, Cambridge, 1–8.

James, M.R. (1917) 'Lives of St Walstan', *Norfolk Archaeology*, XIX, 238–67.

Jewell, H.M. (1972) *English Local Administration in the Middle Ages*, Newton Abbot.

Johnson, F. (1925) 'The Chapel of St Clement at Brundall, Norfolk', *Norfolk Archaeology* 22, 194–206.

Johnson, M. (1996) *An Archaeology of Capitalism,* Blackwell, Oxford.

Kealhofer, L. (1999) 'Creating social identity inthe landscape: Tidewater, Virginia, 1600–1750' eds W. Ashmore and A.B. Knapp *Archaeologies of Landscape: Contemporary Perspectives*, Blackwell, Oxford, 58–83.

Kerridge, E. (1973) *The Farmers of Old England*, Allen and Unwin, London.

Kinnes, I. (1998) 'From ritual to romance: a new western' ed. A. Gibson and D. Simpson *Prehistoric Ritual and Religion*, Sutton Publishing, Stroud, 183–190.

Knapp, A. B. and Ashmore W. (1999) 'Introduction' eds W. Ashmore and A.B. Knapp *Archaeologies of Landscape: Contemporary Perspectives*, Blackwell, Oxford.

Kreider, A. (1979) *English Chantries: The Road to Dissolution,* Harvard University Press, Cambridge and London.

Kumin, B. (1996) *The Shaping of a Community: the Rise and Reformation of the English Parish c.1400–1560*, Aldershot.

Laqueur, T.W. (1989) 'Crowds, carnivals and the state in English executions, 1604–1868' eds A.L. Beier, D. Cannadine, J.M. Rossenheim *The First Modern Society: Essays in English History in Honour of Lawrence Stone*, Cambridge University Press, Cambridge, 305–55.

Lawson, A.J., Martin, E.A., and Priddy, D. (1981) 'The barrows of East Anglia', *East Anglian Archaeology* 12.

Lawson, A.J. (1983) 'The archaeology of Witton', *East Anglian Archaeology*, 18.

Lawson, A.J. (1986) 'Barrow excavations in Norfolk, 1950–82', *East Anglian Archaeology* 29.

Leake, G.F. (1991) *The Commons of East and West Runton*, Norwich.

Lee-Warner, Rev. H.J. (1879) 'The Walsingham "Wishing Wells", *Norfolk Archaeology*.

Leslie, M. and Raylor, T. (eds) (1992) *Culture and Cultivation in Early Modern England: Writing and the Land,* Leicester University Press, Leicester.

LeStrange, R. (1973) *Monasteries of Norfolk*, King's Lynn.

Liddiard, R. (1999) 'The distribution of ridge and furrow in Norfolk: ploughing practice and subsequent land use', *Agricultural History Review* 47, 1–6.

Lucas, R. (1997) 'Brickmaking on Norfolk commons' *Norfolk Archaeology* LXV, 457–468.

McRae, A. (1992) 'Husbandry manuals and the language of agrarian improvement' eds M. Leslie and T. Raylor, *Culture and Cultivation in Early Modern England: Writing and the Land,* Leicester University Press, Leicester, 35–62.

McRae, A. (1996) *God Speed the Plough: The Representation of Agrarian England, 1500–1660*, Past and Present Publications, Cambridge University Press, Cambridge.

Manning, R.B. (1988) *Village Revolts: Social Protests and Popular Disturbances in England 1509–1640*, Oxford University Press, Oxford.

Marsh, C. (1998) *Popular Religion in Sixteenth-century England*, Macmillan, London.

Marsh, C. (2005) 'Order and place in England, 1580–1640: the view from the pew', *Journal of British Studies* 44, 3–26.

Marshall, P. (2002) *Beliefs and the Dead in Reformation England*, Oxford University Press, Oxford.

Meskell, L. (2001) 'Archaeologies of identity', ed. I. Hodder

Archaeological Theory Today, Polity, Cambridge, 187–213.

Messent, C. (1934) *The Monasteries of Norfolk and Suffolk*, Hunt, Norwich.

Morphy, H. (1993) 'Colonialism, history and the construction of place: the politics of landscape in northern Australia', ed. B. Bender *Landscape, Politics and Perspectives*, Berg, Oxford.

Morris, R. (1989) *Churches in the Landscape*, Dent, London.

Muir, R. (1999) *Approaches to Landscape*, Macmillan, London.

Muir, R. (2000) 'Conceptualising landscape' *Landscapes* 1:1, 4–21.

Muir, R. (2004) *Landscape Encyclopaedia*, Windgather Press, Macclesfield.

Neeson, J.M. (1993) *Commoners: Common Right, Enclosure and Social Change in England, 1700–1820*, Cambridge University Press, Cambridge.

Newman, R. (2001) *The Historical Archaeology of Britain c.1540–1900*, Sutton Publishing, Gloucestershire.

Oakey, N. (2003) 'Fixtures or fittings? Can surviving pre-Reformation ecclesiastical material culture be used as a barometer of contemporary attitudes to the Reformation in England', in D. Gaimster and R. Gilchrist, *The Archaeology of Reformation 1480–1580*, Maney, 58–72.

Oestmann, C.H.K. (1994) *Lordship and Community: The Lestrange Family and the Village of Hunstanton, Norfolk, in the First Half of the Sixteenth Century*, Woodbridge.

Ogden, A. (2002) *The Profits of Pilgrimage in Medieval East Anglia* (unpublished MA dissertation, UEA).

Overton, M. (1996) *Agricultural Revolution in England: The Transformation of the Agrarian Economy 1500–1850*, Cambridge University Press, Cambridge.

Owen, D. (1975) 'Medieval chapels in Lincolnshire', *Lincolnshire Archaeology and History* 10, 15–22.

Parker Pearson, M. (1999) *The Archaeology of Death and Burial*, Stroud.

Parsons, W.L.E. (1937) *Salle: The Story of a Norfolk Parish its Church, Manors and People,* Norwich.

Pevsner, N. and Wilson, B. (2002a) *The Buildings of England: North-East Norfolk and Norwich*, second edition, Yale University Press.

Pevsner, N. and Wilson, B. (2002b) *The Buildings of England: North-West and South Norfolk*, second edition, Yale University Press.

Philips, J.R. (1973) *The Reformation of Images: Destruction of Art in England, 1535–1660*, Berkeley.

Phythian-Adams, C. (1987) *Re-Thinking English Local History*, Department Of English Local History Occasional Papers, Fourth Series, 1, Leicester University Press, Leicester.

Phythian-Adams, C. (1993) *Societies, Cultures and Kinship, 1580–1850: Cultural Provinces and English Local History*, Leicester University Press, Leicester.

Phythian-Adams, C. (2000) 'Frontier valleys', ed. J. Thirsk, *The English Rural Landscape*, Oxford University Press, Oxford.

Platt, C. (1984) *The Abbeys and Priories of Medieval England*, Secker and Warburg.

Postgate, M.R. (1973) 'Field Systems of East Anglia', eds A.R.H. Baker and R.A. Butlin *Studies of Field Systems in the British Isles,* Cambridge, 281–324.

Pounds, N.J.G. (2000) *A History of the English Parish*, Cambridge University Press, Cambridge.

Pred, A. (1985) 'The social becomes the spatial, the spatial becomes the social: enclosures, social change and the becoming of places in Skåne', eds D. Gregory and J. Urry *Social Relations and Spatial Structures,* Macmillan, London, 137–65.

Puhvel, M. (1976) 'The mystery of the cross-roads', *Folklore* II, 167–78.

Rackham, O. (1976) *Trees and Woodland in the British Landscape*, J.M. Dent, London.

Rackham, O. (1986) *The History of the Countryside*, J.M. Dent, London.

Rasmussen, L. (2003) 'Why small monastic houses should have a history', *Midland History*, 28, 1–27.

Rawcliffe, C. (1995) *Medicine and Society in Later Medieval England,* Sutton Publishing, Stroud.

Rawcliffe, C. (2005) 'The earthly and spiritual topography of suburban hospitals' in K. Giles, and C. Dyer (eds) *Town and Country in the Middle Ages: Contrasts, Contacts and Interconnections, 1100–1500*, Maney, 251–74.

Reid, A.W. (1984) 'Some medieval road and place names in Ashill', *Bulletin of the Norfolk Research Committee* Sept, 18–21.

Reid, A.W. (1979) 'The process of parliamentary enclosure in Ashill', *Norfolk Archaeology* 37, 169–77.

Reynolds, A. (1997) 'The definition and ideology of Anglo-Saxon execution cemeteries', eds De Boe and F. Verhaeghe *Death and Burial in Medieval Europe: Papers of the "Medieval Europe Brugge 1997" Conference Vol 2*, Brugge, 33–41.

Reynolds, A. (1999) *Later Anglo-Saxon England: Life and Landscape*, Stroud.

Roffey, S. (2003) 'Deconstructing a symbolic world: the Reformation and the medieval parish chantry' eds D. Gaimster and R. Gilchrist *The Archaeology of Reformation 1480–1580*, Maney, 340–55.

Rogerson, A. *Fransham: An Archaeological and Historical Study of a Parish on the Norfolk Boulder Clay*, unpublished PhD Thesis, Centre of East Anglian Studies, University of East Anglia.

Rogerson, A., Davison, A., Pritchard, D. and Silvester, R, (1997) *Barton Bendish and Caldecote: Fieldwork in South-west Norfolk*, East Anglian Archaeology 80, East Dereham.

Rollison, D. (1992) *The Local Origins of Modern Society: Gloucestershire 1500–1800*, Routledge, London.

Rollison, D. (1999) 'Exploding England: the dialectics of mobility and settlement in early modern England', *Social History* 24, 1, 1–16.

Rosser, G. (1991) 'Parochial conformity and voluntary religion in late medieval England' *Transactions of the Royal Historical Society,* 6th series, I, 173–89.

Rosser, G. (1994) 'Going to the fraternity feast: commensuality and social relations in Late medieval England', *Journal of British Studies* 33, 4, 430–46.

Rosser, G. (1996) 'Religious practice on the margins' eds J. Blair and C. Pryah, *Church Archaeology: Research Directions for the Future,* The Council for British Archaeology, 75–84.

Rutledge, P. (1995) 'The dispute of Litcham Lyngs' ed. A. Longcroft and R. Joby *East Anglian Studies,* Norwich, 238–42

Rye, W. (1920) 'Hundred courts and mote hills in Norfolk', in *Norfolk Handlists,* 1st series ed. W. Rye, Norwich.

Scarfe, N. trans. and ed. (1988) *Francois de la Rochefoucauld: A Frenchman's Year in Suffolk, 1784,* Suffolk Records Society 30, Woodbridge.

Semple, S. (1998) 'A fear of the past: the place of the prehistoric burial mound in the ideology of middle and later Anglo-Saxon England', *World Archaeology* 30:1, 109–126.

Shagan, E.H. (2003) *Popular Politics and the English Reformation,* Cambridge University Press, Cambridge.

Shaw-Taylor, L. (2001) 'Labourers, cows, common rights and parliamentary enclosure: the evidence of contemporary comment, c.1760–1810', *Past and Present* 171.

Shepard, A. (2003) *Meanings of Manhood in Early Modern England,* Oxford University Press, Oxford.

Simpson, J. (1986) 'God's visible judgements: the Christian dimension of landscape legends', *Landscape History* 8, 53–56.

Simpson, J. (1991) 'The local legend: a product of popular culture', *Rural History* 2, 25–35.

Skipper, K. (1989) *Wood-pasture: The Landscape of the Norfolk Claylands in the Early Modern Period,* unpublished MA thesis, Centre of East Anglian Studies, University of East Anglia.

Slack, P. (1990) *The English Poor Law, 1531–1782,* Cambridge.

Smith, A. (1968) 'The image of Cromwell in folklore and tradition', *Folklore* 79, I, 17–40.

Smith, A.H. (1956) *English Place-Name Elements,* English Place-Name Society, XXV–XXVI, Cambridge.

Smith, H. (1974) *County and Court: Government and Politics in Norfolk, 1558–1603,* Clarendon Press, Oxford.

Snell, K.D.M. (1985) *Annals of the Labouring Poor: Social Change and Agrarian England, 1660–1900,* Cambridge.

Sommerville, C.J. (1992) *The Secularization of Early Modern England: from Religious Culture to Religious Faith,* Oxford University Press, Oxford.

Stagg, F.N. (2003) *Salthouse: the Story of a Norfolk Village,* Salthouse History Group.

Sussams, K. (1996) *The Breckland Archaeological Survey 1994–1996,* Suffolk County Council.

Swales, T.H. (1966) 'The redistribution of monastic lands in Norfolk at the Dissolution', *Norfolk Archaeology,* 34, 14–44.

Tarlow, S (2003) 'Reformation and transformation: what happened to Catholic things in a Protestant world?' eds D. Gaimster and R. Gilchrist *The Archaeology of Reformation 1480–1580,* Maney, 108–121.

Taylor, C. (2000) 'Fenlands' ed. J. Thirsk *The English Rural Landscape,* Oxford University Press, Oxford, 167–187.

Thirsk, J. (1990) 'Agricultural Policy: Public Debate and Legislation, 1640–1750' ed. J. Thirsk *Chapters from the Agrarian History of England and Wales, 1550–1750,* Cambridge, 125–213.

Thirsk, J. (1967) 'The farming regions of England' ed. H.P.R, Finberg *The Agrarian History of England and Wales V. IV: 1500–1640,* Cambridge University Press, Cambridge, 1–109.

Thirsk, J. (1967) 'Enclosing and engrossing' ed. H.P.R, Finberg *The Agrarian History of England and Wales V. IV: 1500–1640,* Cambridge University Press, Cambridge, 200–240.

Thirsk, J. (1985) *The Agrarian History of England and Wales V.II: 1640–1750 Agrarian Change,* Cambridge University Press, Cambridge.

Thirsk, J. (1987) *England's Agricultural Regions and Agrarian History 1500–1750,* Macmillan, London.

Thomas, K. (1971) *Religion and the Decline of Magic,* Weidenfeld and Nicolson, London.

Thomas, K. (1984) *The Perception of the Past in Early Modern England,* Creighton Trust Lecture, London.

Thomas, J. (2001) 'Archaeologies of place and landscape' ed. I. Hodder *Archaeological Theory Today,* Polity, Cambridge, 165–186.

Thompson, E.P. (1991) *Customs in Common,* Merlin Press, London.

Tilley, C. (1994) *A Phenomenology of Landscape: Places, Paths and Monuments,* Oxford.

Tilley, C. (2004) 'Round barrows and dykes as landscape metaphors' *Cambridge Archaeological Journal* 14:2, 185–203.

Turner, M. (1994) 'Parliamentary enclosure' ed. P. Wade-Martins, *An Historical Atlas of Norfolk,* 2nd edition, Norwich, 124–125,

Ucko, P.J., and Layton, R. eds (1999) *The Archaeology and Anthropology of Landscape,* London.

Underdown, D. (1985) *Revel, Riot and Rebellion: Popular Politics and Culture in England 1603–1660,* Blackwell, Oxford.

Vallance, A. (1920) *Old Crosses and Lynchgates,* Batsford, London.

Van De Noort, R. (1993) 'The context of early medieval barrows in western Europe', *Antiquity* 67, 66–73.

Wade Martins, S. and Williamson, T. (1999) *Roots of Change: Farming the Landscape of East Anglia, c. 1700–1870,* Exeter.

Wales, T. (1984) 'Poverty, poor relief and the life-cycle:

some evidence from seventeenth-century Norfolk', ed. R.M. Smith, *Land, Kinship and Life-Cycle* Cambridge, 351–404.

Walters, H.B. (1941) 'Inventories of Norfolk church goods (1552)', *Norfolk Archaeology*, vols 26–33.

Warner, P. (1986) 'Shared churchyards, freemen, church builders and the development of parishes in eleventh century East Anglia', *Landscape History* 8, 39–52.

Webb, D. (2000) *Pilgrimage in Medieval England*, Hambledon, London.

Whitelock, D. (1954) *The Beginnings of English Society*, Harmondsworth.

White, F. (1854) *White's Directory*, Sheffield.

Whittle J. (2000) *The Development of Agrarian Capitalism: Land and Labour in Norfolk, 1440–1580,* Clarendon Press, Oxford.

Whyte, N. (2003a) 'The after-life of barrows; prehistoric monuments in the Norfolk landscape', *Landscape History* 25, 5–16.

Whyte, N. (2003b) 'The deviant dead in the Norfolk landscape', *Landscapes* 4;1, 24–39.

Whyte, N. (1997) 'Landscape, memory and custom: parish identities' *Social History* 32;2, 166–186.

Whyte, N. (forthcoming) 'Comanded by their mother: women and custom in early modern rural England'.

Williams, H.M.R. (1997) 'Ancient landscapes and the burial of the dead: The reuse of prehistoric and Roman monuments as early Anglo-Saxon Burial Sites' *Medieval Archaeology,* XLI, 1–32.

Williams, H.M.R. (1998) 'Ancient monuments and the past in early Anglo-Saxon England', *World Archaeology* 30:1, 90–108.

Williams, H.M.R. (2006) *Death and Memory in Early Medieval Britain*, Cambridge.

Williamson, T. (1993) *The Origins of Norfolk*, Manchester.

Williamson, T. (1995) *Polite Landscapes: Gardens and Society in Eighteenth-Century England*, Sutton Publishing, Gloucestershire.

Williamson, T. (1997) *The Norfolk Broads: a Landscape History*, Manchester University Press, Manchester.

Williamson, T. (1998) 'Questions of preservation and destruction', ed. P. Everson and T. Williamson, *The Archaeology of Landscape*, Manchester University Press, Manchester, 1–24.

Williamson, T. (2000a) 'Understanding enclosure', *Landscapes* 1:1, 56–79.

Williamson, T. (2000b) 'The rural landscape 1500–1900, the neglected centuries' ed. Hooke, D, *Landscape the Richest Historical Record,* Society for Landscape Studies, supplementary series 1, 109–117.

Williamson, T. (2002) *The Transformation of Rural England: farming and the Landscape 1700–1870,* University of Exeter Press, Exeter.

Williamson, T. (2003) *Shaping Medieval Landscapes: Settlement, Society, Environment*, Windgather Press, Macclesfield.

Winchester, A.J.L. (2000) *Discovering Parish Boundaries*, Shire, Haverfordwest (second edition).

Winchester, A.J.L (1997) 'Parish, township and tithing: patterns of local administration in England before the nineteenth century', *The Local Historian*, 27:1, 3–17.

Winchester, A.J.L. (2000) 'Dividing lines in a moorland landscape: territorial boundaries in upland England', *Landscapes* 1:2, 16–32.

Withington, P. and Shepard, A. (2000) *Communities in Early Modern England: Networks, Place, Rhetoric*, Manchester University Press, Manchester.

Wood, A. (1996) 'Custom, identity and resistance: English free miners and their law c.1550–1800', eds P. Griffiths, A. Fox, and S. Hindle, *The Experience of Authority in Early Modern England,* Macmillan, London, 249–286.

Wood, A. (1997) 'The place of custom in plebeian political culture: England, 1550–1800', *Social History* 22:1, 46–60.

Wood, A. (1998) 'Custom and the social organisation of writing in early modern England', *Transactions of the Royal Historical Society*

Wood, A. (1999) *The Politics of Social Conflict: The Peak Country 1520–1770*, Cambridge.

Wood, A. (2002) *Riot, Rebellion and Popular Politics in Early Modern England*, Palgrave, Hampshire.

Wood, I.N. (1987) 'Anglo-Saxon Otley: an archiepiscopal estate and its crosses in a Northumbrian context', *Northern History* 23, 20–38.

Woodforde, J. (1924) *The Diary of a Country Parson*, ed. J. Beresford, 6 vols, Oxford.

Woodward, D. (1998) 'Straw, bracken and the Wicklow Whale: the exploitation of natural resources in England since 1500', *Past and Present* 159.

Woolf, D.R. (1988) 'The "common voice": history, folklore and oral tradition in early modern England', *Past and Present* 120, 26–52.

Woolf, D.R. (1991) 'Of Danes and Giants: popular beliefs about the past in early modern England', *Dalhousie Review* 71, 166–209.

Wrightson, K. (1982) *English Society, 1580–1680*, Hutchinson, London.

Wrightson, K. (1996) 'The politics of the parish in early modern England' eds P. Griffiths, A. Fox, and S. Hindle, *The Experience of Authority in Early Modern England,* Macmillan, London, 10–46.

Wrightson, K. (2000) *Earthly Necessities, Economic lives in Early Modern Britain*, Yale University Press, London.

Wymer, J. (1996) 'Barrow Excavations in Norfolk 1984–1988', *East Anglian Archaeology* 77.

Yates, E.M. (1981) 'The Dispute of the Salt Fen', *Norfolk Archaeology* 38, 73–78.

Index